# organising the european parliament

## the role of committees and their legislative influence

### Nikoleta Yordanova

**ecpr** PRESS

Table 2.1:Summary of Models is reproduced from Competing Principals: Committees, Parties, and the Organization of Congress, Forrest Maltzman (Ann Arbor: The University of Michigan Press, 1998). Reproduced with kind permission from The University of Michigan Press.

Committee Assignments in the European Parliament: Distributive, Informational and Partisan Rationales', European Union Politics, 2009, 10(2): 253–280. Reproduced with kind permission from SAGE Publications.

'Inter-institutional Rules and Division of Power in the European Parliament: Allocation of Consultation and Codecision Reports', West European Politics, 2011, 34(1): 97-121. Reproduced with kind permission from Taylor & Francis.

The ECPR Press is the publishing imprint of the European Consortium for Political Research (ECPR), a scholarly association, which supports and encourages the training, research and cross-national cooperation of political scientists in institutions throughout Europe and beyond.

ECPR Press
University of Essex
Wivenhoe Park
Colchester
CO4 3SQ
UK

Typeset by ECPR Press

Printed and bound by Lightning Source

British Library Cataloguing in Publication Data

A catalogue record for this book is available from the British Library

Paperback ISBN: 978-1-907301-39-1

www.ecpr.eu/ecprpress

**ECPR – Monographs**
Series Editors:
Dario Castiglione (University of Exeter)
Peter Kennealy (European University Institute)
Alexandra Segerberg (Stockholm University)
Peter Triantafillou (Roskilde University)


**Other books available in this series**
*Agents or Bosses?* (ISBN: 9781907301261) Ozge Kemahlioglu

*Causes of War: The Struggle for Recognition* (ISBN: 9781907301018) Thomas Lindemann

*Citizenship: The History of an Idea* (ISBN: 9780954796655) Paul Magnette

*Coercing, Constraining and Signalling: Explaining UN and EU Sanctions After the Cold War* (ISBN: 9781907301209) Francesco Giumelli

*Constraints On Party Policy Change* (ISBN: 9781907301490) Thomas M. Meyer

*Contesting Europe. Exploring Euroscepticism in Online Media Coverage* (ISBN: 9781907301513) Pieter de Wilde, Asimina Michailidou & Hans-Jörg Trenz

*Deliberation Behind Closed Doors: Transparency and Lobbying in the European Union* (ISBN: 9780955248849) Daniel Naurin

*Democratic Institutions and Authoritarian Rule in Southeast Europe* (ISBN: 9781907301438) Danijela Dolenec

*European Integration and its Limits: Intergovernmental Conflicts and their Domestic Origins* (ISBN: 9780955820373) Daniel Finke

*Gender and Vote in Britain: Beyond the Gender Gap?* (ISBN: 9780954796693) Rosie Campbell

*Globalisation: An Overview* (ISBN: 9780955248825) Danilo Zolo

*Joining Political Organisations: Institutions, Mobilisation and Participation in Western Democracies* (ISBN: 9780955248894) Laura Morales

*Paying for Democracy: Political Finance and State Funding for Parties* (ISBN: 9780954796631) Kevin Casas-Zamora

*Policy Making In Multilevel Systems: Federalism, Decentralisation, and Performance in the OECD Countries* (ISBN: 9781907301339) Jan Biela, Annika Hennl and Andre Kaiser

*Political Conflict and Political Preferences: Communicative Interaction Between Facts, Norms and Interests* (ISBN: 9780955820304) Claudia Landwehr

*Political Parties and Interest Groups in Norway* (ISBN: 9780955820366) Elin Haugsgjerd Allern

*Regulation in Practice: The de facto Independence of Regulatory Agencies* (ISBN: 9781907301285) Martino Maggetti

*Representing Women? Female Legislators in West European Parliaments* (ISBN: 9780954796648) Mercedes Mateo Diaz

*To Bartek,*
*my best friend and husband*

# contents

# | list of figures and tables

# | list of abbreviations

**Standing committees of the European Parliament**

| | |
|---|---|
| AFCO | Constitutional Affairs |
| AFET | Foreign Affairs |
| AGRI | Agriculture |
| BUDG | Budgets |
| CONT | Budgetary Control |
| CULT | Culture and Education |
| DEVE | Development |
| ECON | Economic and Monetary Affairs |
| EMPL | Employment and Social Affairs |
| ENVI | Environment, Public Health and Food Safety |
| FEMM | Women's Rights and Gender Equality |
| IMCO | Internal Market and Consumer Protection |
| INTA | International Trade |
| ITRE | Industry, Research and Energy |
| JURI | Legal Affairs |
| LIBE | Civil Liberties, Justice and Home Affairs |
| PECH | Fisheries |
| PETI | Petitions |
| REGI | Regional Development |
| TRAN | Transport and Tourism |

**European party groups**

| | |
|---|---|
| ALDE | Group of the Alliance of Liberals and Democrats for Europe |
| EPP | Group of European People's Party |
| EPP-ED | Group of European People's Party (Christian Democrats) and European Democrats |
| EUL/NGL | Confederal Group of the European United Left – Nordic Green Left |
| G/EGA | Group of the Greens/European Free Alliance |
| IND/DEM | Independence/Democracy Group |
| UEN | Union of Europe of the Nations Group |
| PSE | Socialist Group in the European Parliament |
| na | Non-attached members |

Other
CNS        Consultation procedure
COD        Codecision procedure
COREPER  Committee of Permanent Representatives (Council of Ministers)
EC          European Community
EP          European Parliament
EU          European Union
MEP        Member of European Parliament
TEC        Treaty establishing the European Community
TEU        Treaty of the European Union
TFEU       Treaty on the Functioning of the European Union

# | acknowledgements

Foremost, I am grateful to my parents for their love and support throughout my studies without which I would not have reached this far.

I am indebted to Bartek, who was always there for an insightful discussion, endured all my ups and downs in the long writing process, gave me motivation and strength at times of self-doubt, and always believed in me. This is why I dedicate this book to him.

I am thankful to my supervisors – to Adrienne Héritier who always supported me and read thoroughly countless drafts of my doctoral thesis, which this book is based on; to Simon Hix who left me inspired with new ideas after every meeting and made the MEP roll call vote and survey data available to me; and to the late Peter Mair who was always available at incredibly short notice when I needed his advice – his premature death was indeed a great loss for political science and for me. Special thanks go to Mark Franklin from whom I learnt a lot about research methods. I am further grateful to Markus Jachtenfuchs who sparked my interest in political science and encouraged me to pursue doctoral studies as well as to David Farrell for serving as an external examiner in my defence.

This book would not have been possible without the generous support of the Italian Ministry of Foreign Affairs and the European University Institute (EUI). The EUI offered a motivating working environment and was a great place to meet a lot of renowned scholars and make life-long friends. In particular, I feel privileged to have discussed my work with visiting scholars and post-doctoral researchers such as Barry Weingast, Bernard Steunenberg, Anne Rasmussen, Gail McElroy, Gaye Güngor and Björn Lindberg, to whom I am grateful for their time and thoughtful suggestions. Thanks go also to my friends at the EUI who have facilitated my work in various ways, including Michaël Tatham, Bram Lancee, Julia Langbein, Chris Hanretty, Franca van Hooren, Sergi Pardos-Prado, Elias Dinas, Till Weber and Christel Koop; to my discussants in supervisees' colloquia at the EUI, including Anna Kristin Müller-Debus, Wojtek Gagatek, Costanza Hermanin, Mads Christian Dagnis Jensen, Christian Thauer, Daniela Piccio, and Umut Aydin; as well as to all participants of the monthly Colloquium on Political Behaviour at the EUI.

Parts of this book have been presented at various conferences such as the European Consortium for Political Research General Conference (2007) and Joint Sessions (2008), the European Union Studies Association Biennial Conference (2009), and the American Political Science Association Annual Meeting (2009). This book would not have been the same without the expert advice I received at these venues from the participants and the discussants of my papers, namely Thomas König, Bjørn Høyland, Michael Kaeding, Amie Kreppel, Mark Pollack, Michael Th. Greven, Royce A. Carroll, and Monika Mühlböck.

I would like to thank my colleagues at the European Parliament (EP) in the Policy Department on Budgetary Control, who made fruitful and memorable my internship and research activities there in 2008. During my time at the EP I gathered the interview data for this project. I am grateful to the MEPs and EP staff members who agreed to answer my questions.

I am thankful to SAGE Publications, Taylor & Francis and Michigan University Press for their permissions to reproduce copyrighted material here. Finally, I would like to thank the staff at ECPR Press, and in particular its editor Dario Castiglione, for making this publication possible.

Nikoleta Yordanova
June, 2013

# | preface

The European Parliament (EP) acts as an equal co-legislator with the Council of Ministers in adopting many policies that affect over 500 million European citizens on a daily basis. However, despite its profound consequences for EU policies and policy-making, our knowledge of the parliamentary legislative organisation is limited. Addressing this gap, this book studies the internal setup and legislative impact of the EP committees.

Drawing on congressional literature, I adapt and confront distributive, informational and partisan theoretical approaches to answer the research questions of this project, namely whether and why the EP committees and their legislative output are dominated by preference-outlying legislators with special interests, experts serving the informational needs of the plenary, or loyal members of the working majority party group (coalition). Statistical analyses of committee assignments, allocation of legislative tasks, and adoption of committee reports in plenary are conducted using data on the 6th European Parliament (2004-2009). They are complemented with evidence from semi-structured interviews.

The results show that, depending on the predominant character of a committee's legislative output (distributive or regulatory), legislators' special interests or expertise play a dominant role in the formally regulated committee assignment process. In contrast, party group affiliation and loyalty shape the allocation of important legislative tasks in committees, owing to the informal allocation process. Furthermore, committee reports are more successful on the floor if drafted by rapporteurs from the working majority party group – perhaps a natural consequence of the EP's open amendment rule. Thus, the parliamentary legislative output is ultimately controlled by the working majority party group and not the committees. The congressional theories fail to account for the committees' legislative influence when an informal early agreement is reached with the Council of Ministers. This occurs increasingly often, rendering decision-making in committees largely obsolete.

The observed regularities are used to advance the theoretical literature on legislative organisation by identifying conditions under which each of the main existing rationales can explain committee setup and influence, namely: 1) the policy areas a committee covers; 2) the parliamentary rules regulating committee-party and committee-plenary relationships; and 3) the balance of power and mode of negotiation between the legislative chambers.

More substantively, the EP committees are not conducive for pursuing particularistic policies. Instead, they promote left-right party politics. This has important implications for EU legislative politics, interest representation, legitimacy, and more generally the EU democratic deficit.

# chapter one | introduction

Parliaments are essential, if not the most important, institutions in democratic political systems (Lijphart 1991: ix). The internal set-up of a parliament is crucial to its ability to perform its tasks effectively and efficiently, and shapes the adopted policies. Thus, a large body of literature has been dedicated to the study of legislative organisation. The organisation of the European Parliament (EP), however, has not received due scholarly attention. While that is slowly changing, the EP has been ignored for a long time on the grounds that it is a weak institution.[1] However, despite the fact that it is a relatively young legislature, over the past thirty years the EP has been given substantive powers in an attempt to reduce the democratic deficit of the European Union (EU). These powers include discretion over the EU budget, control over the EU executive, i.e. the European Commission, and, crucially, the power to determine the content of most EU policies, which affect over 500 million European citizens on a daily basis. Thus, for the most part, the EP now acts as an equal co-legislator in the bicameral EU legislature together with the Council of Ministers, which represents member state governments. That makes very timely the study of its internal structures, dynamics and decision-making mechanisms, which affect the quality of EU legislation and how representative this legislation is of the views of EU citizens. This book focuses on the study of the standing EP committees in recognition of the general agreement that it is within these committees that the parliamentary legislative positions are *de facto* developed.

For a legislature situated in the context of the European Union, the EP is puzzlingly different from any other international assembly or national parliament in Europe and very similar to the US Congress instead. It thus presents an interesting empirical case and an important opportunity to refine the theoretical literature on legislative organisation, which constitutes the second aim of this book.

## The case of the European Parliament and its committees

The European Parliament provides a unique laboratory for the study of legislative organisation. It has been developing dynamically since its establishment in 1957 as a joint parliamentary assembly of the European Coal and Steel Community, the

---

1. While in some theoretical literature 'institutions' are referred to as 'sets of rules that structure social interaction' and organisational actors are defined as 'sets of actors united in pursuit of a common goal' (North 1990: 3), the convention in the literature on the European Union is to refer to bodies such as the EP, the European Commission and the Council of Ministers as institutions (Farrell and Héritier 2003: 596, note 4; see also Héritier 1999). The latter convention is adopted throughout the book.

European Atomic Energy Community, and the European Economic Community, and subsequently as the Parliament of the European Union (1992). During the past two decades its powers increased with each EU treaty (Collins *et al.* 1998). The EP thus transformed quickly from a symbolic assembly meeting once a year into a fully-fledged parliament, comparable to and in some respects, notably policy influence, more powerful than a national legislature (Scully 2000; Corbett *et al.* 2007; Ringe 2009).

### Powers of the European Parliament

The European Parliament was first given budgetary powers in two consecutive treaty amendments in 1970 and 1975, allowing it to decide together with the Council of Ministers on the non-compulsory expenditure in the EU budget. This parliamentary veto power was recently extended to the adoption of the entire EU budget when the Lisbon Treaty (or the Treaty of the European Union (TEU) and the Treaty of the Functioning of the European Union (TFEU)) came into force in 2009. In 1979, the EP became the first directly elected international assembly. While hitherto appointed by their national legislatures, its members were for the first time elected in each EU member state by their countrymen. Yet, the EP had only rather symbolic legislative power under the so called 'consultation procedure' at that point. This changed with the introduction of the 'cooperation procedure' and the 'assent procedure' in the Single European Act (1987)[2], the 'codecision procedure' in the Treaty of the European Union (1992), and the extension of the latter procedure to ever more areas in the Amsterdam (1999), Nice (2003) and Lisbon (2009) treaties, which gradually placed the EP on an equal footing with the Council of Ministers in shaping most EU legislation (Hix 2002b).[3] Under

---

2.   The 'cooperation procedure' gave the EP the right to reinstate its opinion in a second reading. A rejection of a legislative proposal by the EP at that point required a unanimous Council to over-rule. The cooperation procedure originally covered legislation related to the creation of the Single Market but its scope of application was severely limited in favour of the codecision procedure in the Amsterdam Treaty, while the Lisbon Treaty abolished it altogether. The assent procedure gave the EP veto powers but it was applied only to very few policy areas, such as the signing of international treaties. In the Treaty of Lisbon, it was renamed as 'consent' and brought together with the 'consultation' procedures under the 'special legislative procedure'. This special procedure now applies to legislation in some areas of justice and home affairs (policy cooperation, approximation of criminal laws and regulations), budget (own resources, multiannual financial framework, etc.), taxation (harmonisation of legislation on indirect taxation, movement of capital to or from third countries), environmental measures of a fiscal nature, research and technological development programmes, combating discrimination, social security and social protection for workers, membership of the Union and methods of withdrawal from it.

3.   After prolonged debates, most scholars have converged on the opinion that the EP and the Council of Ministers now stand on equal footing under the codecision legislative procedure. The study of Hagemann and Høyland (2010) presents an exception. They show that the Council of Ministers has the advantage of a conditional agenda-setting power due to the change of the majority threshold needed to adopt legislation in the Parliament between the first and the second reading of the

the codecision procedure, to adopt EU legislation both institutions have to agree on the legislative proposals of the European Commission (which retains the exclusive right to initiate legislation) at first reading, second reading or, if not possible, in a Conciliation Committee (see König *et al.* 2007). Until 2009, the codecision legislative procedure was applied primarily to legislative proposals related to the functioning of the EU internal market, but also to proposals in the areas of transport, environment, employment and social policy, culture, public health, consumer protection, industry, and development. With the Lisbon Treaty ratification, the powers of the EP increased further as the codecision procedure became the 'ordinary legislative procedure' of the EU and was extended to more than twice as many policy areas (forty new articles), including agriculture, fisheries, structural funds, international trade, and some justice and home affairs policies.[4] The parliamentary legislative empowerment has important, yet largely unexplored, substantive implications because the adopted EU legislation is binding in all member states and supreme to national law.

Finally, while the EP does not select a government as national parliaments do and is not subject to a governmental vote of confidence (Huber 1996), it exerts executive oversight over the European Commission. The Commission is the closest equivalent to an executive in the EU and while its members are selected by the member states, they are expected to be politically neutral and act in the general interests of the Union and its citizens. Besides its powers to censure the European Commission as a whole, introduced already in the Treaty of Rome (1958)[5], since the Amsterdam Treaty the appointment of the President of the European Commission and the College of Commissioners must be approved by the EP (European Parliament 2009b, Rule 105 and Rule 106).[6] The EP has been able to strategically use its power of investiture and censure of the European Commission to further its institutional goals (for an overview see Judge and Earnshaw 2008; see also Gabel and Hix 2002; Hix *et al.* 2004, 2006b).[7]

---

codecision procedure. Thus, the authors argue that the Council still holds the upper hand in the legislative process even under codecision.

4. The 'ordinary legislative procedure' is outlined in Article 294 of the TFEU, which is also ex Article 251 of the Treaty establishing the European Community (TEC).

5. The European Parliament can censure the European Commission as a whole by double majority, consisting of an absolute majority of its votes and two-thirds of the votes cast (Article 234 TFEU, ex Article 201 TEC).

6. The European Parliament elects the EP President suggested by the Council of Ministers by a majority of its component members. If it fails to approve the candidate, the Council, acting by a qualified majority, has to suggest a new one within a month. The EP also gives its consent on the final composition of the Commission (Article 17, point 7 TEU).

7. The European Parliament has been creative in inventing other mechanisms to exercise scrutiny over the European Commission. For instance, recent research demonstrates that opposition parties in the EP use the written parliamentary questions to specific Commissioners as a means of exerting inexpensive executive scrutiny (Proksch and Slapin 2011).

### *Jurisdictions and role of the committees*

Overall, most of the parliamentary time is spent on drafting legislation. Therefore, this book concentrates on studying how the internal EP organisation allows the Parliament to fulfil its legislative tasks and influences the character of legislation it endorses. A substantial part of the EP's legislative tasks are performed in its committees (Collins *et al.* 1998: 6). The standing committees have been developing dynamically both in terms of number and jurisdictions. Most of the parliamentary powers of delay and amendment are exercised there (Corbett *et al.* 2005). Still, the EP committees have no gate-keeping powers in the broad sense. They have to examine the legislative proposals of the European Commission that are referred to them by the plenary, while their own legislative initiatives require the permission of the EP Conference of Presidents and have no binding effect. The parliamentary committees do not control their own timetables or redraft governmental bills, nor do they have the right to remove committee members. In that sense, they may seem to have little say in the legislative process. However, there is a broad agreement in the literature that after a legislative proposal has been made by the Commission, it is in the EP committees that the '[p]arliament's positions are in most cases decided in practice', before the plenary stage (Mamadouh and Raunio 2003: 348; see also Bowler and Farrell 1995; McElroy 2001; Neuhold 2001; Kreppel 2002a; Hix *et al.* 2003b; Ringe 2005, 2009). Hence, the standing committees have agenda-setting power within the EP. Furthermore, it seems uncommon for committee proposals, i.e. their reports based on the Commission's legislative initiatives, to be heavily modified or rejected in plenary (Bowler and Farrell 1995: 234). Overall, the EP committees are more powerful than their counterparts in most European national parliaments and more like the committees of the US Congress (Ringe 2009).[8]

Besides their procedural empowerment, the EP committees are attributed further importance owing to the functional needs of the EP. Due to its limited staff and the need to obtain supermajority support to pass legislation in the late stages of the codecision procedure[9], it is largely the internal EP organisation that shapes the extent to which it can effectively exploit its resources and institutional powers and, thus, exert influence in the EU framework (Bowler and Farrell 1995). Committees' structural resources and members' specialisation facilitate drafting well-informed parliamentary legislative proposals, thus improving the standing of the EP in the legislative negotiations with the Council of Ministers and the European Commission (Raunio 1997; Mamadouh and Raunio 2003). The success of the EP in the EU legislative process is also contingent upon its ability to build stable majorities. '[T]he bargaining power of the EP is weakened by its internal

---

8.  See Mamadouh and Raunio (2003) for a comparison of the powers of the EP committees *vis-à-vis* those of their counterparts in the national parliaments of EU member states.

9.  The EP needs an absolute majority of its members to amend the Council common position or to reject it in the second reading of the codecision, or the ordinary, legislative procedure (Article 294 TFEU).

division' (Kreppel 1999: 523). For instance, the adoption of the EP draft reports by the other EU legislative institutions under the cooperation procedure was shown to be positively correlated with the internal EP unity (Kreppel 1999). Before being able to act as a unitary agenda-setting actor (Tsebelis 1994, 1995), the EP has to manufacture this unity (Bowler and Farrell 1995). This is a difficult task in a legislature composed of more than 150 national party delegations sitting in seven party groups (during the 6th parliamentary term). In fact, no single party group has ever held an absolute majority of parliamentary seats. The lack of a stable majority in the EP means that a majority needs to be crafted anew for each legislative proposal. While this has not been a problem when it comes to institutional matters such as increasing the parliamentary powers, on which most members of the European Parliament (MEPs) tend to agree, it is more challenging when voting on substantive policy issues. The committees serve as arenas for developing majorities on a case by case basis, thus solving collective action problems (Neuhold 2001).

Overall, informational and majority formation needs are strongly pronounced in the EP. This is due to the organisational set-up of the EU, the EU legislative procedures (especially the codecision procedure), and the functions, powers, and resources allocated to the EP. The EP committees are meant to facilitate solving these collective action problems, and, thus, improve the ability of the Parliament to develop a strong majority position and uphold it in its negotiations with the Council of Ministers. It is this central legislative role of the parliamentary committees that is examined in this book. Rather than outlining how the EP committees have gained power and come to play such an important legislative role – a topic discussed at length elsewhere (Whitaker 2011) – this book focuses on the way and extent to which the committees are able to shape the parliamentary legislative positions.

## Research questions

Although there is a broad agreement that committees, in general, facilitate coping with collective action problems that emerge in the larger legislative chamber, there is no consensus in the theoretical literature on how specialisation and majority formation occur. Following the main current theories of legislative organisation – the distributive (Ferejohn 1974; Shepsle and Weingast 1987; Weingast and Marshall 1988), informational (Gilligan and Krehbiel 1987, 1989a, 1990; Krehbiel 1991), and partisan (Kiewiet and McCubbins 1991; Rohde 1991; Cox and McCubbins 1993, 2007) rationales – specialisation takes place due to, respectively, the special interests of legislators; a committee-plenary arrangement serving information needs of the plenary; and party interests and incentives. There are also alternative views on how collective support for committee legislative proposals is obtained on the floor: via logrolls between committees composed of homogeneous high-demanders (Shepsle and Weingast 1987; Weingast and Marshall 1988); due to acceptance by non-committee members of committees' expert legislative proposals reflecting the median preferences on the floor (Krehbiel 1991); or as a result of the majority party holding the majority of seats in both committee and plenary

(Cox and McCubbins 1993, 2007). The ultimate answers to the questions of what factors cause specialisation and majority formation in a parliament lie in establishing who controls the legislative committees, i.e. whether they are bodies 1) independent of the larger chamber serving the special interests of their homogeneous preference-outlying members; 2) agents of the chamber serving its information needs; or 3) tools of political party leaders for controlling party members.

This book addresses these questions in the study of the EP by confronting adapted distributive, informational and partisan rationales in the study of its legislative organisation and legislative output. The broad research question is: *do the EP committees serve special interests outside the Parliament, the interests of the overall plenary or those of the working majority party group (coalition)?* Since none of the three theoretical rationales is expected to provide the full answer, the primary aim is to establish the conditions under which the predictions of each rationale hold. Hence, this book examines at the micro level: when and why are legislative committees dominated by legislators with special interests (distributive rationale), by specialists producing outcomes favouring the plenary median (informational rationale), or by loyal members of the working majority party group (coalition) (partisan rationale)? These questions could not be fully answered if we did not ask in this book also the following: *under which conditions are the EP committees successful in determining the parliamentary legislative positions?*

The answers to these questions are expected to be multifaceted. A multitude of national and supranational actors are now affected by the legislation that the EP adopts and, hence, are interested in shaping it by influencing MEPs. These actors include national and regional constituencies, national political parties, European party groups, various national and supranational interest groups and organisations, the Commission and the Council of Ministers, etc. It has become difficult to determine the extent to which each of these impacts on the work of the EP. As the EP position is negotiated and largely formed already at the committee stage of the parliamentary legislative process (Corbett *et al.* 2005: 348), the EP committees have become the main subject of internal and external pressure.

## Contributions

This book has three main goals. The first one is to add to the empirical literature on the EP. Although most of the parliamentary work is conducted in the standing committees, yet despite their functional importance, they have not received much attention, unlike the historical development, institutionalisation, and operation of the EP (Fitzmaurice 1978; Westlake 1994; Kreppel 2002b; Corbett *et al.* 2003b; Judge and Earnshaw 2003, 2008; Kreppel 2003; Rittberger 2005; Corbett *et al.* 2007). The focus of most extensive research has been, firstly, the parliamentary level of influence in the EU legislative process and, secondly, party politics in the EP. The former stream of research has investigated the changes in the legislative power of the EP *vis-à-vis* the European Commission and the Council of Ministers following treaty modifications of the legislative procedures (Tsebelis 1994; Scully 1997;

Kreppel 1999; Crombez 2000; Crombez *et al.* 2000; Rittberger 2000; Tsebelis and Garrett 2000; Corbett 2001; Tsebelis *et al.* 2001; Hix 2002a; Kreppel 2002b; Shackleton and Raunio 2003; Kasack 2004; Selck 2004; Selck and Steunenberg 2004). The latter has examined more generally the European party groups (Hix and Lord 1997; Raunio 1997; Kreppel 2002a; Hix *et al.* 2007; McElroy and Benoit 2007, 2010) and, in particular, party group cohesion (Brzinski 1995; Faas 2003), voting behaviour (Attina 1990; Hix 2001, 2002b, 2004; Han 2007), coalition formation (Kreppel and Tsebelis 1999; Kreppel 2000; Hix *et al.* 2003a; Kreppel and Hix 2003) and dimensions of political contestation (Noury 2002; Thomassen *et al.* 2004; Hix *et al.* 2006a; McElroy and Benoit 2007; Hix and Noury 2009; Schmitt and Thomassen 2009; Voeten 2009; Proksch and Slapin 2010). These studies have reached near consensus that, not unlike in national legislatures, decision-making in the EP is largely orchestrated by competitive political parties and is structured mainly along the traditional left-right ideological dimension.[10]

However, there is much less scholarly understanding of the legislative organisation of the EP which has precipitated and, in turn, been shaped by this left-right party politics. Why is the EP organised into committees? Initially, research on the EP committees was mostly descriptive in character (Kirchner 1984; Corbett *et al.* 1990, 1992, 1995, 2000, 2003a, 2003b, 2005, 2007; Judge and Earnshaw 1994, 2003, 2008). Only recently have the EP committees become the subject of analytical research. Owing to their increasing importance, they have become the target of a growing number of empirical studies on the composition and assignments of the standing committees (Bowler and Farrell 1995; McElroy 2001, 2006; Whitaker 2001, 2011), the composition of the conciliation committee (Rasmussen 2008), the allocation of legislative reports (Kreppel 2002a; Mamadouh and Raunio 2002, 2003; Kaeding 2004, 2005; Benedetto 2005; Hausemer 2006; Høyland 2006a; Lindberg 2008; Yoshinaka *et al.* 2010), the voting behaviour within committees (Settembri and Neuhold 2009), the voting behaviour of committee versus non-committee national party contingents (Whitaker 2005, 2011), and the role of committees in formulating legislators' individual policy preferences (Ringe 2005, 2009). However, the results obtained by the various studies and their explanations are often inconsistent and it is not clear what lies behind these differences. This book aims to resolve this puzzle by revisiting previous research with the intention of identifying the underlying pattern among different empirical findings. For this purpose, the effect of alternative explanatory factors under varying conditions is examined.

This leads to the second contribution this project envisions, which is to add to the theoretical literature on legislative organisation. Instead of delving into the building of a new theory with a scope bounded to the unique characteristics of the

---

10. Examining the dimensionality of conflicts portrayed in parliamentary speeches, Proksch and Slapin (2010) showed that these speeches reflect party positions on EU integration and national issues rather than left-right divisions. This finding contrasts with the conclusions of studies based on roll call votes and expert surveys.

EP, in this book I employ the highly elaborate existing theories and seek to enhance their general applicability. The large similarities between the US Congress and the EP allow for exploring the congressional theories in a new context upon an informed adaptation. Furthermore, although in the US Congress the explanatory power of the three main approaches over time has been extensively evaluated, the present study further allows for analysing their propositions in a different institutional setting. The EP offers a new arena for testing the congressional theories and establishing the conditions under which each of them holds. This project aspires to bring new insights to the theoretical literature on legislative organisation by identifying these conditions.

Last but not least, in this book I hope to shed more light on how effective the legislative organisation of the EP is in facilitating the legislative work of the EP and enhancing the extent to which it can uphold its position in the negotiations with the Council of Ministers. How well informed or ideologically biased is the legislation committees produce? When is their organisation and work guided by consensual and when by majoritarian principles? How representative are they of the heterogeneity of interests present both inside and outside the plenary?

In Chapter Two, an overview of the main current theories of legislative organisation is provided. Upon scrutinising their applicability to the present study, the distributive, informational and partisan congressional theories are adapted to the context of the EP. The following three chapters address the research questions empirically. They include statistical analyses, the data for which has been collected from primary sources, including the EP website, the EP Legislative Observatory, parliamentary minutes and debates, etc. These analyses are complemented by semi-structured interviews with MEPs and EP staff members, which I conducted in the period January – February 2008. The focus in Chapters Three and Four is on those aspects of the committee organisation that are most consequential for the type of legislation committees adopt and the support this legislation attracts. These are committee assignments and the allocation of legislative tasks to individual committee members. In Chapter Five, the level of success of committee legislative proposals on the floor is examined, i.e. the legislative impact of committees. They are briefly outlined below.

Firstly, the rationale behind committee assignments is examined in Chapter Three. Following the distributive, informational and partisan rationales, I analyse whether the committee assignment system is designed to 1) serve special interests outside the EP, 2) bring informational benefits to the plenary or 3) promote partisan interests. The expectation is that there will be a difference in the extent to which each theoretical rationale is able to explain committee assignments among the different types of committee. This expectation is justified by the significant differences among committees in their power and the type of legislative output most often associated with the policy areas in which they operate (distributive or regulatory). The hypotheses are examined on a representative sample of different types of committee, using an original data set of MEPs' profiles and committee assignments in the first term of the 6th European Parliament (2004–2007) that was compiled for the purpose of this book.

Secondly, in Chapter Four the rationale behind the distribution of the most influential legislative tasks among committee members is studied, i.e. the allocation of legislative reports to individual committee members who are charged with drafting the parliamentary positions on proposals originating from the European Commission. This chapter aims to evaluate the impact of external incentives arising from the EU institutional context on the internal organisation of the EP. This is done by comparing the determinants of the allocation to committee members of legislative tasks (writing committee reports) on policy proposals falling under the codecision legislative procedure, which grants the EP and the Council of Ministers equal legislative powers, and policy proposals falling under the consultation procedure, which presents the EP with consultative powers only. The assumption is that there is higher competition both between party groups and individual legislators for codecision than for consultation reports. Combined with the informal EP rules on report allocation, this provides incentives for strategic behaviour of party group leadership in report allocation, which is expected to lead to different explanatory factors behind the allocation of consultation and codecision reports. The analysis is performed on data on the codecision and consultation reports allocated in the period 2004–2007.

Thirdly, in Chapter Five the focus is shifted away from the study of the committees' organisation to the study of their legislative impact. How successful are the committee reports on the floor? That is, to what extent does the plenary draw its legislative positions on the basis of committees' proposals by taking on board proposed committee amendments and rejecting alternative amendments by party groups and groups of legislators? Given the *EP open amendment rule* in committee and plenary, committees are expected to be more successful if the legislators drafting their reports have no special outlying interests, have relevant expertise, and are affiliated with big party groups. Additionally, committee-plenary interactions are expected to be heavily influenced by the newly arisen and increasingly common decision-making mode in secluded informal trilogue meetings outside the committees between a limited number of members of the EP, the Council of Ministers and the European Commission. In particular, the committees' impact is likely to be substantially weakened when an informal early agreement is reached with the Council of Ministers. Hence, the variation examined in this chapter is between the committees' legislative impact in the cases in which no informal agreement was reached and the cases in which one was reached (the so called 'fast track legislation'). For the purpose, an original data set of all codecision dossiers that had first reading during the 6th EP (2004–2009) has been compiled.

A common theme to these three empirical chapters is that the aim in all of them is to discover the conditions under which the distributive, informational or partisan rationales explain the organisational aspects of the EP. For the purpose, hypotheses are offered in each chapter about the extent to which these theories are expected to hold in different circumstances, namely across different types of committee (Chapter Three), levels of power of the EP (codecision versus consultation) (Chapter Four), and formal and informal intra- and inter-institutional rules (Chapter Five). The goal is to establish how the explanatory power of the alternative theories varies with context. Other empirical aspects of the committee organisation could have been examined to that effect too, such as the appointment of committee chairs and vice-chairs, MEPs' own initiative reports, or questions to the European Commission. Such aspects, however, do not directly affect the content of committees' legislative proposals and their success on the floor. The empirical examinations are chosen in view of the main topic of this book – the legislative role and power of the EP committees.

In Chapter Six, I summarise and discuss the main findings of the analyses in the preceding three chapters and their substantive implications. This is followed by a discussion of the contribution of this book to the theoretical literature on legislative organisation in Chapter Seven, which culminates in the formulation of new theoretical propositions. In the concluding Chapter Eight, suggestions are offered for future research and a brief overview is provided of the main achievements of the book.

# chapter | theoretical framework on
# two | legislative organisation

In this chapter, the notion of legislative organisation is defined, followed by a discussion of the importance of committees in modern legislatures. Subsequently, the main current theories of legislative organisation borrowed from the congressional literature are presented and their applicability to the study of the European Parliament is examined. The discussion demonstrates that these theories are not pure types and none of them alone seems to explain or fit the EP case perfectly. Therefore, they require certain adaptation to the context of the EP before being able to inform hypotheses in its study. Furthermore, they need to be examined in conjunction due to their quasi-competing, quasi-complementary character. The modified assumptions of the distributive, informational and partisan theories as applied to the EP case are specified at the end of this chapter. This is followed by a brief overview of the derived alternative hypotheses about committees' organisation and legislative output, which are developed and tested in the subsequent empirical chapters.

## Legislative organisation and committees

In this book, the definition of legislative organisation proposed by Strøm (1998: 23) is used: 'Legislative organization defines a set of privileged groups, subgroups of parliamentarians with specific powers, and a set of procedures that specify the powers of these sub-groups with respect to the functions that legislatures perform'. There are important implications of a legislature's organisation, which affects not only the representativeness and quality of legislation, but also the relative power of the legislature in the governing process (Krehbiel 1991: 2).

It is common for legislatures to organise themselves into specialised committees. A 'legislative committee is a sub-group of legislators, normally a group entrusted with specific organizational tasks' (Strøm 1998: 22). Committees are a central element of legislatures in democratic systems globally (Longley and Davidson 1998: 1; Shaw 1998: 225). They are considered to be one of the most important organisational elements of modern parliaments (Copeland and Patterson 1994; Mattson and Strøm 1996: 303; Strøm 1998: 21; Longley and Davidson 1998) and exist in most countries, irrespective of whether they have separated-power or parliamentary political systems (Shaw 1998: 225). Committees serve as the main arenas for organising legislation and parliamentary oversight of the government (Longley and Davidson 1998: 2).[1] They enhance legislative effectiveness by

---

1.    Even the British House of Commons, which is controlled by a single-party government, has been

encouraging the division of labour (Mezey 1979: 64), and hence, specialisation and expertise, which is needed for the legislature to cope with highly technical and complex problems (Judge and Earnshaw 2003: 177). Furthermore, legislative committees are an organisational design solution to the collective action problems that are likely to arise on the floor, such as the formation of coalitions and required majorities (Weingast and Marshall 1988).

Overall, it is believed that committees increase the efficiency of parliaments via the distribution of tasks to legislators, enabling the latter to specialise in certain areas and more easily reach agreements on the floor. However, there is a disagreement in the theoretical literature on how specialisation and majority-formation is induced by committees.

**Existing theories and their fit to the case of the European Parliament**

All theories of legislative organisation discussed below are derived from the literature on the US Congress. 'The focus on parliamentary committees was, in the political science tradition of the past 50 years, almost exclusively an American one.' (Longley and Davidson 1998: 3). Thus, research on the EP has relied mostly on the theories developed in the context of the US Congress. There are a large number of similarities between the Congress and the EP in that both legislatures operate in separated power systems and bicameral institutional environments, have highly developed committee systems and their members are subject to weaker partisan control than the members of the national parliaments of most EU member states. However, the EP functions in a unique multi-national, multi-partisan environment as opposed to the two-party, single-national Congress (Hix *et al.* 1999: 3).[2] One could argue that the US Congress operates in a similar multi-state environment where both local and national parties play a role and do not always have the same interests. While these similarities 'make for relatively easy comparison, [...] it is perhaps the differences, such as the lack of an electoral connection, that will be most instructive' (McElroy 2007b: 446). These differences can serve as a basis for discussion of the general explanatory power and adaptability of the congressional theories to a new context. Such a discussion is offered in the following pages, examining the fit of the congressional theories to the case of the EP.

In particular, this book employs the distributive (Shepsle and Weingast 1987; Weingast and Marshall 1988), informational (Krehbiel 1991), and partisan (Cox and McCubbins 1993, 2007) congressional rationales. They have dominated the recent debate in the US literature and their propositions set the agenda for research beyond the Congress (Mattson and Strøm 1996; Strøm 1998: 56; Longley and Davidson 1998; Shaw 1998). All three are positive theories of legislative

---

subject to recent institutionalisation through the use of specialised committees (Norton 1998).

2.  See McElroy (2007a) for a discussion of the similarities and differences between the EP and the US Congress.

organisation assuming rational individual behaviour and endogenous institutional structures, procedures and rules, determining the distribution of legislative powers and hence shaping policy (Strøm 1998).

Before the emergence of these theories, broader micro and macro organisational approaches prevailed in the study of legislative organisation. Some background information on these approaches can help the reader better understand not only their limitations and the subsequent shift toward a new theoretical framework, but also the foundations of this new framework. Furthermore, the micro and macro approaches have already been applied in a unique in-depth study of the institutional development of the EP and its party system by Kreppel (2002a). Therefore, they will be briefly presented below before embarking on the discussion of theories this book employs.

### *Older macro and micro theoretical approaches*

The macro approach is largely developed by Polsby (1968). It treats internal organisational change as a consequence of changes in the external environment. The institutional adaptation to increased powers and workload is expressed in improved organisational efficiency, which is associated with collective benefits. Furthermore, 'the cost of *not* adapting to environmental changes is essentially institutional failure and eventual replacement' (Copeland and Patterson 1994: 152–3; Kreppel 2002a: 15).

The micro approach, in contrast, offers individual level explanations. It holds that organisational adaptation driven by external environmental changes reflects the preferences of rational actors within the organisation. The internal organisational changes mirror the self-interest of actors. Not collective benefits, but rather empowerment of the majority to the disadvantage of the minority is expected (Cooper and Young 1989; Gamm and Shepsle 1989; Binder 1996). Perhaps the most prominent application of the micro model is offered by Mayhew (1974) in his book *Electoral Connection*. He claims that the primary goal pursued by legislators is re-election, which guides their behaviour within the legislature.

These two approaches have often been tested in combination (Fenno 1973; Cooper and Young 1989; Gamm and Shepsle 1989; Sinclair 1989). Particularly relevant for this book is the work of Kreppel (2002a, 2003), who applies both approaches in studying the development of the EP and its transnational party groups. She describes how the EP has strategically used its internal Rules of Procedure upon each European Community (EC)/EU treaty revision in order to increase its powers *vis-à-vis* the Council of Ministers and the European Commission. The underlying logic is that for the EP to be able to affect the distribution of inter-institutional power, it first has to create an appropriate internal working environment (Kreppel 2003). Kreppel (2003) concludes that once the initial collective striving of legislators for parliamentary institutional empowerment is satisfied, they turn to improving the internal parliamentary efficiency and to fulfilling their policy goals via rule revisions. Thus, internal reforms are no longer egalitarian but rather benefit the big party groups (Kreppel 2002a: 7).

The macro and micro approaches, especially when combined, introduce a time dimension into the study of committees. However, their application has some drawbacks, too. Although prescribing a logical and chronological response of internal legislative organisation to external environmental changes, the macro approach, as Kreppel (2002a: 15) holds, 'lacks [...] a successful method of predicting the character of the internal reforms that result from these external demands'. This makes the approach difficult to test or falsify. For instance, bearing in mind the numerous EC/EU treaty changes, any revisions of the EP committee system could be attributed to external environmental shocks regardless of the direction of these revisions. The micro approach, on the other hand, does not specify how the character of the self-interest of legislators will affect legislative organisation. Thus, there is a need to theorise about the implications of this self-interest – be it re-election, certain policy or office – for institutional set-up.

Indeed, the micro and macro approaches can bring valuable insights to the study of legislative organisation. Following the macro approach, specialisation and consensual majorities are expected to occur because the legislative organisation is conducive to acquiring collective benefits and improving organisational efficiency. However, it is not clear how the pursuit of these collective benefits is induced. Alternatively, the micro approach predicts that specialisation will occur only if it goes along with the individual legislators' goals, i.e. if it is a part of their self-interest. Legislators that are part of the majority will pursue their own interests at the expense of the minority. The micro approach, however, does not specify when specialisation is in one's interest, or how individual legislators come together to form a majority.

Overall, it seems necessary to go beyond the micro and macro approaches in order to understand the underlying mechanisms driving legislative organisation. Rational choice approaches may provide the solution. They allow the formulation of falsifiable hypotheses about when committees serve the collective parliamentary interests or the interests of particular subgroups within the parliament. While specialisation is essential in rationally structured organisations (Gilligan and Krehbiel 1989b: 295), the congressional theoretical approaches presented below suggest different mechanisms through which committees precipitate specialisation (Mattson and Strøm 1996: 251; Strøm 1998). Furthermore, although all these approaches envision an important role of committees in finding majority support for legislation, there is no consensus on how a majority is formed, be it via 1) committees' logroll (Shepsle 1978); 2) a special committee-plenary relationship (Krehbiel 1991); or 3) control of committee work by the majority party (Cox and McCubbins 1993, 2007).

Maltzman (1997: 31) offers a comprehensive summary of the distributive, informational and partisan approaches, reproduced here in Table 2.1. I now turn to the detailed presentation of the congressional rationales, followed by a discussion of their applicability to the study of the EP. The important differences between the US Congress and the EP that affect the applicability of each congressional theory to the new case are *italicised* in the text.

*Table 2.1: Summary of Models*

| Model | Independent-Committees | Party-Dominated | Chamber-Dominated |
|---|---|---|---|
| Committee's principal | Outside of the institution | Party caucus | Chamber |
| Policy-making process | Logroll/distributive | Political | Informative |
| Rationale for Model | Individual members secure re-election by appeasing outside constituencies. | Electoral outcomes depend primarily upon party record. Members seek to belong to majority party. | Chamber's informational and workload needs. |
| Committee role | Facilitate trade | ??????[b] | Provide information/ expertise |
| Committee assignments | Self-selecting | Party-selection | Chamber-selection |
| Committee preferences | Committee median distinct (biased) from the chamber as a whole[a] | Committee party contingents are either aligned or more extreme than their caucus. | Committee's median reflects floor's median; committee and floor have similar distribution. |
| Types of expected procedures | Rules (such as *ex post* veto) that ensure committee autonomy | Rules that ensure and encourage committee compliance with preferences of majority caucus. | Rules that encourage members to specialise. Rules will not infringe on chamber median's capacity to shape outcomes. |
| Committee behaviour | Committee members act without regard to the preferences of their colleagues. | Committee members act in a manner consistent with the preferences of their caucus. | Committee members act in a manner consistent with the preferences of the chamber's median. |
| Principal author(s) | Weingast, Marshall, Baron, Ferejohn, Shepsle, Mayhew | Cox, McCubbins, Kiewiet | Maas, Krehbiel, Gilligan |
| Antecedents | Wilson (1885), Goodwin (1970), Lowi (1969) | Silbey (1967), Brady (1973), Hasbrouck (1927), Rohde (1991) | Fenno (1966), Robinson (1963), Cooper (1970), Alexander (1916) |

[a] The bias can result from committees whose members have preferences that are homogeneous or bipolar extremes.
[b] There is no apparent reason why bipartisan policy outcomes have been created.
*Source*: Table taken in its entirety from Maltzman (1997: 31).

### Distributive rationale

Some of the most prominent contributions to the development of the distributive rationale include the work of Shepsle and Weingast (1987) and Weingast and Marshall (1988). This rationale requires the existence of heterogeneous policy preferences and multidimensional policy choices in a legislative chamber. It holds that nearly autonomous committees composed of relatively homogeneous high demanders are formed or, in other words, '[c]ommittees are decentralised decision-making units composed of those legislators with the greatest stake in their jurisdictions.' (Weingast and Marshall 1988: 147). Self-selected members seek re-election from their constituencies and have personal notions of good policy. They seek to further their special interests in the politics of distribution, and pursue their previously fixed preferences favouring specific policy. These preference outliers are delegated significant influence to capture the legislative process. Members work under non-restrictive committee rules and restrictive amendment procedures in the chamber, which facilitate logrolling and gains from trade (exchange of influence). Furthermore, adjustment mechanisms assure continuity of committees' powers. The preset structural arrangements make continuous strategic interactions possible. Committees serve to minimise the transaction costs of trade and assure equilibrium in logrolling at the plenary stage. In the end, each legislator reaps disproportional benefits on issues he or she values as being of high importance. Due to the scarcity of resources, the self-interested policies pursued by legislators, geared towards their constituencies, may lead to inefficient outcomes and reduced aggregate welfare as a result of excessive spending.

Although not explicitly, this rationale suggests that committees promote specialisation and information accumulation as they are composed of members with special interests in the respective legislative area, who thus potentially have relevant knowledge and experience. However, there are no incentives for the committee members to draft policies following the interests of the plenary median or to sincerely share their information on the floor. Legislative majority is formed on the basis of logrolls, or trade, between committees, i.e. non-committee members support a committee's legislation in an area they do not strongly care about in exchange for support for their own legislation. Repeated interactions promote cooperation and discourage defection.

### Applicability to the European Parliament

The application of the distributive rationale to the study of the EP committees is problematic for a number of reasons. Most importantly, *the special interests of MEPs linked to their electoral constituencies and the motivation of legislators to appeal to their constituencies are not as clear as in the case of the US Congressmen.* While in the congressional context there are well defined regional electoral districts, in the European elections the electoral constituencies and their characteristics are not so easily identifiable, especially given that there is a weak regional division in many EU member states. Perhaps it is then more appropriate to conceive of MEPs' countries as their constituencies (Ringe 2009: 95). However, while MEPs' national interests most likely do shape legislators' policy preferences, research has shown that the main dimension of conflict in the EP is the traditional left-right dimension and not the national one (Raunio 1997; Kreppel and Tsebelis 1999; Hix 2001; Thomassen *et al.* 2004; Hix *et al.* 2007; Van der Brug and Van der Eijk 2007). Additionally, not only is the notion of a constituency unclear (McElroy 2007b), but also the electoral connection of MEPs to their constituencies is generally weak. One reason for this is the 'second-order' character of the European elections (Reif and Schmitt 1980; Van der Eijk and Franklin 1996; Marsh 1998; Hix and Marsh 2007; Van der Brug and Van der Eijk 2007)[3], in which voters are not presented with clear and coherent alternative European programmes (Ferrara and Weishaupt, 2004) but rather vote on the basis of policy and party concerns back home.[4] Thus, the work of MEPs within the EP has, at best, only a marginal effect on electoral outcomes, which weakens their incentives to please electoral constituencies with certain performance in the EP. Instead, MEPs are highly dependent on their national parties for re-election due to the prevalent closed list, proportional representation electoral systems and centralised candidate selection rules of the European elections in most of the member states (Hix 2004). Thus, the MEP candidates can rarely appeal directly to a certain territorially defined electorate and often do not have incentives to do so (Whitaker 2001; Mamadouh and Raunio 2003; McElroy 2007a). That is not to say that MEPs do not have special interests. Alongside the priorities of their countries, such interests can be linked to their previous or current membership in a certain interest group, which reflects the views of legislators themselves. Thus, examining the effect of potential high demand of some legislators for particularistic policy, and hence the predictions of the distributive rationales, should not be discarded solely on the grounds of a weak electoral connection to narrowly defined territorial constituencies.

Another objection to the application of the distributive rationale in the present study is the fact that *the EP's jurisdictions are limited to a narrow range of policy areas, most of which have no pronounced distributive implications*. Indisputable exceptions are areas like agriculture and fisheries, the operation of which entailed only limited parliamentary discretions until recently, i.e. until the Lisbon Treaty brought these policies under codecision (the 'ordinary legislative procedure') in 2009.[5] This claim, however, is not entirely justified since there are many other

---

3. Specifically, the broadly supported predictions of the 'second order' model are that, as opposed to national elections, the turnout at the EP elections will be lower, large parties will do worse and small parties better, and the parties in government will suffer losses.

4. Yet, research findings show that political parties without a clear stance on the EU suffer electoral losses at the EP elections (Ferrara and Weishaupt, 2004) and parties which place 'high quality' candidates on their EU electoral ballot are rewarded by voters (Hobolt and Høyland 2011).

5. The requirement of EP approval of the EC/EU budget introduced in the 1970s gave the EP some control over the Community funds. However, these powers were limited until the Treaty of Lisbon (2009) as the Parliament had a say only over the non-compulsory spending of the EC/

policy areas that are linked to distributive outcomes of the adopted legislation, such as industry, employment and social policies, and environment.

A third objection to the application of the distributive rationale is that *the self-selection of MEPs to their preferred committees is not always possible due to the strong proportionality principal in the EP.* Committee seats are first divided among party groups in proportion to their number of members. Within each group, individual seats are assigned to legislators based on the sizes of their national party delegations within the group. Thus, it is improbable that committees will be composed of homogeneous high demanders because their membership is likely to reflect the plurality of partisan, ideological and national interests in the overall plenary. Reaching an outlying unitary committee position, with which to trade with the other committees in logrolls, is therefore difficult. So, the distributive theory may not be equipped to explain how majority is formed in the EP. These concerns, however, are subject to empirical evaluation and do not constitute established facts.

Similarly, the theory *fails to account for the appearance and influence over committee members of cohesive European party groups.* Yet, not much research has been done on the degree to which party groups shape the structure, division of tasks and output of committees.

Finally, *the EP committees have not been granted restrictive rules and all the legislation in the EP goes through an open amendment rule in the plenary.* Indeed, this clearly reduces the potential for logrolling and particularistic policies but it is less clear if it eliminates these practices altogether.

For these reasons, the application of the distributive theory to the study of the EP is largely contested, especially given that the main underlying assumptions of a strong electoral connection of legislators to narrowly defined territorial constituencies has no firm grounds in the EP context. Yet, to test this theory here we only need to show that MEPs' behaviour can be driven by the pursuit of particularistic policies. The source of their policy interests is of secondary importance. For instance, the special interests of legislators for certain policy could arise from their interest group ties. While interest groups do not necessarily influence the electoral fortunes of legislators in a similar fashion as in the US Congress, they may nevertheless improve the re-election chances of legislators or expand their career options outside politics. Making a justifiable assumption about the source of legislators' special interests is sufficient to utilise the predictions of the theory in informing the hypotheses of the study.

---

EU, including expenses on structural funds, internal policies, and administrative costs. Thus, the EP had no influence over the amount devoted to compulsory spending, meant to fulfil treaty obligations, which included the funding of agriculture, external relations, aid to member states, and a part of the EU development aid.

## *Informational rationale*

The informational rationale offers quite a different explanation for the existence of strong legislative committees. It has been developed by Krehbiel (1991), while previous contributions include those of Austen-Smith and Riker (1987), Gilligan and Krehbiel (1987, 1989a, 1990), and Austen-Smith (1990). The informational rationale underlines the uncertainty about the link between legislative decisions and policy outcomes in a setting without a majority party, which legislators can mitigate through policy specialisation (Strøm 1998: 26). In order to acquire information, the legislature creates institutional incentives for its members to pursue specialisation and share information sincerely with the chamber. These incentives include certain structural resources and parliamentary rights, which are needed to stimulate the building of expertise, information sharing even between legislators with competing distributive interests, and the reconciliation of individual interests with collective goals. Committee formation is driven by the need to bring collective benefit from specialisation to the legislature as a whole. Committee members have heterogeneous policy preferences and are easily able to become specialists at a relatively low cost. They reflect as closely as possible the diversity within the chamber, or more specifically the median policy preference on the floor. As committees are microcosms of the chamber, their legislative output is ideologically balanced. Seniority rights are observed because 'stable assignments enable members to invest time and energy in acquiring expertise in their policy areas and building up personal networks' (Strøm 1998: 40). Deliberation and communication as a whole are means of aggregating and disseminating information about the relationship between policies and their outcomes. Delegation is a means of production, not of allocation. The outcomes are of collective benefit, namely informed decision-making in the plenary, and, hence, improved standing of the legislature *vis-à-vis* the executive.

To summarise, collective information is accumulated as a result of committees being composed of members who can easily become specialists due to their background, and who, subsequently, are given incentives to share their knowledge with non-committee members. Majority is formed around the expert legislative proposals coming from committees, as they reflect the policy preferences of the median member in the overall chamber.[6]

---

6. The process of information-sharing between committee and non-committee members is similar to the one Ringe (2009) proposes in his 'policy preference coherence' model. The main difference lies in the way legislators' policy preferences are aggregated. According to the informational model of Krehbiel (1991), the committee position is adopted on the floor because committees are microcosms of the larger chamber and strongly represent the preferences of its median member. In contrast, Ringe suggests that it is within political parties that committee information and policy preferences transfer to non-committee members, shaping plenary decisions.

*Applicability to the European Parliament*

The informational theory can be applied more readily in the EP context for a number of reasons. There is a pressing need for information in the EP due to its limited staff and resources as compared to the European Commission and the Council of Ministers. Furthermore, there is high uncertainty about the impact of European policies, many of which are not based on existing legislation.

Nevertheless, this theory also does not encompass the whole range of influences that have shaped the EP committee system. Once again, *the appearance and consolidation of European party groups and their influence over committee work is not accounted for*. Since MEPs are in practice allocated to committees by party groups, expertise may not always be the main determinant of committee membership. In addition, previous studies have shown that seniority is not a strong predictive factor of committee assignment (Bowler and Farrell 1995). *Turnover rates in the EP have been traditionally high* and most commonly MEPs have not served on the same committee for more than 10 years (Mamadouh and Raunio 2003).

As a whole, however, the informational theory has strong potential to explain the legislative organisation of the EP, although it does not explain the formation of influential European party groups. An explanation for that is sought in the partisan theory instead.

**Partisan rationale**

The party dominance rationale takes a different perspective and looks at the influence parties have over committees (Kiewiet and McCubbins 1991; Rohde 1991; Cox and McCubbins 1993, 2007). Legislators seek re-election, which is conditional upon not only their own merits but also the collective reputation of their party. In order to improve this reputation, members delegate to party leaders the rights to assure party cohesion around common policy objectives via giving them the monopoly over the allocation of office positions and resources, although that limits members' individual powers. Party leaders utilise committees to discipline party members in order to bolster the collective party reputation with the electorate and thus increase the number of party seats in the next parliamentary term. Rules and procedures are designed in a way that leads to differential empowerment of the majority party, and no procedural changes are expected if there are no changes in the sizes of parties between parliamentary sessions (Cox and McCubbins 1997: 1380). The theory stipulates that the majority party largely controls the committee assignment, and, hence, legislators seek to belong to it. Committee proposals consequently reflect the position of the majority party, which dominates committee agenda, while the minority party uses the plenary as an arena to make amendments.

The partisan rationale is not concerned with the informational needs of the plenary, and, thus, makes no explicit predictions about the way expertise is accumulated. Implicitly, party members will specialise in certain areas to fulfil the collective party need of information.[7] Furthermore, since the allocation of committee positions serves as a means for party leaders to discipline party members, the theory suggests that legislators will obtain seats on the committees whose work they care most about in exchange for their party loyalty. Majority in committee and plenary is formed by the majority party, while the minority party is largely isolated from the legislative process.

*Applicability to the European Parliament*

The EP is more complex than the Congress because *the MEPs are influenced by political parties operating at two levels – national and European.*

On the one hand, MEPs depend on their national parties for re-election, as national parties place them on the electoral list in the nation-wide elections to the EP. Thus, at least in theory, the electoral fortune of most MEPs depends on whether they represent their national parties' policy interests in the EP. Hence, the policy interests of MEPs are often shaped not by the specificities of their regional electoral districts but by national party leadership. In this respect, *the electoral dependence of legislators on their national parties is much stronger than in the case of the US Congress,* where parties affect the re-election of congressmen only to the extent that collective party reputation contributes to an individual's re-election chances. However, arguably *the reputation of national parties with the electorate is not strongly affected by the performance of their members in the EP,* as the European citizens tend not to be interested in the decision-making within the EP and even the overall legislative process in the EU. Therefore, it is not so much the reputation of their national parties that MEPs are interested in, but rather the support of their national party leaders to put them back on the electoral list. There is, however, a further complication in the application of the partisan theory, which is that *national parties are themselves not interested in, or have not developed a systematic way of controlling, the daily work of their members within the EP* as they have limited resources. They are more concerned with national politics and the performance of the national government at the European level. Arguably, with the EP empowerment, the policy positions of MEPs have started to affect national parties back home. The EU policies the EP adopts can restrict the policy choices available to national political parties and a disagreement between a party's MEPs and MPs can harm the party reputation among voters (Whitaker 2011: 51; Kiewiet and McCubbins 1991). Given the general detachment of national parties from decision-making within the EP, though, it is the members of the national

---

7.   Ringe (2009) suggests mechanisms via which parties facilitate the informational needs of the legislature. His theory states that policy positions are 'party-based in the sense that joint partisanship promotes and facilitates the creation of policy agreement through information provision from experts to nonexperts' (2009: 9). Hence, he sees no conflict between strong informational committees and the realisation of party policy goals. Ringe's predictions are evaluated in light of the findings of the book in the concluding chapter.

party delegations within the EP that monitor each other and make sure that the party delegations follow the policy lines favoured by the party leadership back home (Scully 2001; Whitaker 2011), explaining the high cohesion of national party delegations within the EP. National party delegations are more cohesive than party groups as is evident from roll call votes (Hix *et al.* 2007).[8] When it comes to the legislative organisation of the EP, according to some studies, national party delegations, and not party groups, have arguably the biggest say on committee assignments (Kreppel 2002a; Mamadouh and Raunio 2003). Such an application of the partisan rationale obviously deviates from the original theory describing behaviour in a bipartisan legislature. Nevertheless, it links the legislative behaviour of parliamentarians to the policy objectives and organisational structure of the parties that elect them to the EP.

On the other hand, while they have no control over the electoral process, *the European party groups control committee assignments and the allocation of legislative tasks and resources within the EP.* It is difficult for non-attached members to get a seat on their preferred committee and it is very rare that they hold high parliamentary positions such as president, vice-president, chairman, or vice-chairman. Thus, MEPs are dependent on their national parties for re-selection, but on their European parties for their office within the EP.

Additionally, while the Congress is a bipartisan legislature, *the EP is characterised by a multi-party group, multi-national party environment.* In order to pursue the policy goals of their national parties, MEPs need a way of obtaining majority support for their policy positions. According to the partisan rationale, the majority party forms the majority in the Congress. However, *no national party delegation or European party group has ever held the majority of seats within the EP.* In fact, even the biggest national party delegations within the EP (e.g. Christian Democratic Union, Germany; Socialist Party, France; Conservative Party, UK) held no more than between twenty and thirty seats out of 732 in the sixth EP term (2004–2009). At different times, the largest party group has been the European People's Party (EPP)[9] or the Socialist Group in the European Parliament (PSE), but they never obtained an absolute majority of the seats. Thus, *there is no party or party group in the EP corresponding to the majority party in the US Congress.* Alternatively, the majority party referred to in the partisan

---

8.   Hix *et al.* (2007: 132–145) demonstrated that when the MEPs' national party delegations and European party groups disagree, members are more likely to vote with their national party delegation in the respective roll call votes. In a recent article, though, Coman (2009) found that the opposite becomes more likely as the ideological distance between the two principals increases. Furthermore, his study shows that MEPs from the new Central and East European EU member states are more likely to side with their European party groups. However, his findings are based on the analysis of only a sample of votes in which the national and European groups held different positions.

9.   The EPP was named Group of European People's Party (Christian Democrats) (EPP-ED) in the 6th EP due to its expanded membership.

rationale can be conceived of as the working majority party group (coalition) in the EP. While there is no stable coalition in the EP, for the partisan rationale to be applied, a working majority coalition can be operationalised as the coalition that could be formed between the biggest party group at the time and its most likely coalition partner group. National party delegations are not big enough to form a sustainable coalition by themselves. The ideological position of a coalition partner group should be close to that of the working majority party group for the partisan rationale to apply, as it is ideological proximity that predisposes to the pursuit of common policies. A majority coalition could be formed for purely organisational purposes, such as controlling the allocation of parliamentary resources and office. The grand coalition often formed in the past by the two biggest party groups on the centre-left and centre-right in the EP can be seen as a procedural coalition, incongruent with the predictions of the partisan rationale that exacts intra-party cohesion and inter-party conflict. However, Hix *et al.* (2007) argue that EPP and PSE used to vote together more often than they do nowadays not due to purely organisational purposes but because their ideological positions used to be much closer before the British Conservative and Unionist Party joined EPP. With the divergence of the two biggest groups in the past two parliamentary terms, the EPP-ED and PSE have started voting together less and less often. Today, the applicability of the partisan theory is growing due to the increasing party group cohesion and inter-group conflict. Roll call vote analysis shows that EPP-ED and PSE are voting together with the Group of the Alliance of Liberals and Democrats for Europe (ALDE), who are situated between their ideological positions on the traditional left-right spectrum, increasingly more often than with each other (Hix *et al.* 2007).

To sum up, the partisan theory as it stands is not directly applicable to the EP context. However, it can be applied after modifying the underlying assumption about legislators' motivation, linking the policy goals of national parties and party groups and redefining the majority party in the Congress as the working majority party group (coalition) in the EP. Indeed, these are substantive modifications. Yet, the general logic behind Cox and McCubbins' theory (1993, 2007) forms the basis for the theoretical innovation proposed here.

## Adapted theoretical framework and research design

As should have become clear from the presentation above, none of the three approaches alone perfectly fits to and can fully explain the EP case. However, instead of rushing into theory-building, creating a combined model or an utterly new one, a better contribution to the comparative study of legislative organisation can be offered by adapting and testing the highly developed existing theories of legislative organisation and evaluating the pros and cons of testing them beyond the congressional setting. Thus, in this section I turn to adapting the distributive, informational and partisan congressional theories to the context of the EP, specifying the revised assumptions and outlining the derived new hypotheses about legislative organisation and committees' legislative impact. The latter are developed and discussed in detail in the following empirical chapters. Clear patterns emerging from the results of the empirical analyses are used to develop new theoretical propositions for future research in Chapter Seven.

Before adapting the congressional theories to the EP, it is important to note that there is a substantial disagreement in the congressional literature itself about the extent to which these theories are distinct, exclusive or complementary. There exists an irreconcilable conflict between the supporters of the distributive, informational and partisan legislative approaches. Empirical evidence has shown that each of them can be useful in explaining the rationale behind the existence of committees and the purpose they serve, and there has been no agreement so far on which of them best accounts for the legislative behaviour of congressmen in committees. It is difficult to separate the rationales as they are not mutually exclusive: 'in spite of their distinct labels, theories of legislative organisation are more like hybrids than purebreds' (Krehbiel 2004: 127); they are 'partly competing and partly complementary' (Strøm 1998: 25). Scholars have come to the near consensus that 'no one model fully captures the role performed by congressional committees' (Maltzman 1997: 2) and '[e]ach of these committee models provides partial explanation of the committee system as a whole, but none fully captures every committee's responsiveness to its full range of political forces' (Campbell and Davidson 1998: 130). Although the rationales are not exclusive, they cannot be merged as they rest on different assumptions about the dimensionality of the policy space and actors' interests. Hence, they lead to distinct predictions with regard to causal mechanisms that are not necessarily associated with distinct empirical outcomes. Therefore, they must be considered simultaneously to capture not only the array of alternative determinants of a certain feature of legislative organisation but also the underlying causal mechanisms. While indeed in some cases one theory may be better equipped than the others to explain a certain outcome, in general the three approaches are rather complementary.

What the distributive, informational and partisan theories share is that all three are positive theories of legislative organisation, and as such they are based on rational choice assumptions. These include assumption of *rational individual behaviour*. However, all three theories make different assumptions regarding the self-interest of legislators, who are constrained in pursuing their preferences by the organisational framework in which they are situated. Yet, as the second assumption holds, the *institutional structures, procedures and rules are endogenous* rather than exogenously fixed. Hence, those actors who manage to organise and shape them would in turn be allocated disproportionately more power and resources over time than the rest, and their preferences will be favoured in institutional outcomes. A further assumption is that the informational and partisan rationales share *uni-dimensional policy space*, while the distributive theory assumes *multi-dimensional policy space*

In the two sub-sections below, the assumptions of the congressional approaches regarding the dimensionality of the policy space and the legislators' interests are adapted to the case of the EP. Thereafter, the alternative predictions they lead to are discussed. They are summarised in Table 2.2, inspired by Maltzman (1997: 31).

*Assumptions regarding the dimensionality of the European Parliament policy space*

The European party groups are organised on the basis of party families. They consist of national party delegations with similar policy positions and any group switching is driven primarily by the pursuit of minimal intra-group policy incongruence (McElroy and Benoit 2010). Thus, socialist national party delegations join the PSE, Christian democratic parties join the EPP-ED, liberal parties join ALDE, etc. Party groups give their members voting instructions and are more cohesive in roll call votes than national delegations. This holds true especially for the bigger party groups and the pattern has strengthened over time (Raunio 1997; Kreppel and Tsebelis 1999; Noury 2002; Thomassen *et al.* 2004; Hix *et al.* 2005; in Carrubba *et al.* 2006).

As a result of the party politics in the EP, numerous studies based on voting patterns (Raunio 1997; Kreppel and Tsebelis 1999; Hix 2001; Hix *et al.* 2007) and survey data (Thomassen *et al.* 2004; McElroy and Benoit 2007) have found that the main dimension of conflict in the EP is the traditional left-right dimension. It explains about 90 per cent of the roll call votes in the 5th EP, where the explanatory power of the second identified dimension, which broadly speaking captures the positions on European integration and government-opposition conflicts (Hix *et al.* 2006a), has diminished from 20 per cent to only 8.5 per cent since the first directly elected Parliament (Hix *et al.* 2007). This reveals that voting in the EP has become increasingly one-dimensional, which fits with the assumption of unidimensionality of both the informational and partisan rationales.

*Assumptions 1a and 1b (informational and partisan rationales): There is one main policy dimension of conflict in the European Parliament.*

However, the single left-right dimension simplifies the reality by collapsing the existing multiple policy dimensions into a single one. Although it is a practical solution to plotting the preferences and positions of legislators on numerous issues, it inevitably leads to a loss of information regarding the stances of legislators on any given policy. While two MEPs may have the exact same left-right position, they may have utterly different views on issues in a certain policy area. Representing legislators' views on a multi-dimensional space avoids having to assume that there is a link between, for instance, one's views on environment and employment. What the distributive theory adds to that is the assumption that in the multi-dimensional policy space some legislators care strongly about one policy area, while others care about another policy area, which allows for logrolling and gains from trade. It is perfectly conceivable that the legislators in the EP sitting in the committee on agriculture are more interested in farming than others. While this is indeed a special committee, a similar argument can be made about the committee on environment, employment, civil liberties, industry, etc. This leads to the assumption of the distributive theory regarding dimensionality of the policy space in the EP:

*Assumption 1c (distributive rationale): There are multiple policy dimensions of conflict in the European Parliament.*

Table 2.2: Adaptation of the distributive, informational and partisan theories to the case of the European Parliament

| | Distributive rationale | Informational rationale | Partisan rationale |
|---|---|---|---|
| Underlying assumption | MEPs seek particularistic policy (policy serves their special interest). | MEPs seek 'good' European policy (policy outcomes favour their countries and the EU as a whole). | MEPs seek party policy (policy outcomes preferred by their national party leadership and promoted by party groups). |
| Committees serve | Special interests outside EP | EP plenary | Working majority party group (coalition) |
| Committee assignments | Self-selection | Plenary selection | Party group selection |
| Committee composition | Homogeneous members with special interests. | Heterogeneous members who can easily become experts. | Loyal party group members. Over-representation of the working majority party group (coalition) on important committees. |
| Committee preferences | Outlying from the plenary median. | Balanced around the plenary median. Committee distribution similar to plenary distribution. | Close to the median of the working majority party group (coalition). |
| Legislative tasks allocation | High-demanders self-select on tasks addressing their special interests. | Experts undertake important tasks. | Loyal party group members undertake important tasks. Over-representation of majority coalition in the allocation of important tasks. |

| | Distributive rationale | Informational rationale | Partisan rationale |
|---|---|---|---|
| Committees' legislative output | Outlying from the plenary median. | Close to the plenary median. | Close to the median of the working majority party group (coalition). |
| Rules and procedures | Protect committee output from plenary amendments. Facilitate logrolling between committees. | Encourage members to specialise. Rules do not infringe the plenary median's capacity to shape outcomes. | Ensure the congruence of committee output with the preferences of the working majority party group/coalition. |
| Majority formation | Logroll between committees. | Consensual majority cutting across ideological cleavages around the committee report. | Minimal winning majority coalition of party groups based on ideological proximity. |
| Policy | Outlying: reflects special interests | Median of the EP plenary | Median of the working majority party group (coalition) |
| Results/outcome | Subtotal, disproportional benefits | Collective benefit | Working majority party group (coalition) benefits |

*Note*: Table inspired by Maltzman (1997: 31).

## *Assumptions regarding the MEPs' goals*

To explain the creation and organisation of legislative committees in the EP, which are not mandated by the EU treaties, it is crucial to understand what motivates MEPs. Yet, the distributive, informational and partisan theories differ in their assumptions about the specific character of the self-interest that drives individual rational behaviour. It has been suggested that legislators primarily seek re-election (Mayhew 1974; Shepsle 1978; Cox and McCubbins 1993), policy (Shepsle 1978; Cox and McCubbins 1993), 'good' policy or information (Krehbiel 1991), or office (see Hix *et al.* 1999). The attractiveness of the different assumptions can vary with systemic characteristics such as the electoral system, the institutional framework, the strength of political parties, etc., or there may be no systematic pattern in individual interests as they depend mostly on the individuals themselves rather than the external environment. Furthermore, it is difficult to identify one most important goal pursued by all legislators as one and the same individual may have multiple interests, and these may change over time. 'It is not necessary to assume that legislators pursue only one goal and one goal alone. At different points in time, in response to different stimuli, and faced with different strategic choices, politicians may favour one set of goals over others' (Hix *et al.* 1999: 13). For instance, as the EP powers increase, more and more MEPs are likely to pursue a career in the EP, which would be expressed in a greater number of legislators with re-election and office goals (see Scarrow 1997). The EP would also offer them more and more opportunities to pursue certain policy goals.

Nevertheless, for any theorising, hypothesis building and empirical testing to be possible, the reality needs to be simplified by making clear assumptions about the incentives driving individual behaviour. The distributive, informational and partisan theories rely on different assumptions about this main incentive driving legislative behaviour: the search for particularistic policy favouring legislators' special interests, 'good' policy or well-informed policy, and coherent party-prescribed policy, respectively. Below, each of these assumptions is adapted to the EP case, accompanied by a discussion of the predictions it leads to (see Table 2.2).

## *Adapted assumption of the distributive rationale: MEPs seek particularistic policy*

The main assumption of the distributive rationale (Shepsle and Weingast 1987; Weingast and Marshall 1988) following the work of Mayhew (1974) is that legislators seek re-election. Thus, committees serve special interests outside the legislative body, where those interests are generally linked to the electoral constituencies of committee members. What is important, though, is not so much the source of legislators' special interests but that those interests are homogenous within a committee, i.e. that all members in a committee pursue similar policy. Furthermore, this policy should differ across committees to facilitate logrolling between committees in the multi-dimensional policy space, where each committee is concerned primarily and nearly exclusively with its own policy area. In other words, gains from trade become possible where each committee supports the policy proposals of other committees in exchange for support for its own policy proposals.

As discussed above, the re-election motive is not very strong in the EP, which is characterised by high turnover of its members. More importantly, the electoral connection of MEPs to their regional constituencies is weak, and in some cases non-existent, due to the lack of strong regional divisions in many EU member states. Differences between member states do not seem to systematically determine MEPs' specific policy preferences, either, as decision-making in the EP is based not on national but on ideological lines. Assuming that MEPs' national parties determine their special interests may seem like a good alternative. However, political parties usually promote coherent programmes of policy issues. Thus, party members are bound together by the overall party programme, while they may have divergent stances on particular policy issues. For instance, in a Christian democratic party one member may have extreme views on environmental protection as compared to the party median member, while another member may have extreme views on industry protection. Thus, party affiliation is not always a good proxy for individual policy preferences. Alternatively, MEPs' individual special interests may reflect their personal ideological convictions or the policy preferences of the interest groups they have been affiliated with. Many legislators have certain interest group ties.[10] MEPs may have different motivations to pursue the policy preferences of interest groups. For instance, interest groups can enhance legislators' re-election chances by increasing their national party's vote share (e.g. trade unions), or improve their future career prospects outside politics (e.g. industry and business groups). They may also address issues that legislators genuinely care about. Thus, instead of discarding the distributive rationale on the grounds of a weak or unclear electoral connection to territorial constituencies, it is assumed here that *interest group ties reflect the underlying special interests of MEPs and affect their policy choices.*

*Assumption 2a (distributive rationale): MEPs seek particularistic policy in line with their special interests.*

The predictions regarding the EP's legislative organisation following this assumption are akin to those in the original congressional theory. Similarly minded policy-driven MEPs self-select to the same committees, which target their special interests. This leads to the formation of homogeneous preference-outlying committees in the EP, which promote policies away from the ones preferred by the plenary median. In the distribution of legislative tasks within the parliamentary committees, the high-demanders self-select on tasks addressing their particular interests. Such members pursue within their committees and on the floor particularistic policy, which favours their own special interests, in order to signal their

---

10. Legislators' links to interest groups can increase the access of these groups to decision-makers – an indicator used in the lobby literature to measure pressure groups' influence (Austen-Smith 1993; Bouwen 2004).

support for certain groups external to the EP. While they are bound to have more expertise than the average member in the respective policy area of their interest, they have no incentives to share their information sincerely with the plenary. Majority in the plenary is formed on the basis of logrolling between committees. The resulting policies are different from the ones preferred by the parliamentary median and, hence, lead to disproportional benefits for some legislators and subtotal overall outcomes.

*Adapted assumption of the informational rationale: MEPs seek 'good' European policy*

The main assumption of the informational theory is that legislators want re-election and, hence, seek 'good' policy because they are judged by their electorate on the basis of policy outcomes and not just their policy positions. A direct translation of this assumption to the EP context is justifiable. *Because EU policy-making is rarely advertised to voters, they are likely to judge MEPs (and their parties) based on the outcomes of EU policies rather than on their policy positions while in the EP.* Furthermore, political parties fail to offer voters clear choices regarding European issues in the elections to the EP (Van der Eijk and Franklin 1996). Therefore, irrespective of their political affiliation, most legislators are likely to be guided by the pursuit of 'good' European policy (or non-policy).

*Assumption 2b (informational rationale): MEPs seek 'good' European policy.*

Based on this assumption, the informational theory offers clear predictions of how the EP would be organised, not unlike those of the original theory. Legislators have a strong notion of what constitutes a good policy outcome. Yet, they have little information on how to achieve it due to the high uncertainty about the link between policies and outcomes, aggravated by limited EP staff and resources. This uncertainty motivates MEPs to specialise in committees in order to gather information on the possible consequences of European policies on the domestic level. To promote information gathering and its sincere communication to the plenary, the parliamentary rules would assure that committees are staffed with heterogeneous members with relevant expertise.[11] Yet, members with outlying interests can serve the informational needs of the plenary only if counterbalanced within a committee. So, the median policy positions of the EP committees and the plenary should overlap. Given the absence of a majority party in the EP, majority in plenary is expected to emerge around the expert committee reports representing

---

11. Legislator's expertise generally stems from their educational and professional background or parliamentary seniority. Their special interests, or more specifically their interest group ties, can be seen as another source of expertise. However, links to interest groups are also associated with strong preferences for particularistic policy, which the plenary median does not share. This creates incentives for committees to make outlying policy proposals and not to share sincerely their information with the plenary. As a result, the latter is likely to incur high costs of amending committee proposals rather than derive informational benefits. Expertise can only become a collective good if balanced committee membership is assured.

the plenary median. As the committees are microcosms of the Parliament, the legislation they propose is seen as information-driven rather than ideologically biased, and as promoting the public rather than the private good. Thus, it can easily attract support from both sides of the left-right political spectrum, which facilitates the building of large consensual majorities.

### Adapted assumption of the partisan rationale: MEPs seek party policy

The main assumption of the partisan rationale is also that legislators seek re-election. While congressmen are elected directly by their constituencies in clearly defined territorial districts, their electoral chances still depend on the collective reputation of their parties. Therefore, they delegate the power to allocate legislative positions and resources to party leaders, who can use this power to discipline members, i.e. to reward or to punish them for their level of party loyalty. This is the mechanism via which party cohesion and reputation are enhanced.

It is not just collective party reputation with the electorate that influences the electoral chances of legislators in the EP. MEPs depend on their national party leadership for their re-selection to the party list in the next elections and even for their position on that list in closed list electoral systems. Therefore, they have strong incentives to fulfil their national parties' preferences while in the EP in order to keep the support of party leadership.

> Assumption 2c (partisan rationale): MEPs seek party policy (preferred by their national party leadership and promoted by party groups).

This assumption is qualified due to the presence of both national parties and European party groups in the EP, which necessitates further adaptation of the partisan theory. Consequently, the predictions about the EP's legislative organisation also deviate from the original ones. This is discussed below.

Firstly, the pattern of interactions between legislators and their electoral political parties in the EP are very different from the US Congress. Driven by the same policy incentives, members of national party delegations appear to vote quite cohesively in the Parliament. Thus, it seems that national parties retain a high level of influence over the voting behaviour of their MEPs and, arguably, European party groups look highly cohesive only when their constituent national party delegations decide to vote together (Hix 2002b: 696). Yet, it is well known that national parties back home do not engage in monitoring their MEPs on a frequent basis due to their limited resources and other (more) salient domestic matters. Furthermore, in the 2006 MEP Survey (Farrell et al. 2006a) only 36.1 per cent of MEPs said that they met their national party executive at least once a week, while 37 per cent reported they did so at least once a month (see Table 2.3). This level of contact seems unlikely to be sufficient for party leaders back home to control the positions of their MEPs on each and every legislative EP vote. Therefore, it is argued here that *national party leaders judge party members based on policy outcomes rather than policy positions*. This diverges from the prescriptions of the original partisan theory but is necessary to make the link between the MEPs' legislative behaviour and the preferences of their national parties back home.

*Table 2.3: Frequency of the MEPs' contact with their national party executive*

| At least once a week | At least once a month | At least every three months | At least once a year | Less often/ No contacts | N |
|---|---|---|---|---|---|
| 36.1 % | 37.0 % | 18.3 % | 4.3 % | 4.3 % | 208 |

*Source:* 2006 MEP Survey (Farrell *et al.* 2006a).

Secondly, in comparison to the congressional majority party, even the biggest party delegations within the EP are negligibly small. Therefore, *to achieve the policy outcomes preferred by their party leadership back home, national party delegations have incentives to coalesce with similarly minded delegations into party groups.* Thus the formation of the European party groups can be explained. Besides the policy influence benefits, however, the association into party groups implies also certain power concessions. As the EP has gained more powers, the party groups have consolidated their influence over the parliamentary organisation and work (Kreppel 2002a). Perhaps this explains why, although national parties' interest in their members' work may have increased, studies find weak or no evidence of their enhanced control over the allocation of committee positions and tasks over time (Yoshinaka *et al.* 2010; Whitaker 2011). National party delegations have conferred and inadvertently lost to party groups the power to assign parliamentary office and resources, which the latter use to enhance group cohesion. However, while the partisan theory prescribes that this cohesion will be induced by rewarding and punishing party members for their level of loyalty to the party leadership, it is unreasonable to expect such disciplining by party group leaders in the case of the European party groups which are staffed with heterogeneous national parties coming from members states with sometimes differing national interests. Therefore, *it is moderate positions close to the party group median rather than their own positions that group leaders can promote to increase their group's cohesion and, hence, impact on policy.* [12] This is another modification of the partisan theory necessary to adapt it to the EP context.

Finally, party groups in the EP need to form coalitions with one another to assure majority in the plenary because no group holds the majority of parliamentary seats. There is no stable majority coalition, either, and one has to be formed anew for every single issue. This difference from the bi-partisan Congress calls for yet another modification of the partisan rationale. Specifically, it is necessary to *equate the role played by the majority party in the Congress to the role of the working majority party group (coalition) in the EP.* Following the logic of the

---

12. In practice, these two ideal points are likely to overlap because the party group leadership is generally composed of representative of the national party delegations within a group.

theory, the working majority is likely to be formed by the biggest party group in the Parliament at the time (referred to as the working majority party group from here onwards) and the minimal number of party groups closest to its position in the uni-dimensional policy space, which is required to assure a majority in plenary. This proximity in the policy space is needed due to the assumption that MEPs seek to further the policy interests of their national parties as closely as possible. That would be compromised if they were in a coalition with party groups pursuing substantially different policies. Therefore, minimal winning coalitions of party groups based on ideological proximity are expected to control the parliamentary decisions. Additionally, the committee assignments and composition, the distribution of committee tasks, and the legislative output of committees are expected to favour the working majority party group (coalition).

## *List of hypotheses*

Relying on these different assumptions, the distributive, informational and partisan theories lead to different predictions about the legislative organisation of the EP. The aspects examined in this book are 1) the committee assignments; 2) the allocation of committee legislative tasks falling under different legislative procedures (i.e. the assignment of individual rapporteurs to the drafting of codecision and consultation legislative reports); and 3) the success of committee reports on the floor depending on the profiles of individual rapporteurs who drafted these reports in committee. While the hypotheses of the three rationales related to each of these aspects are developed in the following three empirical chapters, they are briefly outlined below and listed in Table 2.4 to provide the reader with a map of the empirical content of the book.

According to the distributive rationale, committees serve the special interests of their members. Committees, and especially those operating in primarily distributive policy areas, are thus expected to be staffed with members with outlying preferences in a certain policy area. These preferences need to be homogeneous for the committee to be able to further the goals of its members. Subsequently, in the division of legislative tasks, members with special interests would self-select in the drafting of legislative reports that address their interests. However, this is expected to be possible only for the less important reports, i.e. reports falling under the consultation procedure, for which there is less competition and less surveillance on behalf of party group leadership as to whether selected rapporteurs have outlying preferences or not. Finally, since there are no restrictive rules on amendment but rather any changes can be made to committee reports at the EP plenary stage, logrolls between committees are difficult to enforce. Therefore, it is expected that a committee will be less successful in having the plenary adopt its proposed amendments if the rapporteur has special interests. This is, of course, given that the legislation passes through the normal decision-making procedure and is not subject to an informal agreement with the Council of Ministers, struck outside the committee.

According to the informational rationale, the main role of parliamentary committees is gathering information on the link between policies and outcome, which they share sincerely with the plenary. Hence, committees are expected to be composed of MEPs who are or can easily become specialists in the respective policy areas, i.e. MEPs with previous experience in the committee area, for instance due to educational or professional background or parliamentary seniority. Members' affiliation to related interest groups can also serve as a source of expertise provided that the set of special interests in a committee is heterogeneous, so that outlying preferences are balanced. The most important legislative reports are then to be written by MEPs with expertise in the respective area. Finally, since committees are expected to have drafted expert legislative reports reflecting the views of the plenary median, proposed committee amendments would be more successful in the plenary if drafted by rapporteurs with relevant expertise.

According to the partisan rationale, the main role of committees is to increase group cohesion. This is achieved by providing the party group leaders with valuable seats and resources to allocate, which they can use to discipline group members. For instance, leaders can punish disloyal members by not assigning to them seats on powerful committees or on the committees they prefer, and vice versa. Furthermore, the majority coalition members are expected to be privileged in the seat assignment to powerful legislative committees and in the allocation of (important) legislative reports. Proposed committee amendments would tend to be rejected in plenary if the rapporteur of the respective committee report does not belong to the working majority party group (coalition).

The following three chapters constitute the empirical part of this book. The explanatory value of the distributive, informational and partisan rationales is tested in the study of the legislative organisation of the EP, by examining the committee assignments (Chapter Three) and the allocation of legislative tasks (reports) (Chapter Four). Subsequently, the rationales will be tested in the analysis of the legislative output of committees (Chapter Five).

*Table 2.4: List of the research hypotheses derived from the adapted theoretical approaches and tested in the empirical chapters*

| | Distributive theory | Informational theory | Partisan theory |
|---|---|---|---|
| Committee assignments | **H1**: The likelihood of being assigned to an interest-driven or mixed committee is increased by having relevant special interests, and the set of such interests is homogeneous. | **H2a**: The likelihood of being assigned to an information-driven or mixed committee is increased by having relevant expertise or parliamentary experience.<br>**H2b**: The likelihood of being assigned to a mixed committee is increased by having relevant special interests, and the set of such interests is heterogeneous. | **H3a**: The likelihood of being assigned to a powerful committee increases with party group loyalty.<br>**H3b**: The likelihood of being assigned to a powerful committee increases with party group and national party seniority. |
| Reports allocation | **H4a**: Having interest group ties decreases the number of codecision reports a committee member/ substitute is allocated.<br>**H4b**: Having interest group ties increases the number of consultation reports a committee member/substitute is allocated. | **H3**: Having committee-specific expertise increases the number of reports allocated to a committee member/substitute.<br>**H3a**: This effect is weaker in the allocation of codecision reports. | **H1a**: Membership in one of the three biggest European party groups – EPP-ED, PSE and ALDE – increases the number of codecision reports allocated to a committee member /substitute.<br>**H1b**: Membership in one of the three biggest European party groups – EPP-ED, PSE and ALDE – decreases the number of consultation reports allocated to a committee member/substitute.<br>**H2**: Party group disloyalty decreases the number of reports allocated to a committee member/substitute.<br>**H2a**: This effect is stronger in the allocation of codecision reports. |
| Plenary adoption of committee reports | **H2**: A committee report is less successful/subject to more changes in plenary if it has been drafted by a rapporteur with relevant special interests. | **H3**: A committee report is more successful/subject to fewer changes in plenary if it has been drafted by a rapporteur with relevant expertise. | **H4**: A committee report is more successful/subject to fewer changes in plenary if it has been drafted by a rapporteur affiliated to one of the three biggest party groups – EPP-ED, PSE or ALDE. |

# chapter three | the rationale behind committee assignment

A natural starting point in the study of legislative organisation is the committee assignment system. Although the committees can largely affect the type of legislation the European Parliament adopts, it is still not clear how representative they are of the overall Parliament. While proportionality to party groups is provided for in the EP Rules of Procedure (European Parliament 2009b, Rule 186, ex Rule 177), the latter assures neither that national party delegations and member states are proportionally represented, nor that committee composition reflects the diversity of policy preferences present in the plenary. Although party group leaders are the ones deciding on individual committee assignments, they may do so on the basis of MEPs' special interests, expertise, loyalty, seniority, or any combination of those, while at the same time being constrained by the wishes of national party delegations within their groups. Thus, it is difficult to discern what the main driving factor behind individual assignments is. This leads to the primary question of this chapter: what factors determine assignment to the standing committees of the EP?

As the 2006 MEP Survey shows, the most important factors affecting MEPs' committee assignments are their personal interests (54.7 per cent) and professional expertise (53.9 per cent), followed by the importance of issues the committee covers (50.2 per cent) (Farrell *et al.* 2006b). Nevertheless, Bowler and Farrell (1995) and McElroy (2006) concluded that committees reflect the ideological composition of the plenary, basing their conclusions on committees' party group composition and roll call votes (used as a proxy of ideology), respectively, thus downplaying the impact of MEPs' special interests on committee assignments, which they also observed. In contrast, this study argues that some committees are staffed with high demanders and preference outliers that could potentially drive policy outcomes away from the plenary median. As demonstrated below, party groups do not reward or punish members for their loyalty in the committee assignments but rather allow them to self-select based on their own special interests. This has broader implications for the informational role of the committees, party group cohesion and the representative role of the EP as a whole. It links to a series of more general questions, such as why do parliamentary committees exist, whose interests do they serve and what is their impact on policy? This chapter aims to contribute to our understanding of the organisational principles of the EP and the nature of the legislation that committees produce.

The basic hypotheses in the study, derived from the distributive, informational and partisan positive theories of legislative organisation, state that committees 1) serve interests outside the chamber, 2) bring informational advantage to the legislature as a whole or 3) serve party interests. A new classification of the EP committees based on their output and power is proposed, which allows for qualifying these hypotheses according to the type of committee. The hypotheses are tested on an original data set of all the MEPs in the 6th European Parliament collected for the purpose of this study.

On the following pages, an overview of the EP committee assignment system and committee composition precedes a review of relevant literature. Thereafter, the hypotheses are developed and the methodology of the empirical analysis of the study is outlined, followed by a presentation of the results. A discussion of the results and conclusions close the chapter.

## Overview of the committee assignment system and composition

There are twenty standing committees in the 6th EP. They differ in size, power and prestige and it is difficult to draw clear demarcations between their competences (Corbett *et al.* 2005). Various classifications of the congressional and EP committees have been offered. For instance, Bach and Smith (1988: 114) have divided the Congress into power and prestige committees, policy interests committees, and constituency-oriented committees. Adler and Lapinski (1997) alternatively have classified them based on the type of output they produce into 'private goods' providing, 'public goods' providing, and mixed committees (or policy committees reaching broad groups of constituencies). Similarly, Cox and McCubbins (1993) have differentiated between committees with targeted, uniform or mixed externalities. Specifically, the EP committees are classified by McElroy (2001) based on the level of competition for their seats and by Whitaker (2005) – following the lines of Cox and McCubbins (1993) – based on their relation to territorial constituencies.

While building on these classifications, a more comprehensive categorisation is proposed here dividing committees on two dimensions. Firstly, committees are classified based on their jurisdictions and output as stated in the EP Rules of Procedure (European Parliament 2007b, Annex IV), into: 1) information-driven with predominantly regulatory output, 2) interest-driven with predominantly distributive output, and 3) mixed ones. While the European Union has limited budget and ability to directly redistribute monetary resources, some of the policies it adopts clearly affect certain groups more than others, or even at the expense of others. As Majone (1996: 28) argued:

> [e]fficiency-oriented policies attempt to increase the aggregate welfare of society, while redistributive policies are designed to improve the welfare of one particular group in society at the expense of other groups.

For the purpose of classifying committees, a policy is considered distributive here if it affects specific constituencies or organised homogeneous interests outside the EP. Alternatively, if it has broader implications it is considered regulatory. Secondly, committees are differentiated into more or less powerful ones based on their influence over the EU budget and legislation (see Table 3.1). Thus, the Budgetary Affairs committee is classified as more powerful. So are the committees that in the examined period drafted the largest number of reports falling under the codecision procedure (see European Parliament 2004; Corbett *et al.* 2005: 132), in which the EP has equal legislative powers with the Council of Ministers.

Party groups and MEPs are aware of the different levels of influence of committees. When asked about the reasons for committee choice in his national party delegation, a member of PSE responded directly: 'We want the committees with most legislative power' (Personal interview 1, 27th February 2008).

A member of the EPP-ED gave a similar answer:

> Committees that do a lot of legislation are inclined to attract members I think generally [...] – codecision legislation. Consultation is not really legislation [...] because we give our opinion but it does not have to be taken on board by the Council of Ministers as you know, or the Commission. But in codecision the European Parliament's opinion must be accommodated. (Personal interview 2, 6th February 2008)

The sample studied here (highlighted in bold in Table 3.1) is chosen to cover different types of committee while focusing attention on the more powerful ones.

*Table 3.1: Classification of EP committees based on their policy output and power*

| | More powerful committees | Less powerful committees |
|---|---|---|
| Information-driven committees with predominantly regulatory output | • **Budget (BUDG)**<br>• **Transport and Tourism (TRAN)**<br>• **Internal Market and Consumer Protection (IMCO)**<br>• **Legal Affairs (JURI)** | • **Foreign Affairs (AFET)**<br>• Development (DEVE)<br>• International Trade (INTA)<br>• Budgetary Control (CONT)<br>• Constitutional Affairs (AFCO)<br>• Petitions (PETI) |
| Interest-driven committees with predominantly distributive output | • **Employment and Social Affairs (EMPL)** | • **Agriculture (AGRI)**<br>• Fisheries (PECH)<br>• Regional Development (REGI) |
| Mixed committees | • **Economic and Monetary Affairs (ECON)**<br>• **Environment, Public Health and Food Safety (ENVI)**<br>• **Industry, Research and Energy (ITRE)**<br>• **Civil Liberties, Justice and Home Affairs (LIBE)**<br>• Culture and Education (CULT) | • Women's Rights and Gender Equality (FEMM) |

### Committee assignment system

The majority of MEPs serve on one committee as full members and on another as substitutes. However, there is a variation between active and inactive members (Corbett *et al.* 2005). While some may serve on two, even three committees as full members, and as substitutes on more than one, others may not participate in any (usually the non-attached MEPs). Multiple memberships are possible because the number of available committee seats (861) exceeds the number of parliamentarians (732) and there are some small, rather technical committees, namely Budgetary Control, Women's Rights and Petitions, in which MEPs generally would not specialise exclusively. Officially, committee positions are assigned in a plenary vote every two and a half years. In practice, however, they are distributed before the plenary stage (Bowler and Farrell 1995; Hix *et al.* 2003b; Mamadouh and Raunio 2003). The only reference to committee assignment in the EP Rules of Procedure states that:

> Members of committees and committees of inquiry shall be elected after nominations have been submitted by the political groups and the non-attached Members. The Conference of Presidents shall submit proposals to Parliament. The composition of the committees shall, as far as possible, reflect the composition of Parliament. (*European Parliament 2009b, Rule 186, ex Rule 177*)

Seats are allocated to the EP party groups in proportion to their sizes in the plenary. Subsequently, the party groups decide on individual assignments taking into account the sizes and wishes of their constituent national party delegations. Upon deciding on individual assignments, the groups present the list to the plenary for a vote, at which point the plenary may reject the party groups' proposal should the suggested committee compositions not reflect sufficiently the composition of the EP. There has been no such precedent so far and the plenary vote has always been a formality. The interviews reveal some differences among the party groups in this selection process. In the big groups, once the seats are distributed among the national party delegations, individual seats are assigned within the delegations. The group leadership plays a decisive role in resolving conflicts between delegations, which are settled as package deals (Personal interview 3 with a PSE member, 12th February 2008). In the Liberal group (ALDE), there is 'a rule which says each national delegation shall be allowed one [committee seat], and then if there are any places after that, then they can have a second one' (Personal interview 4 with a member of ALDE, 13th February 2008). After members have expressed their wishes, 'the distribution itself is done more or less by the Bureau of the group' (Personal interview 5 with a member of ALDE, 13th February 2008). A Green group member states that 'it's more or less the individual interests that decide who is going to which committee' (Personal interview 6, 30th January 2008). As a whole, it seems that while the assignment process is more centralised in smaller groups, individual interests are aggregated in all groups.

*Table 3.2: Observed-minus-expected number of seats based on party group size in plenary, July 2004*

| | AFET | DEVE | INTA | BUDG | CONT | ECON | EMPL | ENVI | ITRE | IMCO | TRAN | REGI | AGRI | PECH | CULT | JURI | LIBE | AFCO | FEMM | PETI | TOTAL |
|---|---|---|---|---|---|---|---|---|---|---|---|---|---|---|---|---|---|---|---|---|---|
| EPP-ED | – | | | +2 | | + | – | – | | – | – | – | + | | | +2 | | | | | +1 |
| PSE | | + | | + | | | + | – | + | +2 | – | | – | | – | – | –2 | – | | | +1 |
| ALDE | | – | | + | | + | | | | | | | –2 | | | | +2 | | | | –1 |
| G/EFA | | | | | | | | + | | | | | | | | + | | | | + | +1 |
| EUL/NGL | + | + | | –2 | | – | + | + | –2 | | | + | + | | | – | | – | + | | +1 |
| IND/DEM | + | – | | – | | | – | + | | – | + | + | + | – | | | | + | – | | 0 |
| UEN | | + | | – | | | – | + | | – | + | – | + | + | + | | | + | | | 0 |
| na | – | | | | | | | –2 | | | | | | | | | | | | | –2 |
| Committee size | 78 | 34 | 33 | 47 | 35 | 49 | 50 | 63 | 51 | 40 | 51 | 51 | 42 | 35 | 35 | 26 | 53 | 28 | 35 | 25 | |

*Source:* Own calculations.

*Note:* The figures are rounded to whole numbers. Signs alone indicate a difference of one seat. Abbreviations: AFET: Foreign Affairs; DEVE: Development; INTA: International Trade; BUDG: Budgets; CONT: Budgetary Control; ECON: Economic and Monetary Affairs; EMPL: Employment and Social Affairs; ENVI: Environment, Public Health and Food Safety; ITRE: Industry, Research and Energy; IMCO: Internal Market and Consumer Protection; TRAN: Transport and Tourism; REGI: Regional Development; AGRI: Agriculture; PECH: Fisheries; CULT: Culture and Education; JURI: Legal Affairs; LIBE: Civil Liberties, Justice and Home Affairs; AFCO: Constitutional Affairs; FEMM: Women's Rights and Gender Equality; PETI: Petitions; EPP-ED: Group of European People's Party (Christian Democrats) and European Democrats; PSE: Socialist Group in the European Parliament; ALDE: Group of the Alliance of Liberals and Democrats for Europe; G/EGA: Group of the Greens/European Free Alliance; EUL/NGL: Confederal Group of the European United Left – Nordic Green Left; IND/DEM: Independence/Democracy Group; UEN: Union of Europe of the Nations Group; na: Non-attached members.

Table 3.3: Observed-minus-expected number of seats based on member state size in plenary, July 2004

| | AFET | DEVE | INTA | BUDG | CONT | ECON | EMPL | ENVI | ITRE | IMCO | TRAN | REGI | AGRI | PECH | CULT | JURI | LIBE | AFCO | FEMM | PETI | TOTAL |
|---|---|---|---|---|---|---|---|---|---|---|---|---|---|---|---|---|---|---|---|---|---|
| Austria | | - | - | | + | + | | | | - | 2 | - | | - | + | | - | + | | | 0 |
| Belgium | + | + | | - | | -2 | | | | 2 | + | - | | | - | - | | | | - | -4 |
| Cyprus | | | | | | | | + | | | | 2 | | | + | + | | + | + | | 4 |
| Czech Republic | - | - | - | + | + | - | + | - | + | | | + | - | - | - | | -2 | - | + | - | -4 |
| Denmark | + | + | + | + | + | | + | | + | + | | + | | + | + | + | | | + | | +1 |
| Estonia | + | - | | + | + | | - | - | + | + | | - | | - | + | -2 | + | -2 | - | | 5 |
| Finland | -2 | + | - | + | -3 | 2 | | -2 | + | 2 | | | + | - | 3 | - | -2 | -2 | + | -2 | 2 |
| France | + | + | 3 | + | -3 | -2 | -4 | - | + | - | | -2 | + | + | - | - | -2 | + | - | | -4 |
| Germany | | - | + | + | 2 | -2 | | + | - | + | | | 2 | + | + | - | + | - | + | 2 | -6 |
| Greece | | | | | 2 | | | + | - | - | | + | | | + | | + | - | + | | 4 |
| Hungary | | | | | | + | - | 2 | - | - | | + | | | | | + | + | - | | -1 |
| Ireland | - | - | - | - | - | - | 2 | -2 | - | - | | + | - | - | - | 4 | 6 | + | - | 2 | +1 |
| Italy | -3 | + | - | -2 | - | | 2 | + | 4 | | | | - | | -2 | | + | -2 | -2 | | -3 |
| Latvia | + | | | | | + | | + | - | | | | - | | + | + | + | + | | | 0 |
| Lithuania | + | | - | | + | | + | - | + | | + | | | - | + | + | - | | + | | -2 |
| Luxembourg | - | | | 2 | | 2 | | | + | | | | | | | | 2 | | | | 5 |
| Malta | + | | | - | 2 | 2 | | - | + | + | | - | + | | - | - | -2 | | + | | 5 |
| Netherlands | + | + | - | 3 | 2 | -3 | - | + | -2 | | + | + | 2 | -2 | -2 | - | 2 | + | + | - | 3 |
| Poland | 2 | - | | | -3 | | + | -3 | -2 | | | + | 2 | 2 | + | 2 | -2 | + | - | - | -1 |
| Portugal | - | | | + | | | - | - | -2 | - | - | + | + | - | | - | | - | + | | 0 |
| Slovakia | | | | | - | | | + | + | | | | - | | | | | + | + | | -3 |
| Slovenia | + | + | | | + | - | | + | + | + | - | - | + | + | + | | - | + | | | 5 |
| Spain | + | + | 2 | - | + | - | | -3 | + | - | - | + | + | + | - | | | + | + | 3 | 2 |
| Sweden | | - | 2 | - | + | + | -2 | 2 | - | + | + | + | - | - | | 2 | 2 | - | + | - | +1 |
| UK | -2 | -2 | 2 | -2 | - | + | 2 | - | - | 3 | + | + | - | 2 | -2 | -2 | -2 | + | -4 | 2 | -2 |
| New ms | 3 | + | -3 | 6 | -2 | -3 | -2 | -3 | | -2 | -2 | 6 | - | -6 | + | 2 | -3 | | | -4 | -2 |
| Old ms | -3 | - | 3 | -6 | 2 | 3 | 2 | 3 | | 2 | 2 | -6 | + | 6 | - | -2 | 3 | | | 4 | +2 |
| Committee size | 78 | 34 | 33 | 47 | 35 | 49 | 50 | 63 | 51 | 40 | 51 | 51 | 42 | 35 | 35 | 26 | 53 | 28 | 35 | 25 | |

Source: Own calculations.

Note: The figures are rounded to whole numbers. Signs alone indicate a difference of one seat. Abbreviations: ms: member states; see also the note in Table 3.2 above.

## *Committee composition*

Whether committee membership is proportional to the party group composition of the plenary following the EP Rules of Procedure can be evaluated by examining committee composition. Table 3.2 displays the difference between the observed and the expected number of committee seats per party group based on size in plenary. The difference is zero in most cases and only in a few instances reaches a maximum of two seats, which may result from a deal between groups driven by their policy priorities. For instance, the over-representation of ALDE on the Civil Liberties committee may be strategic. However, in general, party groups tend to observe proportionality and deviations are negligible. This confirms previous findings of proportional representation of the two biggest party groups EPP-ED and PSE (McElroy 2006) and extends them to all groups in all committees.

The Rules of Procedure do not assure that the composition of committees reflects the national composition of the plenary. Bearing in mind that half of the member states have fewer seats in the EP than there are standing committees, inevitably they cannot be represented everywhere. There is mixed evidence in the literature. While Bowler and Farrell (1995: 227) hold that 'the composition of committees generally reflects the national and ideological composition of the chamber', proportionality to national delegation sizes does not seem to be the norm in the study of McElroy (2006). Therefore, the national composition of committees is revisited here. Table 3.3 shows for each committee the difference between the observed and the expected number of seats per member state based on the size of that member state's representation in the EP. Some member states appear to be over- or under-represented on certain committees. For instance, Italy is over-represented on the committees on Industry, Legal Affairs and Civil Liberties as well as Justice and Home Affairs while it is under-represented on Foreign Affairs; France is over-represented on International Trade and Culture, while under-represented on Budgetary Control; Poland is over-represented in the Committee on Budget but under-represented on Budgetary Control, Economic and Social Affairs and the Environment committees. Another curious fact is that the MEPs coming from new member states seem to target, or gain access to, different committees than the MEPs from old member states. Whether these figures portray an underlying bias of member states targeting certain committees (as they may have higher stakes in particular policy fields), or that the number of their representatives on different committees is random, remains a puzzle. However, since the committee assignment is based on party group affiliation and not on nationality, systematic self-selection of members with a certain nationality on a particular committee is highly unlikely. It is reasonable to expect that the seat assignments will not reflect exactly the national parties' composition of the plenary, either, as this is also not directly controlled by the Rules of Procedure. Interestingly, Whitaker (2011) shows that in the assignment of committee seats within EPP-ED and PSE in the beginning of the 6th EP, national party delegations were more likely to be over–represented with one or more seats on the committees whose jurisdictions were of higher salience to them.

While the party group composition of committees is regulated by formal and informal proportionality rules, this does not necessarily translate into proportional representation of the range of policy preferences present on the floor. Thus, only an individual level analysis of factors influencing MEPs' assignments can answer questions such as: Do members with strong interests in the policy areas covered by specific committees self-select to those committees? Do members with specialised knowledge join the respective committees? Do party groups assure they have representative contingents on the powerful committees?

## Literature on European Parliament committee assignments

A number of studies discuss committee assignments directly or indirectly. Bowler and Farrell (1995) produced a milestone study, using the distributive and informational rationales in exploring committee formation in the 3rd EP (1989–1994). They identified occupational and interest group attachments as the only statistically significant determinants of committee membership. In a study concurrent to the present one, Whitaker (2011) confirms that expertise has played a prime role in committee assignments since the first directly elected EP, although the same does not hold for interest group attachments. Similarly, McElroy (2006) showed that policy-specific expertise played a role in the assignment of members to the committees on Environment, Industry and Legal Affairs in the 5th EP, concluding that 'committees are, nonetheless, highly representative of the EP as a whole, in terms of both party and policy representation' (McElroy 2006: 5). In reaching this conclusion, however, MEPs' NOMINATE scores (more on NOMINATE in the methods section) were used as a proxy for policy preferences. Since they are not party-free measures and, as such, probably do not reflect true preferences, their examination is not sufficient to conclude that committees are representative of the EP as a whole in terms of policy preferences. Committees may still be staffed with members with outlying interests, driving policy away from the plenary median. Thus, for instance, Kaeding (2004), in his study on report allocation during 1994–1999, holds that the Environment committee was composed of homogeneous high demanders, often affiliated with Greenpeace and other environmental groups. While interest group ties may be associated with certain expertise, they are often also associated with high demand for a certain policy.

Moreover, it is not entirely clear whether or how party group and national party delegation leaderships control individual assignments and where the boundary between their roles lies. Focusing on the study of report allocation, Mamadouh and Raunio (2002, 2003) stated that 'national party delegations inside the transnational groups are often key gatekeepers in the division of spoils within the groups, with group leaders restricted in their ability to direct the actions of their committee members' (Mamadouh and Raunio 2003: 333; see also Kreppel 2002a: 202–11). Whitaker (2001, 2005, 2011) further argues that as the EP has acquired more legislative powers, national parties have become increasingly interested in lowering agency loss by influencing committee assignments and the work of committees with legislative powers. He showed that 'national parties ensure higher level of responsiveness on committees that have legislative powers' (2005: 5; 2011). Yet, in his study of committee assignments over time and committee chair allocations in the 6th EP, he found no evidence of national party delegations systematically preventing disloyal party members from accruing on any committee[1] or rewarding loyal party members with committee chair positions. Alternative evidence for the influence of party groups is provided by McElroy (2001) who showed that MEPs who voted consistently against the group leadership were more likely to be demoted in the mid-term shuffle of committee seats for the period 1989–1991. In exploring the transnational party groups in the EP, Raunio (1997) also pointed to party groups' control over committees. However, no study so far has explicitly modelled the impact of party groups on the assignment of individual members to committees. In the conclusions of her study, McElroy (2006: 26) drew attention to the fact that 'the role of political groups in the process of committee assignments needs to be examined in greater detail'.

To summarise, while a number of recent studies has largely increased our knowledge about the EP committees, the rationale behind individual committee assignments is not yet clear. Is it guided more by individual preferences and interests or by partisan considerations? As a result, how representative are the committee contingents of the range of preferences present in the EP? This chapter aspires to add to the existing literature by offering a comprehensive examination of the assignments to different types of committee in which a wide array of individual and partisan factors, informed by alternative theoretical rationales, are considered.

*Table 3.4: Adapted predictions of the congressional theories about committee assignment*

| Rationale | Assumptions | Predictions |
|---|---|---|
| Distributive | MEPs seek particularistic policy | Homogeneous preference outliers self-select to committees |
| Informational | MEPs seek 'good' European policy | Non-outliers or heterogeneous (bipolar) preference outliers with relevant expertise assigned to committees by chamber |
| Partisan | MEPs seek party policy | Loyal members rewarded and disloyal members punished by party group leadership in committee assignments |

---

1.   The Environment committee presents an exception in the committee assignments in 2002.

## Hypotheses

The assumptions and predictions of the distributive, informational and partisan rationales about individual committee assignments are summarised in Table 3.4. The hypotheses are developed in greater detail below.

The distributive approach (Shepsle 1978; Shepsle and Weingast 1987; Weingast and Marshall 1988) predicts that legislators seeking re-election from their territorial constituencies self-select 'to those committees that have the greatest marginal impact over their electoral fortunes' (Weingast and Marshall 1988: 145), which results in committees staffed with relatively homogeneous high demanders on a policy dimension.

As discussed in Chapter Two, the electoral link between legislators and their constituencies is much weaker in the EP than in the US Congress. Thus, the work of MEPs within the EP has, at best, only a marginal effect on electoral outcomes, which alone may not be sufficient to induce legislators to specialise in certain areas. Still, MEPs' special interests stemming from their ties to certain groups other than their constituencies can drive them to self-select to some interest-driven committees. Checking whether members with interest group ties indeed work for those special interests is beyond the scope of this chapter. Still, it is not unreasonable to expect that if, for example, the Environment committee is staffed with members with green ties not counterbalanced by members with industry ties then it may propose some policy in the direction of more environmental regulation than preferred by the EP median. Linking the theory to the proposed classification of the EP committees offered in Table 3.1, it is tested whether members with homogeneous special interests tend to accrue on the respective interest-driven or mixed committees.

*H1: The likelihood of being assigned to an interest-driven or mixed committee is increased by having relevant special interests, and the set of such interests is homogeneous.*

Committee assignment is crucial in order to 'achieve maximum feasible informational efficiencies' (Gilligan and Krehbiel 1990: 556). Thus, the informational rationale (Krehbiel 1991; see also Gilligan and Krehbiel 1989a) prescribes that in the pursuit of informational gains the plenary will create institutional incentives for members to specialise. Committees will be staffed with non-outlying legislators or bipolar, hence heterogeneous, outliers 'who can specialise at relatively low cost due to, for example, their prior experience or intense interest in the policies that lie within a committee's jurisdiction' (Krehbiel 1991: 136; see also Gilligan and Krehbiel 1990). Committees are expected to reflect the diversity within the chamber and, hence, its median policy preferences as closely as possible. Seniority rights in the office assignment are observed to encourage the investment of time and energy in acquiring expertise in a given policy area and building personal networks (Strøm 1998: 40).

Specialisation at low cost can be achieved in the EP via committee assignment based on relevant expertise. Hence, the EP committees are expected to be staffed with members who can easily become specialists in the respective area owing to their education or occupational background. Furthermore, MEPs acquire expertise during their service in the EP and, therefore, parliamentary seniority may play an important role, too. As a whole, members with relevant expertise are expected to accrue on the information-driven and mixed committees.

*H2a: The likelihood of being assigned to an information-driven or mixed committee is increased by having relevant expertise or parliamentary experience.*

Although members with strong special interests in a certain area, derived, for instance, from their interest group ties, may have relevant expertise, they may not be assigned to the respective committee by the plenary since high demanders decrease a committee's capacity to perform its informative function. Despite 'the possible relationship between committee preferences and low-cost expertise' (Gilligan and Krehbiel 1990: 543), leading to a correlation of the predictors of the distributive and informational perspectives, self-selection of preference outliers is not likely unless it is rational for the chamber, i.e. unless the benefits of information outweigh the potential costs of outlying policies. Although the EP plenary has reserved the right to revert outlying committee proposals back to the plenary median via the open amendment rule in plenary,[2] heavy amending implies costs for the plenary and reduces committees' incentives to gather information. It is less costly for the plenary to assure via the committee assignment that committees are not preference outliers and that the committee's median reflects the plenary median. Should preference outliers be allowed to self-select to committees, they are to be counteracted by an equal number of preference outliers in the opposite direction if committees are to serve the plenary median. In other words, the special interest of committee members must be heterogeneous – otherwise they will not further the informational goals of the legislature because committees will not have an incentive to share their information sincerely with the plenary, and such information would be biased anyway. This leads to the following hypothesis:

*H2b: The likelihood of being assigned to a mixed committee is increased by having relevant special interests, and the set of such interests is heterogeneous.*

As MEPs are in practice assigned to committees by party groups, expertise may not always be the main determinant of committee membership. Therefore, the alternative partisan rationale of legislative organisation (Cox and McCubbins 1993, 2007) is considered, too. According to this rationale, legislators seek re-election, which is conditional not only upon their own merits but also upon the collective reputation of their party. Therefore, party members delegate to party leaders the responsibility to assure party cohesion around common policy objectives by giving them the monopoly over the allocation of parliamentary

---

2.  Amendments for consideration in Parliament may be tabled by the committee responsible, a political group or at least forty Members' (European Parliament 2009b, Rule 156, ex Rule 150).

office and resources as a disciplining tool. Party leaders use this power to assure that 'important' committees are staffed with loyal members.

Since the aim of party leadership is to increase group cohesiveness, party group leaders in the EP, who control individual committee assignments, are expected to use the latter as a means of disciplining group members, i.e. rewarding loyal members and punishing disloyal ones. The partisan theory prescribes that this cohesion will be induced by giving positive and negative incentives to the party members to vote with the party leadership. However, due to the presence of heterogeneous national parties with differing ideological and national interests within party groups, and the heterogeneity of group leadership itself, it is voting with the group majority rather than group leadership which can be interpreted as loyal group behaviour. It is expected that party group leaders will try to avoid staffing powerful committees with disloyal group members. The underlying assumption is that MEPs prefer to work in the policy areas falling under the codecision procedure where the EP has a strong say on legislation, as this would allow them to advance the policy preferences of their national parties in the adopted European legislation and, thus, increase their own re-selection chances.

*H3a: The likelihood of being assigned to a powerful committee decreases with party group disloyalty.*

While not explicitly suggested by the partisan rationale, senior party group and national party members can be expected to use their position to secure themselves desirable committee seats. Thus, party group leaders may be keeping seats on powerful committees for themselves. Within national party delegations, the senior party members, i.e. those who have held an official party position back home, may be given priority over their party colleagues by the delegation heads. This leads to an additional hypothesis related to the partisan positions of MEPs:

*H3b: The likelihood of being assigned to a powerful committee increases with party group and national party seniority.*

## Research design

This section presents the data, measures and methods used in the empirical analyses.

### Data

For the purpose of this study, an original data set is compiled on the biographies and committee membership of the MEPs from the 6th European Parliament. To verify the reliability of the information, the data is collected from two sources: the official EP website and Eurosource (2005). The data includes all the MEPs in the 6th EP, representing the situation at the time of committee assignment (July 2004). The codebook and descriptive statistics are provided in Appendix A. The unit of analysis is an individual MEP. The results from the statistical analysis of this data are complemented by evidence from the semi-structured interviews with MEPs and EP staff members conducted in the period January – February 2008.

### *Measures*

Firstly, special interests of legislators are accounted for by a number of dichotomous variables. An MEP is ascribed business or industry interest if he or she has been employed as manager or director of a big company or has owned a business. Trade unionists are people with ties to organised trade unions. Affiliation to green interest groups and work as an environmental public or party advisor are expected to be related to a member's special interest in environment. Special interest in farming was assigned to MEPs who have been members of farmers' unions, have owned a farm or have held a ministerial or other public office in agriculture. Finally, MEPs are considered to have social group ties if they are affiliated with social groups or organisations dealing with people and issues such as human rights, women's rights, humanitarian aid, etc. All these special interests are inevitably associated with certain expertise. However, related expertise and special interest measures are not strongly correlated, e.g. not all economists are working in business, not all natural scientists have green ties, not all lawyers are affiliated with groups protecting civil liberties, and the other way round. Furthermore, special interests also imply MEPs' preferences for a policy in a certain direction such as, for instance, less regulation of private enterprises, more social protection of workers, more environmental regulation, more farming subsidies or more humanitarian aid, all of which may drive policy outcomes away from those preferred by the plenary median.

Secondly, variables aimed at addressing the informational rationale include factors of MEPs' biographies that allow for specialisation at low cost. These variables capture pure expertise derived from educational and occupational characteristics that do not imply any clear outlying interest for certain policies. These include legal (law and legal career), medicine (doctors, pharmacists and ex-ministers of health), economics and finance (higher education), transport and telecommunications (local and national level officials in the sector) and engineering and natural sciences (higher education) expertise. Members with international experience are those who have worked in the national foreign ministries, in foreign affairs committees of national assemblies or in international organisations such as NATO, UN or the Council of Europe. Similarly, experience in local level government is considered.[3] EP experience is accounted for by a dummy variable assuming a value of 1 for members with length of service in the EP above their group's mean and 0 otherwise, because EP experience is only relevant in the context of the party

---

3. The effect of experience in national politics was evaluated in the preliminary data analysis, including past membership in national parliament, national executive and public office. By analogy, the effect of having held a high position in the EP was examined. However, none of these factors had a significant influence on committee assignments.

group, within which the individual assignments are made. Another indicator is the retention of senior members on committees, i.e. whether a member is assigned to the same committee(s) as in the last parliamentary term.[4]

Thirdly, partisan measures include dummies for seniority within own national party (previous official position) and own party group (current official group role). Since the larger national parties basically run their party groups (Hix 2002b), they may be privileged in the seat assignment of the most powerful committees. Thus, a variable is included accounting for the relative size of a national party delegation within its party group, calculated as delegation size divided by group size. Additionally, membership in the two biggest party groups, EPP-ED and PSE, is controlled for to see whether they differ significantly from smaller groups due to alternative assignment strategies.[5]

The partisan theory predicts party loyalty to be the most important determinant of committee assignment. However, there is no way of evaluating the party group loyalty of freshmen MEPs in the beginning of a legislative term, and 55 per cent of the members of the 6th EP are freshmen. Hence, one could either look at the loyalty of the incumbent members only, reflected in their voting records in the 5th EP, or use an *ex-post* measure of observed loyalty after the committee assignments as a proxy of expected loyalty, under the assumption that party group leaders had reasons to form such expectations. For the sake of preserving the full sample, the results for the latter case are displayed here, although the analysis on incumbents leads to equivalent results. The *ex-post* measure used here is constructed on the basis of the NOMINATE scores of MEPs, derived via multidimensional scaling (Poole and Rosenthal 1997) of their observed roll call votes during the first year of the 6th EP (collected by Hix *et al.* 2007). Group loyalty is defined as the frequency of voting with the group majority, which is reflected in the absolute distance between a legislator's score and the median of his or her party group on the first NOMINATE dimension.[6] Thus, as this distance grows group disloyalty increases. As Hix (2001: 673) notes, 'the distance between the members within each party group is an indication of the cohesion of the party groups on each dimension'. McElroy (2001: 19) holds that '[l]oyalty cannot be fully captured through roll-call voting but it is undeniable that the most public demonstration of loyalty or dissent is through the process of roll call voting.' Thus, roll call votes are the best available data that can be used to estimate group loyalty. Using only the first dimension, which closely approximates the traditional left-right spectrum, is deemed appropriate here as it explains about 90 per cent of the variation in voting (Hix *et al.* 2006a; McElroy 2006). It has to be noted that true

4. As the EP committees have changed considerably through the years, their number, names and responsibilities have been traced back in compiling the variables on previous committee experience. See Appendix B.

5. Including dummies for all the party groups does not alter any of the results.

6. Measuring group loyalty as the absolute distance between a legislator's NOMINATE score and the median score of his or her party group leadership has not led to different results of the analyses.

MEPs' preferences need not align on the same dimension as their votes. While in previous studies the NOMINATE scores were used as a measure of ideology, preferences or policy positions (Hausemer 2006; Høyland 2006a; McElroy 2006; Rasmussen 2008), there is an inherent problem with such conceptualisation in that they are not party-free measures, as acknowledged in these studies (see also McElroy 2007b: 435). This is not a problem for the disloyalty measure constructed in this study as party groups do not evaluate their members on the basis of their true preferences but rather on their expected or manifested behaviour. A member with outlying preferences may vote perfectly loyally together with his or her group. Nevertheless, the NOMINATE scores are limited in that only about a third of the EP votes are conducted via a roll call (Hix 2001: 667) and there may be strategic motivations of party groups requesting roll call votes such as disciplining and signalling. Research on one year of voting in the 5th EP showed them to be called disproportionately more often on some policy areas, by specific party groups and on resolutions rather than important legislative proposals (Carrubba *et al.* 2006). This could lead to selection bias and potential overestimation of group loyalty. However, Høyland (2009) demonstrated that if only a subsample of the important votes is considered, nearly the same results are obtained, hence proving the NOMINATE scores to be unbiased. Furthermore, Han (2007) showed that the Bayesian method, measuring the uncertainty of the NOMINATE estimates due to missing data and random attendance, leads to results comparable to those produced by the standard NOMINATE method.

A number of control variables are considered, including gender, age and new member state. Age has been coded as 1 for members whose age is above the 75th percentile in their group and 0 for the others.

### *Methods*

It has to be noted that in contrast to McElroy (2006), who examines the assignment strategies of EPP-ED and PSE only, all the party groups' members are included in this analysis, making it more similar to that in Bowler and Farrell's study (1995), with the difference that partisan effects are modelled, too. McElroy (2006 :14–15) argues that in view of the strong proportionality rule and since not all party groups may have members with a certain type of expertise, an aggregated analysis may attenuate statistical results, i.e. lead to insignificant or low coefficients. However, examining the big groups separately in the preliminary analysis did not render the impact of any additional factor significant. Potential problems with an aggregate analysis are ameliorated by the presence of the various types of MEPs' characteristics in most groups in the current data as shown in the descriptive statistics in Appendix A. An advantage of the current method is the ability to include the five smaller groups (constituting 30 per cent of the EP), which could not be studied separately due to the small number (N). More importantly, general conclusions about committee assignments in the EP can be drawn concerning the extent to which special interests and expertise matter beyond partisan affiliation.

The statistical tool employed is logistic regression because of the dichotomous character of the dependent variables on committee membership, coded as 1 for being a member of a named committee and 0 otherwise. While such a model may not be appropriate for highly skewed dependent variables (Long 1997), analysis of deviance did not give a clear indication that a better model fit is offered by an alternative loglog model, assuming significantly more zeros than ones in the binary outcome (Hardin and Hilbe 2007: 148–55). Hence, conventional logistic regression is used here, while the reader may also want to consult Appendix E for the loglog analysis, which leads to comparable results. For each committee, a separate model is constructed composed of general as well as committee-specific variables in accordance with the jurisdictions of the respective committee (European Parliament 2007b, Annex IV). The average marginal effect of each variable on the probability of committee assignment holding all other variables constant is reported in Table 3.5 (see Bartus 2005). The original logistic regression coefficients are presented in Appendix C since they provide information only about the direction but not the size of each effect.

## Empirical analysis of committee assignments

The findings of the quantitative analysis are presented in this section together with some evidence from the semi-structured interviews. The marginal effects displayed in Table 3.5 show that the statistically significant determinants of membership differ across the different types of committee. Consistent with Hypothesis 1, members with special interests have a higher likelihood of being assigned to interest-driven (Agriculture, Fisheries, etc.) and mixed committees (Environment, Industry, etc.). While expertise and committee incumbency increase the likelihood of assignment to both information-driven (Internal Market, Legal Affairs, etc.) and mixed committees, in accordance with Hypothesis 2a, the special interests associated with membership in mixed committees are not heterogeneous, i.e. members serving on these committees are not bipolar preference outliers, contrary to Hypothesis 2b. As the special interests of legislators in mixed committees are not counteracted by interests in the opposite direction, they may serve more than purely informational purposes. Partisan disloyalty and seniority do not systematically affect the likelihood of assignment to a powerful committee, contrary to Hypotheses 3a and 3b. Combined with the lack of over-representation of big party groups or national party delegations on powerful committees, it is hard to find any evidence for the partisan rationale.

In accordance with Hypothesis 1, the empirical analyses show that MEPs with special interests are likely to join a committee whose area of operation addresses these interests, i.e. an interest-driven or a missed committee. Thus, parliamentarians with ties to business or industry are 9 per cent more likely to join the Committee on Economic and Monetary Affairs and 6.5 per cent more likely to join the Committee on Industry, Research and Energy than other MEPs. On average, members with trade union ties have a 17 per cent higher probability of assignment to the Committee on Employment and Social Affairs than other parliamentarians;

members with green interests have an 18 per cent higher probability of going to the Committee on the Environment, Public Health and Food Safety; members with farming group ties have a 34 per cent higher probability to join the Committee on Agriculture and Rural Development, and members with social group ties have a 10.9 per cent higher probability of assignment to the Committee on Civil Liberties, Justice and Home Affairs. As a whole, there is strong evidence that special interests of MEPs derived from their interest group ties do affect their membership in interest-driven and mixed committees whose jurisdictions target these groups.

The significant positive impact of education and professional expertise on the likelihood of membership in information-driven and mixed EP committees requiring technical knowledge corroborate Hypothesis 2a. On average, expertise in economics increases an MEP's likelihood of joining the Committee on Budgets (by 7.5 per cent) and the Committee on Economic and Monetary Affairs (by 5 per cent); in medical science the Committee on the Environment, Public Health and Food Safety (by 12 per cent); in natural science or engineering the latter committee (by 6 per cent) and the Committee on Industry, Research and Energy (by 9 per cent); in transport or telecommunications the Committee on Transport and Tourism (34 per cent); and in law the Committee on Legal Affairs (6 per cent). Furthermore, members of the Committee of Foreign Affairs tend to have experience in international relations, and being an Ex-Head of Executive increases the likelihood of assignment to that committee on average by 21 per cent. Members with knowledge in economics do not seem to be drawn to the Committee on Internal Market and Consumer Protection, nor do lawyers to the Committee Civil Affairs, presumably because the majority of such members are assigned to those committees linked more closely to these areas of expertise. Furthermore, having local government experience has no statistically significant effect on assignment to the Agriculture committee.

However, contrary to Hypothesis 2b, in none of the mixed committees do we observe accruing of members with heterogeneous special interests running in opposite directions, i.e. members with conflicting policy preferences. Thus, members with trade union ties do not tend to go to the committee on Economic and Monetary Affairs, which contrasts with previous findings of Bowler and Farrell (1995), possibly due to the increased competences of the Employment and Social Affairs committee since the early 1990s, leading to such members going there instead. In addition, there is no evidence of members with green ties targeting the committee on Industry or members with industry and business ties targeting the committee on Environment. Similarly, members with farming ties and environmentalists do not target each other's committees and, hence, it is not surprising that Kaeding (2004) finds no impact of links to farmer unions on report allocation in the Environment committee. Since no bipolar outliers are present in these committees, their informational role may be jeopardised despite the expertise present, leading them to advocate policies away from the plenary median preference and, possibly, not even sharing information sincerely in the plenary. As was also suggested in the interviews, the members of such committees tend to have more extreme stances than members in their own party groups:

Often you would see, for instance in the Environment committee, the members would tend to be a little bit more environmental friendly than the rest of their group. A little bit in my group [PSE] but very much so in the EPP and the Liberal group [...] And in general you would see that the members of the committee [are] more on the environment side, are greener than the rest [...] Also, in the Industry committee you would probably see that they are more on the industry side than the rest of their group [...] You choose your committee after interests, and everybody does that more or less, and therefore you would get conflicts when you then have to translate that to the group.[...] On issues like agriculture, fisheries, nuclear power we are divided. (Personal interview 1 with a PSE member, 27th February 2008)

Along the same lines, referring to the legislation on Airline Emissions another MEP commented:

You would have seen, for instance Peter Liese [Environment committee] versus Jarzembowski [Transport committee] coming from the same party but different committees, having completely different views. So, there is a committee specific view, which is quite strong sometimes as well. (Personal interview 7 with an EPP-ED member, 11 February 2008)

Consistently with previous results (Bowler and Farrell 1995; Hausemer 2006), no effect of parliamentary seniority *per se* is observed. EP experience, however, matters in terms of committee incumbency (see also McElroy 2006; Whitaker 2011), reflecting a certain property right of members over their committee seats. This finding confirms the observation of Corbett *et al.* (2005) who hold that less well-known MEPs in their first term are disadvantaged in the committee assignment and there has been a movement towards greater committee specialisation. This finding was also confirmed in the interviews:

Obviously if there is some new member just elected and is on her first day and wants to be on this committee and there is a member who has been around a little bit longer then seniority clearly plays a role. (Personal interview 3 with a PSE member, 12th February 2008)

[...] if I as a senior member say I want to go there [a specific committee], naturally they respect me before someone who came on board in this legislative period, without doubt. (Personal interview 8 with a PSE member, 26th February 2008)

[...] if you are in your second or other mandates, I think a member would be very disappointed they didn't get the committee of their first choice. (Personal interview 2 with an EPP-ED member, 6th February 2008)

Overall, all the findings of the statistical analysis outlined above are supported by the collected qualitative interview data. When asked about the source of committee choice, the members of different party groups gave similar answers – it is shaped by personal interests, expertise and seniority:

> In our group it is more or less the individual interests that decide who is going to which committee. (Personal interview 6 with a Green/EFA member, 30th January 2008)

> The first driving force is always interest. The second one is then, I would say, expertise. Then, I would say seniority but in the terms of having been in the Parliament before. In other words, if you have sat in the committee for a long time it is very difficult to kick you out of there. (Personal interview 7 with an EPP-ED member, 11th February 2008)

> You will separately of course have members who [...] would say I won't be on this committee, I want to be on that committee. Why are they saying that? Because they have a particular expertise, or they have a particular constituency interest, maybe they represent a rural area and they want to be on the Agriculture committee, or whatever. So you usually have volunteers to be on a committee. (Personal interview 3 with a PSE member, 12th February 2008)

There is little evidence for Hypothesis 3b, though. High position in a party group has no effect on assignments while having held an official position in a national party increases the probability of assignment only to the Committee on Employment and Social Affairs and the Committee on Transport and Tourism by, on average, 4 and 5.5 per cent, respectively. This may be explained by the fact that the output of these two committees largely targets the national arena, and thus they can be exploited to pursue national electoral interests. Neither the affiliation to a big party group, nor the relative size of national party delegations within groups disproportionately affects the committee assignments. Thus, there is no indication that committee assignments are guided by explicit partisan considerations.

Being from a new member state has a significant and positive impact only on assignment to the Budgetary Affairs committee, probably reflecting underlying special interests in the Cohesion Funds. In addition, the committee on Foreign Affairs appears to be staffed predominantly with male MEPs. Relative age in party group does not affect committee assignments.

To summarise, in line with the distributive theory, homogeneous special interests affect assignment to both interest-driven and mixed committees, suggesting potential outlying preferences of these committees left unchecked by members with alternative views. Purely information-driven and mixed committees are staffed with specialists as the informational theory prescribes. However, no evidence in support of the partisan theory is found. The latter finding has to be treated with caution, though, due to the difficulty inherent in evaluating the expectations of group leaders about the partisan loyalty of freshmen MEPs.

*Table 3.5: Average marginal effects on the probabilities of committee assignment to an MEP in the first half of the 6th EP in percentage*

| | AFET | BUDG | ECON | EMPL | ENVI | ITRE | IMCO | TRAN | AGRI | JURI | LIBE |
|---|---|---|---|---|---|---|---|---|---|---|---|
| **Special interests** | | | | | | | | | | | |
| Business/Industry | | 9.23** | | -2.16 | -0.75 | 6.53* | 4.43 | | | | |
| Trade union | | 4.73 | | 17.3** | 18.1** | 0.84 | | | | | |
| Green | | | | | | | | | -3.17 | | |
| Farming | | | | | -4.79 | | | | 34.3** | | |
| Social group | | | | | | | | | | | 10.9** |
| **Expertise/seniority** | | | | | | | | | | | |
| International relations | 10.3** | | | | | | | | | | |
| Ex-Head Executive | 21.5** | | | | | | | | | | |
| Economics/Finance | | 7.53** | 5.15* | -1.75 | | | -0.36 | | | | |
| Medicine | | | | | 12.0** | | | | | | |
| Science/Engineering | | | | | 5.76* | 8.79** | | | | | |
| Transport/Telecomm. | | | | | | | | 33.8** | | | |
| Local government | | | | | | | | | 2.08 | | |
| Legal | | | | | | | | | | 6.45** | 2.77 |
| Committee incumbent | 53.4** | 51.4** | 49.4** | 47.5** | 69.9** | 41.8** | 51.2** | 51.1** | 53.2** | 13.8*** | 47.2** |
| EP experience w/n group | -3.31 | 2.62 | -2.14 | -4.17* | -1.72 | -6.22** | -1.46 | -2.44 | -0.07 | -2.15 | -3.17 |
| **Partisan measures** | | | | | | | | | | | |
| EPP-ED | -2.77 | 2.08 | 0.18 | -0.45 | -3.33 | 1.06 | 1.26 | -3.01 | -3.25 | -0.91 | -1.08 |
| PSE | -1.82 | 1.37 | 0.43 | -2.02 | -3.95 | 1.5 | 2.91 | -1.16 | 0.21 | -0.46 | -2.38 |
| Party group disloyalty | -17.3 | -1.71 | -2.66 | 8.66 | 4.3 | -35.4 | 7.37 | 3.96 | 0.87 | -4.98 | -19.4 |
| Holds group office | -3.18 | -1.71 | 3.13 | 1.96 | -4.33 | 0.49 | 5.79 | -4.71 | -4.19 | 1.65 | 1.74 |
| National party size | -0.04 | 11.5 | 6.42 | -24.5 | -20.5 | 12.4 | 9.46 | -11.3 | 4.49 | 7.32 | -30.8 |
| Held national party office | 3.13 | -1.65 | -0.75 | 4.18* | -1.08 | -3.12 | -1.88 | 5.50** | -0.85 | 2.11 | -2.58 |

| | AFET | BUDG | ECON | EMPL | ENVI | ITRE | IMCO | TRAN | AGRI | JURI | LIBE |
|---|---|---|---|---|---|---|---|---|---|---|---|
| **Demographics** | | | | | | | | | | | |
| New member state | 5.27 | 6.74** | -0.54 | -1.3 | -1.15 | -0.23 | 0.31 | 2.3 | 0.58 | 2.57 | -0.49 |
| Male | 6.37** | -0.31 | 1.73 | 0.5 | -0.58 | -0.58 | -4.71* | 2.31 | -0.7 | 1.12 | -1.11 |
| Age in top quartile (EPG) | -2.6 | -2.11 | -0.44 | 1.94 | -3. 86 | -1.28 | 1.04 | -3.08 | -2.04 | 2.74 | -0.38 |
| | | | | | | | | | | | |
| Observations | 695 | 695 | 695 | 695 | 695 | 695 | 695 | 695 | 695 | 695 | 695 |
| Percentage classified | 91.37% | 94.10% | 94.39% | 94.39% | 93.53% | 94.24% | 94.53% | 95.68% | 95.68% | 96.55 | 92.95% |

*Note:* Dependent variable: individual member assignment to the respective committee in 2004. * significance at 10%; ** significance at 5%. See Appendix C for the raw coefficients. Since committee incumbency has the highest average marginal effect on the probability of committee assignment it is further examined in Appendix D.

## Discussion

Examining the committee composition and assignments after the 2004 EU Enlargement, this chapter demonstrates the strong committee specialisation of incumbent members on the same committees on which they have previously served, reflecting the gradual institutionalisation of the EP which has been traditionally associated with high membership volatility. It further shows that while not proportional to the EP's national composition, with minor exceptions the EP committee composition is largely proportional to the partisan composition of the plenary, thus extending the findings of proportionality in previous studies (Bowler and Farrell 1995; McElroy 2006) to all the committees and party groups. However, not all committees are representative of the EP in terms of policy preferences. Members with relevant expertise are assigned to the respective information-driven committees and mixed committees, while interest-driven and mixed committees are staffed with homogeneous preference outliers with special interests not matched by members with opposing interests. Whitaker's (2011) concurrent study of committee assignments confirms these findings in that expertise has always been the main determinant of committee assignment, followed by interest group ties in the last two parliamentary terms. Claims that the committees are representative of the overall plenary in terms of ideological preferences relying on NOMINATE scores only (McElroy 2006) need to be revised since the accrual of homogeneous preference outliers on some committees suggests that they may not be representative of the range of preferences present in the EP. As previous research relying on qualitative interviews demonstrates, 'most members are able to self-select their committee positions and many do so primarily on the basis of their own policy preferences' (Whitaker 2001: 82).

The findings suggest that the distributive theory can bring important insights into the study of legislatures other than the US Congress if considered more broadly and not discarded solely on the basis of weak electoral connection of legislators to territorial constituencies. Special interests of legislators deriving, for instance, from their interest group ties can also lead them to self-select on interest-driven committees, i.e. committees with distributive output, targeted to their specific preferences. Thus, interest groups can increase their representation in the EP by promoting their candidates at elections. If interest groups are conceived of as 'intermediaries between [MEPs'] constituents and themselves' (Katz 1999 :69), MEPs' ties may facilitate better parliamentary representation of certain electoral constituencies. However, drafting particularistic policies reduces aggregate welfare and decreases the parliamentary output legitimacy. In addition, although the accrual of expertise in the specialised committees can facilitate the drafting of well-informed legislation and increase the bargaining powers of the EP in its negotiations with the Council of Ministers, this informed legislation may not always represent the interests of the overall EP or the parliamentary median, especially in interest-driven and mixed committees. The accumulation of biased information in committees can jeopardise not only the informational role of committees, but also the representative functions of the EP or its responsiveness to the policy demands of the broader electorate.

Additionally, there is no evidence in support of the hypotheses of the partisan rationale. Its explanatory power in accounting for committee assignments in a legislature characterised by high turnover of members is questionable. The observed cohesion of party groups, composed of heterogeneous national interests, may call for a different explanation than the one offered by the partisan rationale as leadership disciplining does not occur, at least not when it comes to seat assignment. In normative terms, the proportional partisan composition of committees decreases the likelihood of a high number of amendments in plenary by smaller party groups because none of them seem to be under–represented in committees. This can facilitate reaching required legislative majorities.

Further research is needed to analyse the effects of homogeneous committee membership on legislative behaviour and, more generally, on policy making in the EP committees and plenary. This could be done by examining plenary amendments and votes, which can portray conflicts between committees representing alternative policy views[7] and, more generally, how responsive the committees are of the common parliamentary interest. Such questions are addressed in Chapter Five. The next chapter proceeds with examining the factors driving the allocation of legislative tasks in committees. Perhaps the working majority party group (coalition) regains influence over committee members at this stage?

---

7.   See Burns (2006) for evidence of inter-committee conflict in the EP based on the analysis of the Socrates case.

# chapter four | distribution of legislative tasks

Most of the existing studies on the European Parliament's legislative organisation have examined the internal parliamentary rules and division of resources in isolation from the external institutional environment in which the EP operates. In contrast, this chapter aims at capturing the effect of the inter-institutional locking on the internal EP organisation. It examines how the different inter-institutional legislative procedures shape the internal power struggle and division of tasks among parliamentary groups and individual actors. The factors influencing the allocation of legislative reports falling under the codecision and consultation legislative procedures are compared in light of the substantively different distribution of power between the EP and the Council of Ministers under these two procedures as specified in the European Union treaties.

Committee positions on the legislative proposals of the European Commission are prepared into so-called reports, in which amendments may be proposed for consideration in plenary. Drafting legislative reports on the Commission's proposals by individual committee members constitutes probably the most influential individual legislative task within the EP. The rapporteurs serve *de facto* as the primary intra-institutional agenda-setters and the main parliamentary representatives in the inter-institutional negotiations. Thus, they can largely shape the content of adopted legislative acts. The choice of a rapporteur, therefore, can influence the level of expertise embodied in draft legislation, the breadth of party group and plenary support it attracts, and its representativeness of the preferences of the median member of the EP or bias toward certain interests outside the plenary. Nevertheless, it is not formally governed by the EP Rules of Procedure. Instead, complex informal rules guide the division of reports among party groups and, subsequently, within party groups by their committee coordinators. This procedural ambiguity could lead to violations of the prevalent proportionality norm in the EP and give disproportionate advantage to certain party groups and legislators in obtaining the more competitive reports, i.e. the reports falling under the codecision procedure where the Parliament has equal legislative powers with the Council of Ministers. Thus, the main questions this chapter addresses are whether any systematic differences between the allocation of codecision and consultation reports exist and, if so, who wins and who loses in the division of parliamentary resources.

While stemming from the partisan, distributive, and informational rationales of legislative organisation, as discussed in Chapter Two, the hypotheses developed here are further qualified to unveil the conditions under which each rationale holds. They are centred on the specific incentive structures of MEPs and party group coordinators given the EP rules and the EU's legislative procedures shaping the inter-chamber balance of power.

Following the partisan theory, the primary motivation of party group coordinators in selecting individual rapporteurs is to promote group cohesion. Thus, they are expected to reward loyal members with reports, while avoiding allocating codecision reports to members with special interests and, hence, outlying policy preferences in certain areas. Therefore, such 'interested' members are rather expected to draft more consultation reports. While MEPs with expertise are likely to be advantaged in the report allocation, due to the substantive power of party group coordinators in selecting rapporteurs, partisan considerations take precedence over informational ones. Therefore, expertise is expected to facilitate obtaining mostly consultation reports for which competition is lower.

These hypotheses are examined via count regression models with the use of a data set on the legislative reports allocated during the first term of the 6th European Parliament (2004–2007) and data on the individual MEPs' profiles used in Chapter Three. The semi-structured interviews complement this data. To give the reader a taste of the findings, the results show that indeed the different parliamentary empowerment under the consultation and codecision procedures shaping intra-parliamentary completion affects the division of resources within the EP.

In what follows, background information on the complex system of report allocation is provided, followed by a presentation of the academic literature on the topic. The hypotheses of the study are developed thereafter. Subsequently, the data and methods are described and the results are outlined. The chapter concludes with a discussion of the theoretical and empirical contributions, the limitations of the study and suggestions for future research.

## Role of the rapporteur and the system of report allocation

The legislative powers of the EP vary depending on the inter-institutional procedure required for adopting legislation in a given policy area. Since the introduction of the codecision procedure in the Treaty of the European Union (1993), the extension of its application to ever more policy areas in the Amsterdam (1999), Nice (2003) and Lisbon (2009) treaties, and the gradual abolition of the cooperation procedure, the two main procedures used in adopting EU legislation have become consultation[1] and codecision (renamed since the Lisbon Treaty (2009) to 'ordinary legislative procedure' and 'special legislative procedure', respectively). The balance of power between the EP and the Council of Ministers in the bi-cameral legislative system of the EU varies greatly between the two procedures. Under consultation the EP's powers are confined to giving its opinion, bar the exceptional cases in which it is supported by the Commission and is able to exert limited pressure by delaying proposals or linking them to codecision draft legislation (Kardasheva 2009). In contrast, under codecision the EP has an unconditional veto

---

1. The consultation procedure was merged with the assent procedure in the Treaty of Lisbon (2009) into the 'special legislative procedure'.

power, placing it on equal footing with the Council of Ministers.[2] Not surprisingly, the EP allocates more time to drafting its codecision than consultation legislative positions as a result, at least in the first reading (Rasmussen and Toshkov 2010). The differential powers of the EP under the two procedures influence the level and type of external and internal pressure it attracts. The primary focus of such pressure is on the parliamentary legislative committees, where most of the formal parliamentary deliberation takes place, which are open to the public. The committees draft reports on the Commission proposals in which they propose amendments to the plenary for consideration in formulating the final EP position. However, there are substantial differences in the type and number of legislative reports that each committee writes depending on the policy area it covers.[3] The differences in legislative power between the committees affect the competitiveness of their working environment, the leverage their members have in advancing special interests, and the incentives national parties and party groups have to exert control over them.

Within a committee, usually one rapporteur is assigned to write each incoming draft report. The rapporteurs are the primary legislators responsible for organising discussions and hearings on legislative proposals within the committees, proposing draft amendments and building majority support for their draft reports. They have to present the committee reports to the plenary after the final committee vote and give an opinion on changes proposed on the floor. The rapporteur also follows the report's development through later readings, sits on the conciliation committee if one is formed (in the third reading of the codecision procedure), and – since the Lisbon Treaty came into force or whenever the Regulatory Procedure with Scrutiny applied before that – follows the legislative act in the implementation stage.[4]

In all these activities, the rapporteur is expected to represent the common committee position rather than a personal view or partisan stance. However, limited time resources give the rapporteurs a powerful 'agenda-setting' role. For instance, they can negotiate the parliamentary positions on legislative proposals in secluded trilogue meetings with representatives of the Commission and the Council of Ministers. That sometimes leads to an informal inter-institutional agreement without a clear committee mandate, e.g. before the responsible committee has adopted a draft report on the proposal (Farrell and Héritier 2004; Héritier 2007). To control the development of reports, other party groups appoint shadow rapporteurs, who are normally invited to such meetings. However, the smaller party groups often

2.   See Rasmussen and Toshkov (2010) for a review of the literature on the power of the EP under different legislative procedures.

3.   Some committees do not operate in policy areas falling under the codecision procedure as specified in the EU treaties. In the examined period, about 90 per cent of all codecision reports were drafted by nine standing legislative committees (European Parliament 2007a).

4.   The Lisbon Treaty made the regulatory procedure with scrutiny, which the 2006 Comitology reform introduced (Eurlex 2006), redundant. It introduced Delegated Acts (Article 290 TFEU) that give the EP rights of oversight (Kaeding and Hardacre 2010).

lack the human resources to appoint shadow rapporteurs. Thus, recognising the rapporteurs' substantive powers, interest group representatives and other lobbyists target mostly them in trying to influence the content of legislative proposals, especially in the early stages of drafting a committee report (Mahoney 2008). This holds regardless of whether the rapporteurs' policy preferences match or conflict with those of the lobby group (Marshall 2010).

Despite the influential role of the rapporteurs, report allocation is not regulated by the EP Rules of Procedure (European Parliament 2007b, 2009b). Instead, it is guided by complex and ambiguous rules, which differ between committees. Usually, party groups' coordinators (selected by the groups' committee members) first compete for reports. Then, once a coordinator has won a report, the coordinator decides which member of the group will draft it. This process is described in more detail below.

In the first step, party groups are allocated a number of points based on their respective sizes in the committee, with which their coordinators can bid for reports in closed-door meetings. In some committees, a price may be set for a report based on a common agreement of the party group coordinators prior to the bidding. Alternatively, there is a fixed price for reports based on their type, e.g. one point for own-initiative reports, two points for consultation reports, and three points for codecision reports.[5] Due to their attractiveness, codecision reports are the most expensive, making them difficult to obtain for smaller party groups. Thus, the latter may choose to spend their points on cheaper reports instead. A correcting penalty system may also be in place, whereby if a party group decides to skip its turn and not bid for a specific report, it is fined with one point (e.g. in the Industry, Research and Energy Committee). This is done to prevent the strategic behaviour of party groups saving points for popular reports – a strategy that smaller party groups may be willing to resort to in order to get priority over the bigger party groups in obtaining an upcoming report that is important to them. If no party group wants a report, it may be allocated for no points to the committee chair, who usually serves as a rapporteur of last resort.[6]

Due to its informal character and flexibility, the point system can lead to disproportional representation of party groups and national (party) delegations in the report allocation. This is further aggravated by the lack of transparency, external monitoring or enforcement of proportionality in the allocation process.

Once a party group has won a report, the second step involves the party group coordinator deciding which full committee member or substitute within the group will be the rapporteur. There are no rules on how the coordinators should allocate reports. The lack of any formal procedures assuring the proportional allocation of

---

5.    The example is from the Industry, Research and Energy Committee. See Judge and Earnshaw (2008: 177) and Lindberg (2008: 1189) for alternative pricings of reports in other committees.

6.    In a limited number of cases, the committee decides to consider the report under the procedure without amendments and debate and no rapporteur is assigned (European Parliament 2009b, Rule 46, ex Rule 43).

reports to national (party) delegations gives more freedom to party group coordinators to accommodate individual legislators' interests or use the allocations strategically (Yoshinaka *et al.* 2006: 8). Thus, asking what factors trigger individual allocations and whether those differ according to the type of report – codecision or consultation – is an outstanding empirical question. While the differences between codecision and consultation report allocations has not yet been analysed, a number of studies have addressed the former question.

## Previous research on report allocation

Some scholars argue that the most important factor in report allocation is the interest group attachment of MEPs (Kaeding 2004, 2005), while others emphasise the role of their national party delegations (Kreppel 2002a; Høyland 2006a), party groups (Benedetto 2005; Yoshinaka *et al.* 2006, 2010), or the combination of the latter two (Mamadouh and Raunio 2002, 2003; Lindberg 2008). Despite the valuable insights these studies have brought, their findings are not always reconcilable.

Analysing report allocation in the period 1999–2004, Kaeding (2004, 2005) concluded that it did not proportionally reflect the EP composition. Focusing on the Environment committee, he found that the Liberals, the Greens/European Free Alliance and the European United Left – Nordic Green Left were over-represented in the report assignment, while the European People's Party and the Socialists produced 10 per cent fewer reports than expected from their sizes. He showed that variations also existed between countries, where Italy and France produced only a small number of reports, while Sweden, Belgium and the Netherlands produced twice as many as expected. It appears that MEPs from environmentally conscious and Nordic member states are more active and dominate the committee. Thus, the distribution of reports in the Environment committee is not fully representative of the national and partisan composition of the EP plenary. Kaeding (2005) provided descriptive statistics suggesting that this is also true of the other committees. Considering all the reports allocated in the period 1994–2004, he showed that the two biggest party groups (EPP and PSE) were considerably over-represented in all but the Environment committee, and when member states were considered, Germany and the Netherlands performed well above the average. He concluded that: 'The world of committee reports is one of disproportionality within party groups and national delegations that contradicts the overall principle laid down in the standing rules of procedure of the EP' (Kaeding 2005: 99–100).

In contrast, Benedetto (2005: 80) claims that with the exception of slight over-representation of EPP and PSE, the allocation of codecision reports in the periods 1996–1998 and 1999–2001 was highly proportional to the party group sizes. However, it was not proportional to the sizes of national delegations. On the one hand, this could be ascribed to the influential role played by the large national party delegations (Mamadouh and Raunio 2002, 2003), which tend to be privileged in the report allocation. Mamadouh and Raunio (2003: 333) state that 'national party delegations inside the transnational groups are often key gatekeepers in the division of spoils within the groups.' They further specify that this holds true specifically for the constituent parties of the two biggest party groups – EPP and PSE. On the other hand, Høyland's (2006a) findings suggest that it is MEPs from national parties represented in the Council of Ministers who are the more frequent rapporteurs of the codecision legislation. His analysis demonstrated that the number of codecision reports produced by governing parties is 43 per cent higher than that written by opposition parties. Along the same lines, Benedetto (2005) alludes to some MEPs having privileged access to the Council of Ministers and the European Commission owing to their national party affiliation.

Thus, disagreements regarding the level and causes of disproportionality in report allocation to party groups and national party delegations seem to be ir-resolvable when considering aggregate level data. This has led scholars to turn to individual level explanations. Legislators' individual interests and experiences could be the source of discrepancies. Benedetto (2005) concludes that besides the desire to observe party proportionality, report allocation can be shaped by leg-islators' self-selection and expertise. Similarly, Mamadouh and Raunio (2003: 344) acknowledge that 'policy expertise is a major consideration' when it comes to individual appointments. More concrete evidence of the impact of individual level considerations is given by Kaeding (2005). He finds that having working experience at the European level has a strong positive impact on being allocated a report, as does affiliation to Greenpeace and other environmental groups. The latter observation reflects the Environment committee's composition of mem-bers affiliated with green interest groups (see Chapter Three, see also Bowler and Farrell 1995; McElroy 2006). Furthermore, in their study on report allocation in the Environment committee, Yoshinaka et al. (2006: 19) show that 'expertise, ide-ology, and views on European integration all affect the likelihood that an MEP will be a repeat rapporteur.' In their concurrent with the present study analysis of all report allocations in the 4th and 5th EP terms, Yoshinaka et al. (2010) conclude that, alongside ideological affinity to one's party group median (but not national party delegation median), expertise is a prime determinant of report allocation. Yet, Lindberg (2008) did not find expertise to be a strong explanatory factor of the selection of a rapporteur in the Legal Affairs committee for the services directive – the most salient and politically controversial EP legislative act of the past ten years. Nor did he find clear evidence that leadership of national party delegations or party groups selected the rapporteur based on partisan loyalty or proximity to party leaders' preferences. Similarly, Kreppel (2002a) showed that the most pro-lific rapporteurs during the 3rd and 4th EP terms did not exhibit higher levels of party group loyalty (as reflected in voting) than other legislators.

Potentially, differences in the level of proportionality in report allocation could be detected in the allocations of different types of report. A first step in this di-rection is the study of Hausemer (2006: 254), who shows that MEPs from large national delegations, committee chairs and preference outliers obtain less salient reports than their party group colleagues, defining salience in terms of impor-tance for their own national party as reflected in party manifestos. He attributes this disproportionality to the party group leaderships' concern with maintaining group cohesion. Since smaller national party delegations are disadvantaged in the assignment of high-ranking parliamentary positions, group leaders compensate them with reports of higher salience for them to keep their support in voting. Additionally, he holds that due to the open amendment rule in committee and plenary, MEPs who are not part of the majority coalition (EPP-ED and ALDE) do not have incentives to compete for the most popular reports and, thus, focus on a restricted range of policy areas of particular interest to them.

While the studies surveyed above have greatly enhanced our understanding of report allocation, there is currently no common underlying pattern in their findings. It is argued here that the solution lies in identifying the conditions under which the different factors play a role as prescribed by the inter-institutional context. This chapter proposes to examine the predictions of the alternative congressional theoretical approaches in the parallel study of codecision and consultation report allocations. Are factors such as partisan affiliation, party group loyalty, expertise and interest group ties equally important in the allocation of codecision and consultation reports, or are there systematic differences in their level of influence? When is report allocation guided primarily by party groups' considerations or individual preferences? These questions are addressed by testing the theoretical predictions developed in the next section, which are based on the incentive structures of MEPs and party group coordinators as the ultimate report allocators.

## Hypotheses

The internal parliamentary organisation of the EP shapes its ability to fully exercise its legislative power and advance its position in negotiations with the Council of Ministers. However, the EP's organisation is in turn shaped by the inter-institutional rules governing these negotiations. Hence, it is impossible to fully understand the intra-parliamentary organisation in isolation from the inter-institutional context. Owing to the substantively higher legislative power of the EP under the codecision than under the consultation procedure, there is higher internal competition for codecision reports. Consequently, different factors are likely to shape the allocation of codecision and consultation reports. Thus, the hypotheses on report allocation developed below take into account the type of report under consideration. Although they are based on the specific incentives and interests of party group coordinators and MEPs, the hypotheses are broadly informed by the congressional literature.

While the system of rapporteurs originates in the continental parliamentary practice and does not exist in the US Congress (Corbett *et al.* 2005), hypotheses about report allocation can nevertheless be informed by the congressional theories. Since party group coordinators in the EP are the ones 'purchasing' reports for their groups and selecting individual rapporteurs, it is reasonable to presume that the partisan rationale has the highest explanatory power in accounting for report allocation, while distributive and informational factors would play a role only if they do not clash with the interests of the party leadership, i.e. of the party group coordinators.

The partisan rationale (Kiewiet and McCubbins 1991; Cox and McCubbins

1993, 2007) prescribes that the majority party dominates the work and output of committees while the minority party is neglected. However, as previously discussed and in contrast to the US bi-partisan legislature, a plurality of national parties and European party groups are present in the EP and no single party group has ever held an absolute majority of the parliamentary seats. Thus, it could be expected that a majority coalition of party groups in the European Parliament would dominate the committees' work and division of tasks instead. Yet again, no such permanent majority coalition exists in the EP, which, unlike the national parliaments in the EU member states, does not appoint a government. Thus, legislative majorities have to be created specifically for each issue. There have been two big party groups in the EP – the EPP (EPP-ED during the 6th EP) in the centre-right and PSE in the centre-left of the political spectrum. The EPP-ED held more seats in the 6th EP term. The absolute parliamentary majority (at least half of all MEPs regardless of how many are present at a vote), required in the second reading of the codecision procedure to amend or reject legislative proposals, is difficult to form without assent from both groups. For a long time, grand coalitions between EPP-ED and PSE were commonplace in adopting the EP's legislative position (Hix *et al.* 2007). However, only a simple majority (i.e. 50 per cent of the voting MEPs) is needed to amend legislative proposals under the consultation procedure and in the first reading of the codecision procedure. In these cases, other minimal winning coalitions are more attractive as they are easier to secure. The simple majority rule is applied increasingly more often with 64 per cent of all codecision dossiers during the first term of the 6th EP concluded in first reading (European Parliament 2007a). This gives higher flexibility to EPP-ED, which as the biggest party group is most often the agenda-setter in forming a working majority coalition with either PSE or ALDE. The simple majority rule puts in a powerful position the third biggest party group ALDE, which, being ideologically positioned between EPP-ED and PSE, is a convenient coalition partner for each side in most policy areas. Obtaining the backing of ALDE greatly decreases the interdependence of the larger party groups. Thus, it is any configuration of the three biggest party groups EPP-ED, PSE and ALDE that most often forms an EP majority.[7] They can be expected to dominate the EP committees and their most important legislative tasks. The informal points system governing report allocation favours bigger party groups who own the most points for 'purchasing' reports, giving them higher bargaining power and manoeuvre for strategic behaviour in the bidding for popular reports. Therefore, it is expected that their members be privileged in the allocation of the more competitive codecision reports.

---

7.   Notably, in the period 2004–2007 with 88 members ALDE was much smaller than EPP-ED (288 members) and PSE (200 members) but still twice as big as the next biggest party group.

***H1a:*** *Membership of one of the three biggest European party groups – EPP-ED, PSE and ALDE – increases the number of codecision reports allocated to a committee member /substitute.*

If the bigger party groups are indeed over-represented in the allocation of codecision reports, they spent most of their points on these expensive reports. Logically, this should come at the expense of purchasing fewer consultation reports, since the total number of points per party group is fixed. Therefore, more consultation reports are expected to be written by members of the smaller party groups or, if not wanted, by the respective committee chairs. However, on the whole we can anticipate members of the bigger party groups to write fewer consultation reports.

***H1b:*** *Membership of one of the three biggest European party groups – EPP-ED, PSE and ALDE – decreases the number of consultation reports allocated to a committee member/ substitute.*

Once the competition between party groups has been resolved, reports are allocated to individual legislators by group coordinators. This process is contingent upon the incentives of both individual MEPs and the party group coordinators and, therefore, will be theorised below in view of these incentives. The selection or 'self-selection' of rapporteurs may be influenced by multiple factors such as their partisan loyalty, special interests or expertise, not unlike the committee assignments (see Chapter Three). Furthermore, irrespective of whether legislators seek policy or career (Hix *et al.* 1999), drafting legislative reports can facilitate achieving their goals by increasing their visibility.

Firstly, legislators who are primarily interested in furthering their career in national or European politics depend on their national parties for re-election. Writing reports on matters of interest to their national parties and in accordance with the parties' positions is one of the main ways in which MEPs can increase their 're-selection' prospects.[8] However, national parties are reportedly uninterested in the day-to-day operation of the EP and most of them may only try to 'ensure higher level of responsiveness on committees that have legislative powers' (Whitaker 2005: 5, 2001). Furthermore, most of them have better ways of influencing consultation legislation by directly addressing their respective national governments that sit in the Council of Ministers rather than lobbying the EP. Thus, legislators interested in 'pleasing' their national party leaders would prefer writing codecision reports. According to the predictions of the partisan theory (Cox and McCubbins 1993), party group coordinators would use this intense competition for reports, and especially codecision reports, as a means of enhancing group cohesion.

---

8. MEPs use other means of obtaining the favour of their national party leaders, too. For instance, Slapin and Proksch (2010) hold that alerting their national parties to their compliant behaviour is a major reason for MEPs to choose to give parliamentary speeches in the case of conflict between their national parties and EP groups. The other reason, they suggest, is explaining one's voting defection from the European party group to other group members.

Coordinators have been referred to as party group 'whips' or 'watchdogs' within their committees, whose primary goal is achieving consensus among the committee contingents of their groups (Settembri and Neuhold 2009: 141–2; Corbett *et al.* 2005). Thus, they are expected to reward loyal group members, i.e. members who most often vote with the respective party groups' median members, and punish disloyal members in allocating legislative reports.

*H2: Party group disloyalty decreases the number of reports allocated to a committee member/substitute.*

The negative effect of party group disloyalty is expected to be even stronger in the allocation of codecision reports, for which competition is keener.

*H2a: This effect is stronger in the allocation of codecision reports.*

Secondly, legislators who have specialised knowledge in a particular field may be attracted to writing reports falling within their areas of expertise, or be externally motivated to do so. The need for information could not be stressed more in the case of the EP, which has limited staff and resources to obtain information regarding potential policy outcomes. Thus, it has the freedom, but also the necessity, to build its own expertise. Emphasising the information accumulation role of the committees in a setting of uncertainty due to the lack of a majority party, the informational theory (Krehbiel 1991) predicts that the plenary would create incentives for individual members to specialise. Members who can specialise at low cost due to their educational and professional background would be assigned to respective specialised committees. Indeed, as Chapter Three showed, economists tend to serve on the committees of Economic and Monetary Affairs and Budgetary Affairs; lawyers are concentrated in the Committee of Legal Affairs; members with previous experience in the transport sector are mostly assigned to the Committee on Transport, etc. Another incentive for specialisation that the plenary creates is 'the possibility of repeated appointments as rapporteur' (Yoshinaka *et al.* 2006: 7–8), which is reflected in the flexibility of EP rules with respect to the proportional allocation of reports.

A coordinator has an incentive to announce the names of the potential expert rapporteurs he or she envisions at the stage of allocating the report between the party groups because '[i]f the suggested rapporteur is recognised as a specialist on the issue it is easier to get agreement on his or her nomination' (Corbett *et al.* 2005: 134). Appointing a member with relevant expertise may facilitate the majority formation in committee and plenary. It is cost-free for a party group coordinator to allocate consultation reports to expert members, for which competition is generally low. Thus, experts are expected to write disproportionately many consultation reports. However, expertise is expected to be less of a determining factor in the allocation of codecision reports, for which not only inter-group, but also intra-group competition is stronger. As discussed above, in this case there may be a trade-off between choosing an expert rapporteur and a loyal party group member, in which case the latter factor would be more important for the party group leadership primarily seeking group cohesion.

This leads to the following hypotheses:

**H3:** *Having committee-specific expertise increases the number of reports allocated to a committee member/substitute.*

**H3a:** *This effect is weaker in the allocation of codecision reports.*

Finally, MEPs may be foremost policy-driven and seek policy that advances their own policy preferences, reflected in the interest groups with which they have been affiliated. The distributive rationale (Shepsle 1978) prescribes that committees serve special interests outside the legislative body, be it territorial interests or specific interest groups, on which their members depend for their re-election or future career. Interest groups can enhance MEPs' re-election chances by increasing their national party's vote share (e.g. trade unions), or their future job prospects outside politics (e.g. industry and business groups). While legislators' interest group ties are likely linked to some form of expertise, this expertise is associated with outlying ideological positions in the respective policy areas, which negatively affects their chances of obtaining popular reports.

Being selected by the committee contingents of their party groups, party group coordinators have the incentive to keep the majority of their group members satisfied with the rapporteur selection. Assuming that legislators with special interest tend to have ideal policy positions away from the group median, coordinators would not select them as rapporteurs on important reports. Given the heterogeneous party groups' membership of national delegations with sometimes differing interests, the selection of a rapporteur with median views in a respective area who can draft a report representing the views of most group members within a committee is essential for intra-group majority formation. Thus, in the allocation of codecision reports where a lot is at stake, a group member with special interest group ties is unlikely to be selected irrespective of his or her expertise.

**H4a:** *Having interest group ties decreases the number of codecision reports a committee member/substitute is allocated.*

Nevertheless, the EP is still the interest groups' primary lobbying point due to their limited access to the Council of Ministers. Aiming to represent such groups, MEPs with respective interest group ties would be interested in drafting consultation reports in the specific areas in order to voice their opinion and, thus, signal their support for the respective groups. The open amendment rule in committee and plenary provides further incentives for them to focus on reports of high salience for them but of lower common popularity so that their reports are not heavily modified. Depending on all party groups' contingents in their committees for re-selection, group coordinators have an incentive not to systematically exclude any group members from writing reports, especially those who are single representatives of their national party delegation within the committees. Thus, members with special interests would not be prevented from drafting consultation reports unless they vote systematically against the group, i.e. they are manifestly disloyal and thus unlikely to appeal to the majority within their groups (see Hypotheses 2 and 2a). In order to maintain group cohesion, group coordinators would be willing to allocate to legislators with special interests consultation reports of particular importance for them, but for which there is little general interest and competition (see Hausemer 2006).

**H4b:** *Having interest group ties increases the number of consultation reports a committee member/substitute is allocated.*

## Research design

This section presents the research design of the study on report allocation. The data, measures and methods are presented below.

### Data

The data on the individual profiles of MEPs is based on the information available on the EP website and in Eurosource (2005) (see Chapter Three), while the original data on the codecision and consultation reports was extracted from the Legislative Observatory site of the EP in the period March – July, 2009. The analyses cover report allocations during the first half-term of the 6th EP (22nd July 2004 and 31st January 2007) since committee assignments are reshuffled every two and a half years. Only substantive reports were considered, excluding reports considered under the simplified procedure without amendment or debate (European Parliament 2009b, Rule 46, ex Rule 43), codifications, technical reports meant solely to formalise the new parliamentary powers in implementation due to the entry into force of the regulatory procedure with scrutiny, and reports solely giving a parliamentary mandate to the Commission for the employment of new executives of the European agencies. For such reports a rapporteur is either not assigned or plays a minor technical role. In total, the allocation of 257 consultation and 223 codecision reports is examined in two separate sets of models. Only committees that produced codecision or consultation reports are covered in the respective models. Thus, the analysis of codecision report allocation excludes the Constitutional Affairs and Petitions committees, while the analysis of consultation report allocation excludes the committees on Internal Market and Consumer Protection, Women Affairs and Petitions. Once again, the semi-structured interviews conducted with MEPs and EP staff members are used to complement the statistical analysis.

The unit of analysis required to test the hypotheses on the impact of committee-specific expertise and interest group ties is a committee member (full or substitute). Since an MEP can serve on more than one committee, and most members are full members on one committee and substitutes on another, the data set on individual legislators has been stacked so that each observation in the restructured data (legislator*committee) represents a committee member or a substitute (Van der Eijk and Franklin 1996; for a similar approach see Yoshinaka *et al.* 2010). While demographics and partisan variables stay constant after stacking, the other independent variables are re-coded to reflect the nature of the legislator-committee relationship (e.g. committee-specific expertise). Because one MEP can appear multiple times in the data, such observations are weighted with sampling weights to reflect the real number of legislators in the Parliament (Long and Freese 2003: 73).

### Measures and methods

The two dependent variables represent the number of codecision or consultation reports assigned to a committee member or a substitute. These are discrete variables ranging from 0 to 3, where 3 means an MEP has been allocated three or more reports of the respective type. Since the dependent variables are non-negative counts, count models are most appropriate for the present study. The dependent variable measuring the number of allocated codecision reports is suitable for and modelled with a simple Poisson model. However, the overdispersion in the variable measuring the number of allocated consultation reports, reflected in its conditional variance being substantively higher than its conditional mean, calls for a negative binomial regression model (Long and Freese 2003: 266–7). The latter model only adds one additional parameter to the Poisson model to account for unobserved heterogeneity among observations and, thus, to correct the standard errors, which are otherwise biased downward. Hence, the two used models have the same mean structure and their results are comparable.

Similarly to the previous chapter, dummies for membership in the three biggest European party groups – EPP-ED, PSE, and ALDE – are introduced to test Hypothesis 1. In testing Hypotheses 2 and 2a on the impact of party group loyalty, the 1st dimension NOMINATE scores of MEPs (introduced in Chapter Three) representing the relative positions of legislators based on their voting records are used to calculate the absolute distance of MEPs from the median positions of their party groups. A small distance reflects a loyal voting record, while a large distance is a sign of disloyal behaviour. Notwithstanding the inherent problems of the NOMINATE scores discussed in Chapter Three, they are nevertheless the most suitable proxy for party group loyalty, as it is the observable voting behaviour of legislators that party groups coordinators would be familiar with and base their allocation decisions on.[9] While party group coordinators are supposed to allocate reports proportionally to the sizes of the national party delegations within their groups, this is not necessary the case. To verify, the size of a member's national party delegation in the EP is controlled for in the models. Furthermore, a variable accounting for the proportion of time that a member's national party was in government during the examined period is included in order to address previous research suggesting that national parties in government write more codecision reports than opposition parties (Høyland 2006a). This variable is calculated by dividing the number of months that a legislator's party was in government by the total number of months in the examined period, i.e. thirty.

---

9.  See Chapter Three for a detailed discussion of the NOMINATE scores.

In testing Hypotheses 3 and 3a, information on MEPs' educational and professional background is used to create a new 'committee-specific expertise' variable, signifying whether the expertise of a committee member is relevant for the respective committee on which he or she sits or serves as a substitute. This variable is coded as 1 if a member fulfils the following conditions: has educational and professional experience in economics and sits (as a full member or a substitute) on the Budgets Committee or the Committee of Economic and Monetary Affairs; has a legal education or career and sits on the Committee of Legal Affairs or the Committee of Constitutional Affairs; has experience in international politics and sits on the Committee of Foreign Affairs; has a natural sciences or engineering education and sits on the Committee of Industry, Research and Energy or the Committee of Environment, Public Health and Food Safety; has a medical education and sits on the latter committee; or has professional expertise in the transport or telecommunication sectors and sits on the Committee of Transport and Tourism.

Analogically, to test Hypotheses 4a and 4b, a 'committee-specific interest' variable is created. It is a dummy variable assuming the value of 0 unless at the beginning of the 6th EP term a member: has had farming ties and is on the Agriculture Committee; has had green group ties and is on the Committee of Environment, Public Health and Food Safety; has had trade union ties and is on the Committee of Employment and Social Affairs; has had industry or business ties and is on the Committee of Industry, Research and Energy or the Committee of Economic and Monetary Affairs; or has had ties to social groups and is on the Committee of Civil Liberties, Justice and Home Affairs. In Chapter Three, we saw that members with such interest group ties have higher chances of assignment to the respective committees. Appendix F provides some descriptive statistics on the variables indicating committee-specific expertise and interest.

Additionally, previous membership on the same committee in the last EP term is controlled for to take into consideration the impact of seniority. So is also the number of reports allocated to a member other than the ones measured in the respective dependent variable, serving as a proxy for both the level of workload of legislators and their experience in drafting reports. Due to the crucial role that the party group coordinators play in the allocation of reports, a dummy variable is included to mark whether a committee member is a coordinator or not. Similarly, the effect of being a committee chair is controlled for. All models include dummies for gender and age, as well as fixed effects for committee membership.[10] The latter are included because substantial differences are expected between committees owing, for instance, to the different number and types of report they drafted in the studied period and their different sizes. To address further the intra-group correlation of observations, robust standard errors are estimated to decrease the chances of committing type 1 errors (Hosmer and Lemeshow 2000, Section 8.3).

---

10. A control for the size of one's member state delegation was included in the preliminary data analysis but did not have a significant impact and was dropped from the final analysis.

**Empirical analysis of report allocation**

The findings of the count models are displayed in Table 4.1. The dependent variable in the first three models is the number of allocated codecision (COD) reports, while in the last three models it is the number of allocated consultation (CNS) reports to a full committee member or a substitute. In order to avoid reporting spurious relationships, the independent variables are introduced stepwise, testing first the effect of individual background only, then the effect of party-related factors, and finally all effects simultaneously. Since the observed significant effects in the full models are significant also in the partial models, only the final models on codecision and consultation report allocation are discussed below. For better readability, the fixed committee effects are only displayed in Appendix G. The factor changes in the number of reports allocated to a committee member or substitute for a unit increase in a dichotomous independent variable or a standard deviation increase in a continuous independent variable, holding all other variables constant, are displayed in Table 4.2. The results of the statistical analysis are presented and discussed below together with the evidence from the semi-structured interviews.

The data from MEP interviews is certainly in line with Hypothesis 1a. Asked about the principles guiding report allocation to party groups, members of bigger and smaller groups alike shared the same beliefs:

> You sort of try to balance that the big ones [party groups] get the important reports, the smaller ones have to take the not so important reports, and the smallest get what is left over, ... and sometimes it's just a pure dog fight. (Personal interview 9 with an EPP-ED member, 27th February 2008)

> You can say the biggest groups get the best reports. (Personal interview 10 with an ALDE member, 27th February 2008)

> Sometimes it is simply a question of power. The big groups make a gentlemen's agreement and say – ok, this is coming and let's share it between us. (Personal interview 11 with a member of the EPP-ED secretariat, 27th February 2008)

However, the results of the quantitative analysis only partially confirm Hypothesis 1a. The model on the allocation of codecision reports shows that after controlling for all other factors, being a member of either EPP-ED or ALDE multiplies the predicted number of codecision reports an MEP is allocated by a factor of 1.9 and 1.8, respectively (see Table 4.2). However, this is not the case for the members of PSE. This finding corroborates Hausemer's (2006: 513) claim that 'the distribution of salient reports mirrors coalition dynamics in the Parliament'. Recent roll call vote analysis shows that 'party competition and coalition formation in the European Parliament occur along the classical left-right dimension, and that the two main political groups vote together less than they used to' (Hix *et al.* 2007: 148). In the 4th and 5th EP terms, grand coalitions between EPP and PSE were common and necessary to reach the required absolute parliamentary majorities at the time, a fact reflected in their over–representation in the report allocation

*Table 4.1: Count models of codecision and consultation report allocation during 2004–2007*

| | COD M1 | COD M2 | COD M3 | CNS M1 | CNS M2 | CNS M3 |
|---|---|---|---|---|---|---|
| Committee-related interest group ties | 0.127 | | 0.144 | .280** | | 0.322** |
| | (0.150) | | (0.133) | (.129) | | (0.157) |
| Committee-related expertise | 0.001 | | 0.048 | .424* | | 0.405* |
| | (0.184) | | (0.157) | (.253) | | (0.232) |
| Party group disloyalty | | -3.270** | -3.378** | | -3.232** | -2.541* |
| | | (1.274) | (1.501) | | (1.480) | (1.323) |
| EPP-ED | | 0.531* | 0.641** | | 0.126 | 0.237 |
| | | (0.272) | (0.291) | | (0.383) | (0.481) |
| PSE | | 0.225 | 0.366 | | -0.233 | -0.062 |
| | | (0.286) | (0.289) | | (0.449) | (0.517) |
| ALDE | | 0.596* | 0.593** | | 0.311 | 0.219 |
| | | (0.310) | (0.283) | | (0.511) | (0.508) |
| National party delegation size | | 0.014** | -0.002 | | 0.016** | 0.011 |
| | | (0.007) | (0.008) | | (0.007) | (0.008) |
| Time in government | | 0.120 | 0.092 | | -0.164 | -0.080 |
| | | (0.169) | (0.137) | | (0.171) | (0.192) |
| No. of codecision reports | | | | | | 0.543*** |
| | | | | | | (0.180) |
| No. of consultation reports | | | 0.418*** | | | |
| | | | (0.096) | | | |
| Previously in committee | | | 0.878*** | | | -0.126 |
| | | | (0.148) | | | (0.250) |
| Chair | | | 0.156 | | | 1.189*** |
| | | | (0.526) | | | (0.396) |
| Coordinator | | | .458** | | | 0.574 |
| | | | (0.203) | | | (0.383) |
| Male | -0.480*** | -0.461*** | -0.360*** | -0.173 | -0.126 | -0.134 |
| | (0.106) | (0.097) | (0.121) | (0.171) | (0.145) | (0.144) |
| Age | 0.006 | 0.002 | -0.008 | 0.016* | 0.014 | 0.011 |
| | (0.008) | (0.008) | (0.008) | (0.009) | (0.009) | (0.010) |
| Substitute | -1.822*** | -1.842*** | -1.435*** | -1.062*** | -1.104*** | -0.750*** |
| | (0.292) | (0.283) | (0.262) | (0.238) | (0.240) | (0.241) |
| Committee fixed effects | Yes | Yes | Yes | Yes | Yes | Yes |
| Constant | -3.034*** | -3.254*** | -3.178*** | -3.775*** | -3.339*** | -3.744*** |
| | (0.491) | (0.516) | (0.561) | (0.514) | (0.488) | (0.749) |

|  | COD M1 | COD M2 | COD M3 | CNS M1 | CNS M2 | CNS M3 |
|---|---|---|---|---|---|---|
| Log-pseudolikelihood | -243.0 | -232.2 | -217.3 | -228.2 | -221.8 | -214.5 |
| McFadden ps. Rsq | 0.22 | 0.24 | 0.29 | 0.15 | 0.16 | 0.19 |
| Alpha |  |  |  | 1.767 | 1.479 | 1.005 |
| lnalpha |  |  |  | 0.570 | 0.391 | 0.005 |
| N | 1547 | 1475 | 1475 | 1471 | 1399 | 1399 |

*Note*: Dependent variables: number of codecision (COD M1–3) and consultation (CNS M1–3) reports allocated to a committee member/substitute. Robust standard errors displayed in brackets, * significance at 10%, ** significance at 5%, *** significance at 1%. Full models with the committee fixed effects shown in Appendix G.

(Mamadouh and Raunio 2003; Benedetto 2005; Kaeding 2005). However, a much smaller parliamentary majority is often sufficient nowadays due to the drastic increase in the number of codecision acts concluded in 1st reading since the Amsterdam Treaty (1999).[11] Furthermore, since a centre-right majority holds both the EP and the Council of Ministers since 2004, it has become easier for the EPP-ED to advance its positions with the Council even when it is not supported by PSE when the codecision procedure applies and under qualified majority voting in the Council. Contrary to Hypothesis 1b, membership in none of the three biggest party groups seems to have a significant negative effect on the allocation of consultation reports.

As affiliation to EPP-ED and ALDE facilitates getting codecision reports at the individual level, this must be reflected in the distribution of codecision reports among party groups at the aggregate level. Hence, report allocation in the nine most prolific committees (drafting 90 per cent of all codecision reports in the period) is portrayed in order to see on which committees the members of the working majority party group coalition are over-represented in the writing of codecision reports. The difference between the observed and the expected number of codecision reports per party group based on their sizes in the EP and the total number of codecision reports allocated in the respective committee in the considered period is shown in Table 4.3. There are indeed considerable variations between committees. While the report allocation in the Environment and Legal Affairs committees seems to be relatively proportional to the sizes of the party groups, EPP-ED is over-represented on three committees, namely Industry, Internal Market and Consumer Protection, and Civil Liberties; PSE is over-represented on the Employment, and Culture and Education committees and under-represented on the committees of Economic and Monetary Affairs, and Transport; and ALDE is over-represented on

---

11. The Amsterdam Treaty (1999) abolished the Council's ability to reinstate its common position if no compromise is reached with the Council after the third reading of the codecision procedure and introduced the option of early conclusion of codecision acts already in first reading.

the committees of Economic and Monetary Affairs, Transport, and Civil Liberties. More generally, Table 4.3 shows that indeed EPP-ED and ALDE are over-represented in the total number of codecision reports written by members of the nine committees.

Furthermore, the results of the count models provide strong evidence for Hypothesis 2. Party group disloyalty has a significant negative effect on the number of both kinds of report a member is allocated. Indeed:

> If you see that constantly someone is against the group line you would doubt that he is the right person to represent the group. (Personal interview 11 with a member of the EPP-ED secretariat, 27th February 2008)

*Table 4.2: Factor changes in the expected count of reports for a unit/a standard deviation increase in x*

|                                         | COD m3  | CNS m3  |
| --------------------------------------- | ------- | ------- |
| Committee-related interest group ties   | 1.1546  | 1.3792  |
| Committee-related expertise             | 1.0494  | 1.4997  |
| Party group disloyalty                  | 0.6600  | 0.7282  |
| EPP-ED                                  | 1.8982  | 1.2671  |
| PSE                                     | 1.4418  | 0.9396  |
| ALDE                                    | 1.8092  | 1.2446  |
| National party delegation size          | 0.9765  | 1.1161  |
| Time in government                      | 1.0395  | 0.9669  |
| No. of codecision reports               |         | 1.2759  |
| No. of consultation reports             | 1.2344  |         |
| Previously in committee                 | 2.4070  | 0.8815  |
| Chair                                   | 1.1694  | 3.2835  |
| Coordinator                             | 1.5816  | 1.7761  |
| Male                                    | 0.6979  | 0.8742  |
| Age                                     | 0.9219  | 1.1137  |
| Substitute                              | 0.2380  | 0.4723  |

*Note*: The factor change in the expected count is shown for a standard deviation increase in party group disloyalty, national party delegation size, time in government, No. of codecision reports, No. of consultation reports and Age, holding all other variables at their mean. For all other variables, the factor change in the expected count for their discrete change from 0 to 1 is displayed.

*Table 4.3: Observed minus expected number of codecision reports per party group in % (2004–2006)*

|  | ECON | EMPL | ENVI | ITRE | IMCO | TRAN | CULT | JURI | LIBE | Total |
|---|---|---|---|---|---|---|---|---|---|---|
| EPP-ED | 0.3 | -8.7 | 1.7 | 17.9 | 13.7 | 2.1 | 9.5 | 6.8 | 12.5 | 4.6 |
| PSE | -13.7 | 24.4 | -1.3 | 8.0 | 2.7 | -14.1 | 13.6 | 2.4 | 6.1 | 1.1 |
| ALDE | 17.0 | -5.3 | 1.7 | 6.2 | -0.3 | 29.8 | 0.6 | 0.5 | 12.0 | 6.0 |
| G/EFA | -6.8 | 1.5 | 2.7 | -7.7 | 0.2 | -9.6 | 0.7 | -2.3 | -7.3 | -2.4 |
| EUL/NGL | -6.7 | 1.7 | 0.1 | -7.5 | 0.4 | 4.2 | -7.5 | -2.3 | -7.1 | -1.8 |
| IND/DEM | -5.8 | -5.3 | 1.1 | -6.6 | -6.4 | -8.3 | -6.6 | -2.0 | -6.3 | -3.5 |
| UEN | 8.1 | -4.0 | 0.1 | -4.9 | -4.8 | -1.7 | -4.9 | -1.5 | -4.7 | -1.3 |
| na | 7.6 | -4.4 | -6.0 | -5.5 | -5.4 | -2.3 | -5.5 | -1.7 | -5.2 | -2.7 |
| Total reports | 19 | 14 | 53 | 12 | 17 | 37 | 16 | 15 | 28 | 211 |

*Note:* Abbreviations: ECON: Economic and Monetary Affairs; EMPL: Employment and Social Affairs; ENVI: Environment, Public Health and Food Safety; ITRE: Industry, Research and Energy; IMCO: Internal Market and Consumer Protection; TRAN: Transport and Tourism; CULT: Culture and Education; JURI: Legal Affairs; LIBE: Civil Liberties, Justice and Home Affairs; AFCO: Constitutional Affairs; EPP-ED: Group of European People's Party (Christian Democrats) and European Democrats; PSE: Socialist Group in the European Parliament; ALDE: Group of the Alliance of Liberals and Democrats for Europe; G/EGA: Group of the Greens/European Free Alliance; EUL/NGL: Confederal Group of the European United Left – Nordic Green Left; IND/DEM: Independence/Democracy Group; UEN: Union of Europe of the Nations Group; na: Non-attached members.

It appears that allegiance to one's party group has become a more important factor in the report allocation than shown in past research (see Kreppel 2002a), which Yoshinaka *et al.* (2010) confirm. There is, however, insufficient evidence that this effect is stronger for codecision than consultation reports as suggested by Hypothesis 2a. While the model coefficients (see Table 4.1) as well as the factor changes (see Table 4.2) in the full models imply that the effect of disloyalty is higher on codecision report allocations, this difference may have occurred by chance. In Figure 4.1 the predicted number of report allocations as party group disloyalty increases is displayed for each procedure, holding the remaining variables at their mean. Although the slope is steeper in the first graph, the confidence intervals of the two graphs largely overlap, thus providing no evidence for a systematically stronger negative effect of disloyalty on codecision than on consultation report allocation.

The analyses give mixed evidence regarding Hypotheses 3 and 3a. Committee-specific expertise appears to be unrelated to the number of codecision reports one is allocated, contrary to the predictions of Hypothesis 3a. This may be due to the fact that a member's party group loyalty, being the strongest factor for obtaining codecision reports, shadows the effect of expertise. This is how an MEP from a small party group replied when asked whether an important report would be given to her group instead of EPP-ED if a member of that small group were an acknowledged expert in the respective policy area:

> No, not if the EPP really wants to have it. Then, they would say – you will be the shadow, you will do your comments and amendments but it's from the majority point of view, it's our EPP prerogative to have it and we will have it. And it is a very hard bargaining on that. If they want to have it they are not very generous, they will not give it to us even if it is a person with a lot of experience or knowledge, or something like that. They will not give it. (Personal interview 6 with a Green/EFA member, 30th January 2008)

Nevertheless, in line with Hypothesis 3b, having relevant expertise changes the expected number of consultation reports a member is allocated by a factor of 1.5, holding all other variables constant. Thus, the effect of the trade-off between group loyalty and expertise is weaker for consultation reports, for which intra-group competition is lower.

Having committee-specific special interests does not have a significant negative effect on the number of received codecision reports, contrary to Hypothesis 4a, but neither is the effect positive. Yet the interview data support the theoretical prediction that party group policy outliers will be marginalised in the report allocation:

> The role of the coordinator is to make a choice, also to see who is a good representative of our group, in this case. So, you do not choose somebody who has an extreme position. [...] in the end it is also a decision on whom the coordinator trusts. (Personal interview 11 with a member of the EPP-ED secretariat, 27th February 2008)

> Obviously, the coordinator has to be sensible and not propose, you know, giving all the reports to one person or to a person whose views are totally out of sync with the rest of the group. (Personal interview 3 with a PSE member, 12th February 2008)

> You know if someone is in the Environment committee and they have a consistently different line than the other of us that's in the Environment committee then probably that person wouldn't get many reports. I know of people in the EPP that are very green and environment friendly but the EPP are not, so they just never get reports because they simply don't represent the group. (Personal interview 1 with a PSE member, 27th February 2008)

The Environment committee, however, operates mainly under the codecision procedure. As Hypothesis 4b prescribes, committee-specific special interests do have a significant positive effect on the number of consultation reports allocated to a committee member, which it multiplies by a factor of 1.38. Party group coordinators have an incentive not to completely marginalise certain members from writing of reports. As one interviewee reflected:

Codecision Reports                     Consultation Reports

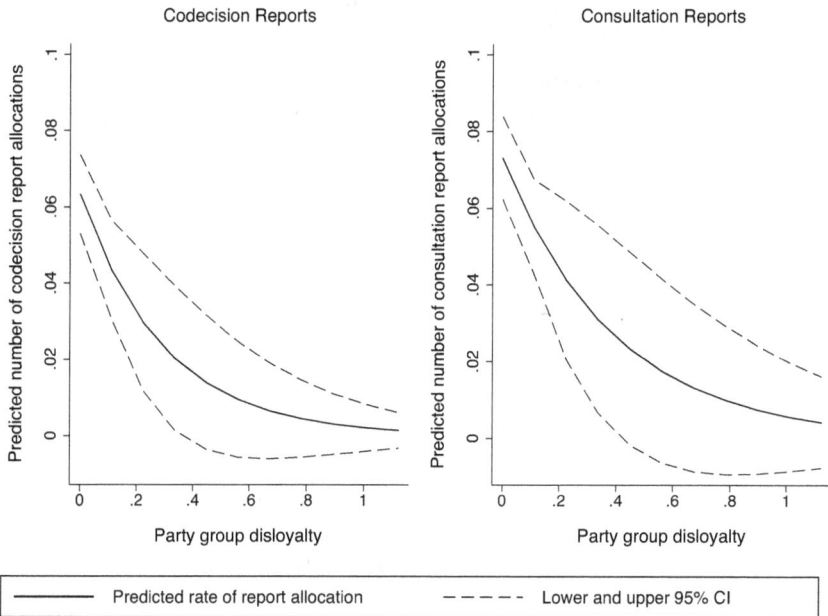

*Figure 4.1: Predicted effect of party group disloyalty on the number of codecision and consultation reports allocated to a committee member or a substitute*

I think coordinators look for [...] over a period of time getting a reasoned balance so that every member of the committee gets the chance at some point during the five years, or the two and a half years, to have a report on something and making sure that there is a reasonable spread. (Personal interview 3 with a PSE member, 12th February 2008)

Among the control variables addressing alternative hypotheses, the size of national party delegations is not a significant predictor of codecision and consultation report allocation. Thus, the results provide no evidence in support of Mamadouh and Raunio's (2002, 2003) expectation that the members of bigger national party delegations are privileged in the report allocation. Nor does the proportion of time a member's national party has been in government in the examined period affect the number of reports the member receives. While admittedly based on individual rather than aggregate data, this finding fails to support the result of a previous study, which held that national parties present in the Council of Ministers write more reports than opposition parties (Høyland 2006a).

The other controls show that being a committee substitute rather than a regular member strongly decreases the number of either kind of report one is allocated. Previous membership in the same committee in the past EP term is a very strong positive predictor of the number of codecision reports one is allocated (increasing it by 141 per cent), while it has no effect on the number of consultation reports. It is arguable whether this effect is due purely to the seniority status of committee members or to their expertise accumulated through the years:

> It's much easier for someone who has been here for a long time to get a report. [...] You really respect people with experience. (Personal interview 8 with a PSE member, 26th February 2008)

> It goes without saying that senior members often have more experience and knowledge. So they don't get a report because of their seniority, they get it because of the competences that they have because of their seniority. It is not enough to have been a member of the Parliament for a long time; if you have never done anything and you haven't shown any results then you won't get the report. (Personal interview 1 with a PSE member, 27th February 2008)

Being a chair more than triples the number of consultation reports one is assigned. This is likely due to chairs serving as rapporteurs of last resort (Corbett *et al.* 2005):

> Chairs write as a rule many more reports than others, basically usually because they are given all the reports no one wants to write. But the committee has to do them. (Personal interview 9 with an EPP-ED member, 27th February 2008)

> When a chair has a report, it is always a small report with no political dynamite in it. (Personal interview 1 with a PSE member, 27th February 2008)

A different explanation holds for the over–representation of party group coordinators, whose position increases by 58 per cent the number of codecision reports they are likely to be allocated, or rather self-allocated, owing to their powerful position. This does not seem to be due to pure chance, but rather reveals an underlying pattern. As MEPs from different party groups reflected in interviews:

> I think that the coordinators in all groups have a very high standing in the hierarchy, meaning if my coordinator wants a report, he would get it, always. There would never be anyone saying 'well I would like that one also'. They have priority. They are sort of *de facto* chairman of the working groups. (Personal interview 1 with a PSE member, 27th February 2008)

> Coordinators usually get a little bit more than the others. This is acceptable because they do have much more work and if they do it well everyone profits. (Personal interview 9 with an EPP-ED member, 27th February 2008)

Being a male member decreases the number of codecision reports one is allocated by 30 per cent. Interestingly, the numbers of codecision and consultation reports a member is allocated seem to be correlated. The more codecision reports one writes, the more consultation reports he or she is allocated, and vice versa. In fact, one third of the MEPs wrote all of the substantive codecision and consultation reports in the studied period. An MEP from the working majority party group EPP-ED explained this:

On each committee there is only, I don't know, maybe thirty per cent of the members that are workers. They really want reports and really want to get down and do it so that's why there's sometimes an impression that the same people are doing more than their share. It's because there's quite a lot of members of committees that really don't want reports. (Personal interview 2 with an EPP-ED member, 6th February 2008)

## Discussion

The purpose of this chapter was to improve our understanding of the legislative organisation of the EP in view of the inter-institutional context of the EU. In particular, it examined how the intra-parliamentary division of tasks is affected by the substantively different legislative powers of the EP under the codecision and consultation procedures. Comparing the factors determining the allocation of codecision and consultation reports, the study demonstrates that the power relations of the EP with the other EU legislative institutions shape the internal parliamentary division of legislative tasks. The higher salience and hence competition for codecision reports as compared to consultation reports combined with the informal rules of report allocation has produced clear winners and losers in the distribution of parliamentary resources among party groups and individual legislators.

Firstly, the different attractiveness of codecision and consultation reports is reflected in their distribution among party groups. Concerns about reaching necessary parliamentary majorities combined with strategic entrepreneurial behaviour have led to a bias in the allocation of codecision reports in favour of members of EPP-ED and ALDE, whose support largely assures the simple parliamentary majority that is increasingly sufficient for adopting legislation. The members of PSE, however, are not enjoying the same benefits of their group's size. Faced with the need to get a simple majority support, EPP-ED is better off forming a centre-right coalition with the Liberals rather than a grand left-right coalition with PSE, in which it would have to make bigger policy concessions. Thus, it is plausible that EPP-ED prefers, and for strategic reasons, facilitates ALDE rather than PSE getting important reports. Logrolling between party group coordinators in the bidding for the most popular codecision reports is made possible by the informal rules governing report allocation, which pull the division of codecision and consultation reports together. Placing the members of the second biggest group, PSE, at a disadvantage in obtaining codecision reports violates the parliamentary norm of proportionality. Given the substantive 'agenda-setting' powers of the rapporteurs, under-representation in the codecision report allocation of any party group can have important normative implications. The actors who write codecision rather than consultation reports are more powerful in asserting their positions in legislation.

Secondly, the different legislative power of the EP under the two procedures also shapes the distribution of reports among legislators within party groups. It affects the incentives of both individual MEPs and party group coordinators, who decide on report allocations. The different salience and competition for codecision and consultation reports combined with the informal rules of report allocation, allowing for substantive manoeuvring in individual appointments, have strengthened the role of party group leadership. Concerned mostly with enhancing the cohesion of their party groups, party group coordinators have utilised their power to discipline group members by allocating all reports on the basis of group loyalty. Furthermore, they give members with portrayed special interests and outlying preferences in the respective committee's policy areas systematic access only to the writing consultation reports. In line with Hausemer's (2006: 254) observation, preference outliers obtain less salient reports. Contrary to previous assertions (Ringe 2009), these findings suggest that the party groups are able to exert systematic control over group members in the allocation of committee resources and rights, and thus potentially shape their future policy choices.

In conclusion, rather than favouring legislators' special interests or 'hiring' experts, it is promoting party group cohesion and coalition-building that appear to be the major mechanisms driving report allocation. As expected, this comes closest to the predictions of the partisan rationale. However, none of the congressional theories anticipated the strong impact of the inter-institutional rules on the division of power and resources within the legislature. Notably, in this chapter it has been demonstrated that there are important differences in the determinants of codecision and consultation report allocation, triggered by the different power of the EP under the two legislative procedures. Thus, the internal EP organisation cannot be fully understood in isolation from the EU inter-institutional context. This observation suggests that the congressional theories may benefit from modelling the incentives and constraints that the inter-institutional relations among the House of Representatives, the Senate and the Presidency provide in addition to the dynamics between different actors and institutions within the House. Such an approach will inform expectations about the conditions under which each theoretical approach is more powerful in explaining organisational outcomes.

In the next chapter how the rapporteur selection influences the procedural development and content of legislation is examined. In particular, the effect of the rapporteurs' background and party affiliation on the level of success of committee reports in plenary under the codecision procedure is analysed.

# chapter five | legislative influence of the committees

While the previous two empirical chapters analysed the factors shaping the composition and internal task allocation of committees, this chapter considers how much they actually affect legislation. In particular, it examines how the choice of a rapporteur and the mode of bicameral European Union negotiations under the codecision procedure affect committees' legislative influence. This is done with a view to identifying the conditions under which the three congressional rationales can explain the parliamentary internal set-up and operation.

The codecision procedure has changed significantly since it was first introduced in the Maastricht Treaty (1992). Most importantly, the Amsterdam Treaty (1999) abolished the ability of the Council of Ministers to reinstate its common position after three readings of unsuccessful negotiations with the European Parliament and allowed for an early conclusion of codecision acts already in the first reading. This option of 'fast track legislation' has had profound impact not only on the legislative process, but also on the internal dynamics of decision-making in the EP. Traditionally, the EP committees have been acknowledged as the main arenas for legislative deliberation and the development of the parliamentary positions, which the plenary adopts for the most part. However, with the proliferation of early inter-institutional agreements, increasingly often the parliamentary stances are negotiated in informal trilogue meetings of representatives of the EP, the Council of Ministers and the Commission, often without a clear mandate from the responsible committees. While these meetings have inevitably increased the agenda-setting power of the actors negotiating on behalf of the EP (mainly the rapporteur and shadow rapporteurs), it is claimed here that they have undermined the legislative role of the parliamentary committees.[1]

To examine this proposition, this chapter first compares in each committee the average extent to which the EP draws its legislative positions on the basis of committee reports when an early agreement is reached with the Council of Ministers after the final committee vote and when no such agreement is concluded. This is done using Monte Carlo permutations on a novel data set of all legislative reports falling under the codecision procedure that had their first reading during the 6th EP (2004–2009).

---

1. It has been argued elsewhere that the informal decision-making mode between the EU's legislative institutions has rather increased the power of the EP's committees *vis-à-vis* both the parliamentary plenary and the Council of Ministers (Marshall 2010: 555). This claim is backed by the fact that the EP has so far not rejected an informal trilogue agreement. Yet, the extent to which compromise agreements reached after the committee stage draw on or conflict with committee reports has not yet been examined – a research gap that this chapter addresses.

As a second step, the variation in the degree to which the plenary adopts individual committee proposals following formal or informal bicameral decision-making and depending on the characteristics of the rapporteurs and properties of the reports is analysed using regression models. Following the distributive, informational and partisan congressional theories and given the open amendment rule in plenary, a larger proportion of the committee reports is expected to be adopted in plenary if the rapporteur has no special outlying interests, has expertise in the subject area, or is a member of the working majority party group (coalition).

This chapter proceeds as follows. After a brief overview of the state of the art, the average success rate of committee reports on the floor is analysed. Subsequently, the hypotheses regarding the level of success of individual reports are developed. Their analysis follows upon a brief presentation of the methodological design. Finally, the legislative role and influence of the EP committees are re-evaluated in light of the findings.

## Role of the European Parliament under codecision and impact of early agreements

The influence of the EP committees over the parliamentary legislative positions has not been examined empirically. There is a common assumption that it is in the EP committees that the '[p]arliament's positions are in most cases decided in practice', before the plenary stage (Mamadouh and Raunio 2003: 348; see also Bowler and Farrell 1995; McElroy 2001; Neuhold 2001; Kreppel 2002a; Hix *et al.* 2003b; Ringe 2005, 2009). Scholars have further claimed that it is uncommon for committee proposals to be heavily modified or rejected in plenary (Bowler and Farrell 1995: 234). Practitioners share this perception. As one senior MEP stated in an interview:

> The chances of having amendments adopted in plenary if they haven't been adopted in committee, are very slim. Normally, most of the work is carried out in the committee and only in very special cases does the plenary change the substance of the reports of committees. Minor amendments can be accepted but the main line is already made in the committee. (Personal interview 12 with a PSE member, 13th February 2008)

These perceptions, though, are based on a snapshot view of the EP committees. Thus, the impact of the dynamically evolving EU inter-institutional context on the committees has been ignored. The growing legislative power of the EP *vis-à-vis* the Council of Ministers has been analysed under the assumption of the former being a unitary actor (Kreppel 1999, 2002b; Tsebelis *et al.* 2001). It is doubtful, however, that the parliamentary structure and dynamics have remained unaffected by the intensified interaction between the two chambers of the now truly bicameral European legislature.

Besides intra-organisational changes, the empowerment of the EP under codecision has brought about a new mode of inter-institutional negotiations. A growing number of legislative proposals are now decided upon in informal trilogue meetings of limited number of representatives of the EP, the Council of Ministers and the European Commission. These trilogues happen behind closed doors outside the traditional decision-making arenas. They 'involve the president of COREPER (which rotates with the presidency) and the chairman of the relevant working group on the Council's side. On the EP's side, they involve the rapporteur, the committee chairman, one of the vice presidents of the EP, and the shadow rapporteurs or coordinators from the various political groups' (Farrell and Héritier 2004: 1197). 'But of course smaller groups many times cannot show up because they cannot really look after every single report' (Personal interview 11 with a member of the EPP-ED secretariat, 27th February 20 08). An expert staff member from the specialised EP Legislative Coordination Unit, DG IPOL, suggested that the rapporteur has 'close links to the Presidency [of the Council of the European Union] if from the same country and then shadow rapporteurs are simply not there (Personal interview 17, 22nd February 2008). He further shared that committee rapporteurs do not always tell when they visit the Commission or the Council, which is linked to problems of reporting back to the committee.

While originally convened to make preparations for upcoming negotiations in the Conciliation Committee (Garman and Hilditch 1998), trilogue meetings have become a common decision-making arena in the early stages of the codecision procedure since the Amsterdam Treaty (1999) made that possible. Statistics show that during the 5th EP (1999–2004) 28 per cent of codecision acts were concluded in first reading (European Parliament 2004). The number grew to 61 per cent in the 6th EP (2004–2009) (European Parliament 2009a).

On the one hand, these developments have been interpreted positively since trilogue meetings have increased the communication and coordination between the EP and the Council of Ministers, thus speeding up the legislative process. Arguably, they have also enhanced the overall legislative influence of the EP. The EP is better able to affect the common position the Council adopts through its prior negotiations with the Council Presidency (Héritier 2007: 98). As a PSE member stated in an interview:

> [Early agreements] increase the power of the Parliament. Actually, I was [there] in the beginning of this process, it was during the Swedish Presidency, it was 1999 and the Swedish presidency introduced informal consultation procedures in 1st reading. So, [...] that has been a big improvement because we talk directly to the Council and the Commission in a very early stage and we save a lot of time. It is working very well – informal consultation procedures in first reading. (Personal interview 12 with a PSE member, 13th February 2008)

Usually, pressure to reach an agreement early in the legislative process comes neither from the EP (since it is more powerful in the 3rd reading under codecision), nor from the European Commission (due to the large number of amendments to its proposals), but from the European Council Presidency (Personal interview 13 with an EP administrator, Codecision and Conciliation Unit, DG IPOL, 22nd February 2008). 'Presidencies try to show their success by how many reports have been finalised during their term. This is a very important part of their performance.'

(Personal interview 18 with an EP administrator, DG Presidency, EXPO, 28th February 2008)

On the other hand, the increase in efficiency may come at the price of decreased quality of legislation. '[S]ometimes one finds to achieve a first reading agreement is more important than the substance of a document' (Personal interview 5 with an ALDE member, 13th February 2008). Similarly, a member of the EPP-ED secretariat explains:

> So, on some reports which have gone very very fast, take Roaming, although it has gone a good way but still very fast, and many people said this is the last time such an exercise may take place. We will no longer play this game of rushing into negotiations. So, it's a question of self-respect for the Parliament, whether we play this game and let the Council drag us into a very early agreement because it will be at the expense of transparency. (Personal interview 11 with a member of the EPP-ED secretariat, 27th February 2008)

Furthermore, trilogue negotiations have been accompanied by a decrease in transparency and a shift in the decision-making process away from the traditional parliamentary arenas of democratic debate. These problems were recognised in the interviews by EP staffers from the specialised Codecision and Conciliation Unit (Personal interview 13, 22nd February 2008; Personal interview 15, 27th February 2008) and the Legislative Coordination Unit of DG IPOL (Personal interview 16, 25th February 2008; Personal interview 17, 22nd February 2008). The EP has made some efforts to counteract the transparency deficit by signing a joint declaration with the European Commission and the Council of Ministers (European Parliament et al. 2007).[2] Among other things, it encourages the Council Presidency to attend committee meetings and, where not bounded by confidentiality, to provide information regarding the potential common position of the Council of Ministers. Furthermore, it invites the chair of COREPER to send a letter to the parliamentary committee chair whenever an informal agreement is reached in the trilogue meetings, thereby expressing the Council's intention to support the EP position if the agreement is adopted in plenary. However, an EP administrator working in the Codecision and Conciliation Unit of the parliamentary secretariat commented in an interview that these non-binding practice guidelines have not been respected much (Personal interview 13 with an EP administrator, DG IPOL, 22nd February 2008). Thus, the asymmetry of information between the parliamentary representatives in the trilogue meetings and the other MEPs regarding the content of legislative acts and the position of the Council of Ministers has remained. Negotiations with the Council are often initiated by the rapporteur without a clear committee mandate, i.e. before the committee has even voted on its draft position

---

2.   In a further effort to address the transparency problems inherent in early agreements, at the time of the present study the EP added a new Annex XX to its Rules of Procedures (European Parliament 2009b) defining the code of conduct to be followed in trilogue negotiation. Examining the impact of this new rule is beyond the scope and time frame of this study.

(Farrell and Héritier 2004). A concerned senior MEP urges in an interview:

> [...] the Parliament really has to organise, to make sure that the whole discussion doesn't only belong to the rapporteur. (Personal interview 14 with a PSE member, 12th February 2008)

The rapporteurs may be obtaining mandates for the concessions they make in trilogue negotiations from their party groups instead of committees. As interviewees affiliated to the two biggest party groups share:

> And then before you go to plenary you have to, of course, convince the working group, being in our case in the EPP for the five committees one working group in which all meet together under the chairmanship of one of our Vice-Presidents, and go through all the reports to be voted in plenary. Also there you need to get a mandate, you need to make a case, you have to make a point and if you want to table amendments you need the support of this working group. (Personal interview 11 with a member of the EPP-ED secretariat, 27th February 2008)

> [B]efore you finalise a negotiation it will be in the group for discussion. When we had REACH on the agenda, for instance, before Sacconi would say ok here we have a [inter-institutional] compromise, he had to have from us a mandate and that mandate was, of course, negotiated in detail also in the group, on group level. (Personal interview 1 with a PSE member, 27th February 2008)

In any case, leading the informal inter-institutional negotiations gives the rapporteur strong agenda-setting powers. While in theory each committee member can propose amendments to be included in the committee report, in practice, '[t]he draftsman can offer a take-it-or-leave-it proposal to the committee.' (Personal interview 20 with an EP administrator, Legislative Coordination, DG IPOL, 25th February 2008) Where an early agreement has already been reached before the committee vote, the report proposed by the rapporteur is composed solely of amendments drawn from that agreement. Such reports end up as the final parliamentary positions, rendering both committee and plenary discussion virtually obsolete. By forgoing the opportunity of adopting and pursuing their own positions, committees weaken the bargaining position of the EP. As an EP staffer explained, committee votes can serve as signals for the Council of Ministers: 'if a committee gets broad support, the EP can negotiate and put pressure on Council' (Personal interview 19 with an EP administrator, Legislative Coordination, DG IPOL, 27th February 2008). Instead, as another staff member pointed out, there is limited debate between political groups and lack of a genuine inter-institutional confrontation whenever an early agreement is struck, be it before or after the final committee report has been adopted (Personal interview 13 with an EP administrator, Codecision and Conciliation Unit, DG IPOL, 22nd February 2008). When an informal trilogue 'works successfully, the Parliament and Council do little more than sign off on an early-agreement deal that has already been negotiated among a small group of actors' (Héritier 2007: 99).

Overall, it is reasonable to conclude that whenever the EP positions are drafted and agreed upon outside the committee arena, the committees' legislative influence is compromised. Early agreements appear to constitute the committee reports if struck before the committee stage, in which case it is difficult, if not impossible, to evaluate the committees' influence over the content of the compromise texts. Alternatively, if struck after the committee stage, trilogue agreements seem to replace committee reports as the basis for the EP's official positions, which the open amendment rule facilitates.[3] To what extent this is indeed the practice is an empirical question, which deserves closer attention. Therefore, it is hypothesised here that whenever a trilogue compromise is reached after the committee stage the plenary is likely to adopt it despite its non-binding character and bypass the committee's report. In other words:

*H1: The EP committees are on average less successful in having the plenary adopt their draft reports if an informal agreement is reached with the Council of Ministers after the committee stage than if no early agreement is reached.*

In order to examine this hypothesis, the average success of committee reports in plenary is examined, first, for those reports on which an agreement with the Council was concluded after the committee stage but before the plenary stage and, second, for those reports on which no early agreement at all was reached in the first reading. For the purpose, a new data set has been compiled, which includes all the codecision proposals that had their first reading in both committee and plenary during the 6th EP (2004–2009) and underwent amendment in the EP. While a total of 487 proposals had first reading in committee and plenary in the period, 88 sustained no EP amendments.[4] Since it is not possible to talk about a committee's success in shaping the plenary legislative positions when it proposed no amendments, such proposals were excluded from the sample. Furthermore, because nine of the twenty EP standing committees produced over 90 per cent of all the codecision reports in the period and no other committee drafted more than six reports, these are the only committees whose average legislative success can be examined (see Table 5.1). Information on the existence and stage of conclusion of early agreements was extracted from committee reports, Commission documents, and debates and amendments in plenary, all of which are available on the EP's website and the EP Legislative Observatory.

Table 5.1 shows the number of codecision reports drafted by each of the nine most prolific legislative committees. It differentiates between reports on which an early agreement with the Council of Ministers was reached before or after the committee stage, i.e. before or after the committee vote in the 1st reading of the

---

3. Amendments for consideration in Parliament may be tabled by the committee responsible, a political group or at least forty Members (European Parliament 2009b, Rule 156, ex Rule 150).

4. Almost all legislative proposals that were not amended either fall under the simplified procedure without amendment and debate (European Parliament 2009b, Rule 46, ex Rule 43), simply introduce the new regulatory procedure with scrutiny to old legislation, or repeal old legislation.

codecision procedure, and reports on which no such agreement was reached. In all committees but Transport and Tourism more than 50 per cent of the committee reports were subject to an early agreement. Furthermore, the vast majority of these agreements took place after the committee vote.[5]

To test Hypothesis 1, the committees' mean success rate in shaping the final parliamentary positions is analysed in the two rightmost columns of the table. For each legislative proposal, the success of a committee is measured as the fraction of amendments adopted in plenary that originate from a committee's report, i.e. the number of adopted committee amendments divided by the total number of amendments adopted in the plenary. The mean success rate for each committee is then calculated separately for legislative proposals on which an early agreement was reached *after* the committee vote and for those on which *no* early agreement was reached.[6]

For all committees, the mean success rate is substantially lower when an early agreement is reached after the committee stage than when no early agreement is reached (see Figure 5.1). To evaluate whether this difference is statistically significant, Monte Carlo permutations have been conducted to establish how extreme those means are with respect to the average success rate of all committee reports in the EP. For each category of report (with and without early agreement after the committee stage), 10,000 samples of size equal to the number of reports a committee drafted that fall in that category were drawn without replacement from the pool of all reports in the EP and the mean success rate was calculated for each sample. The actual mean committee success is considered significantly high or low if it falls within the top or bottom 5 per cent of the 10,000 generated mean success rates, respectively. The significant values are marked with stars in Table 5.1. The results show that when an early agreement is reached after the committee stage, the mean success rates of all nine committees are lower than average, and most of these figures are statistically significant. Conversely, for reports on which no early agreement has been reached, all nine committees exhibit higher than average mean success rates and only one of these means narrowly escapes statistical significance. Thus, there is strong evidence for Hypothesis 1. Committees are significantly more successful when there is no early agreement than when an early agreement is reached after the committee stage.

---

5.    The Committee on Culture and Education and the Committee on Civil Liberties, Justice and Home Affairs present deviations from this trend, accounting for 83 per cent of the early agreements reached before the committee stage in the nine committees. They present interesting case studies for future in-depth research.

6.    In the cases when an agreement was reached before the committee stage (not in table), in line with the discussion above, not surprisingly, in all committees on average more than 99 per cent of the amendments adopted in plenary stemmed from the committee reports. This is simply because such reports *de facto* constitute the early agreement texts and are not necessarily committee products. Thus, their success in plenary cannot be considered as a straightforward committee success or failure without further qualitative research.

Table 5.1: Number of committee reports and their mean success rate on the floor given the existence and stage of an early interinstitutional agreement reported per committee

| Committee | Total number of reports in a committee | Reports with early agreement before comm. vote | Reports with early agreement after comm. vote | Reports with no early agreement | Mean success rate if agreement after comm. vote | Mean success rate if no early agreement |
|---|---|---|---|---|---|---|
| Economic and Monetary Affairs | 39 | 3 (8%) | 30 (77%) | 6 (15%) | 0.11** (0.00) | 0.89 (0.94) |
| Employment and Social Affairs | 23 | 4 (17%) | 10 (43%) | 9 (39%) | 0.74 (0.80) | 0.93* (0.99) |
| Environment, Public Health and Food Safety | 86 | 3 (3%) | 46 (53%) | 37 (43%) | 0.07** (0.00) | 0.82** (1.00) |
| Industry, Research and Energy | 33 | 7 (21%) | 10 (30%) | 16 (48%) | 0.70 (0.74) | 0.94** (1.00) |
| Internal Market and Consumer Protection | 24 | 1 (4%) | 16 (67%) | 7 (29%) | 0.20** (0.00) | 0.90* (0.97) |
| Transport and Tourism | 54 | 6 (11%) | 18 (33%) | 30 (56%) | 0.13** (0.00) | 0.94** (1.00) |
| Culture and Education | 21 | 25 (61%) | 6 (15%) | 10 (24%) | 0.24** (0.02) | 0.91* (0.98) |

| Committee | Total number of reports in a committee | Reports with early agreement before comm. vote | Reports with early agreement after comm. vote | Reports with no early agreement | Mean success rate if agreement after comm. vote | Mean success rate if no early agreement |
|---|---|---|---|---|---|---|
| Legal Affairs | 48 | 3 (6%) | 22 (46%) | 23 (48%) | 0.30** | 0.85** |
| | | | | | (0.00) | (1.00) |
| Civil Liberties, Justice and Home Affairs | 37 | 20 (54%) | 6 (16%) | 11 (30%) | 0.37 | 0.95** |
| | | | | | (0.10) | (1.00) |
| N | 364 | 54 (15%) | 164 (45%) | 146 (40%) | | |

*Note*: The numbers reported in the two rightmost columns present for each committee the mean proportion of amendments in the adopted EP opinions derived from a committee report given an early agreement after the committee stage or the lack of an early agreement. The significance levels are derived from the distribution of the 10,000 committees' means simulated by Monte Carlo permutations for each category; * Significance at 5% one-tailed; ** Significance at 1% one-tailed based on the percentile of the observed mean (displayed in brackets).

Notably, the EP draws its position almost exclusively on the basis of commit-tee reports when no inter-institutional agreement took place. This suggests that the parliamentary committees have lost influence due to the introduction of the 'fast track legislation' option in the Treaty of Amsterdam (1999) and the ensuing practice of informal negotiations with the Council of Ministers. To verify these conclusions, future research needs to evaluate the level of success of committee reports on the floor prior to the treaty changes in 1999.

Table 5.1 also portrays substantial differences between committees in the ex-tent to which they manage to influence the parliamentary legislative positions after the committee stage, especially whenever an early inter-institutional agreement is concluded. This curious observation combined with my interest in explaining vari-ation in the level of success of individual reports in the plenary calls for a shift of analysis from the aggregate to the individual level.

*Figure 5.1: Mean success rate of committee reports on the floor by committee*

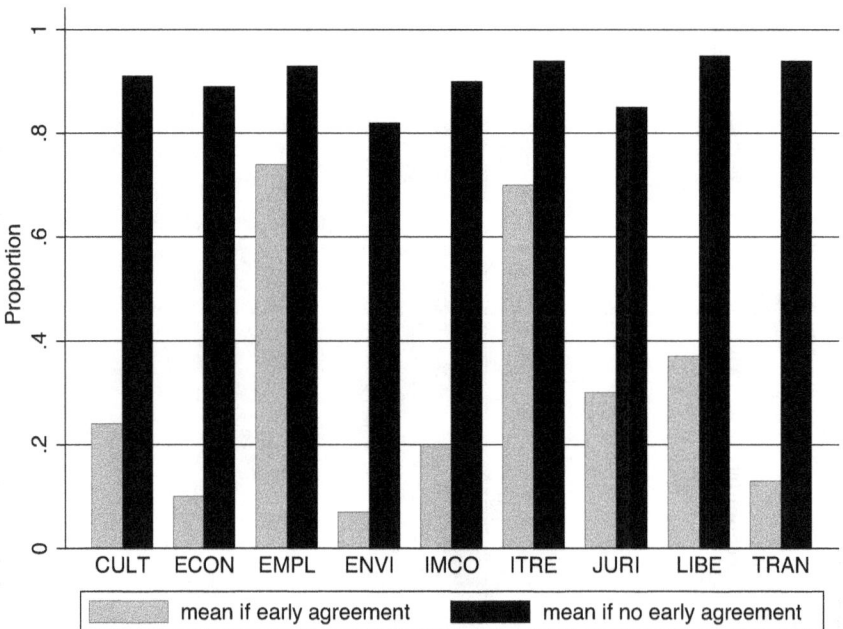

*Note:* The figure shows the mean proportion of amendments in the adopted EP opinions derived from a committee report when an early agreement is reached after the committee stage and when no early agreement is reached. Abbreviations: CULT: Culture and Education; ECON: Economic and Monetary Affairs; EMPL: Employment and Social Affairs; ENVI: Environment, Public Health and Food Safety; IMCO: Internal Market and Consumer Protection; ITRE: Industry, Research and Energy; JURI: Legal Affairs; LIBE: Civil Liberties, Justice and Home Affairs; TRAN: Transport and Tourism.

## Explaining variation in the success of committee reports in plenary

In the concluding remarks of their study, evaluating the conditions under which the EP is successful in getting its amendments accepted by the Council of Ministers, Tsebelis *et al.* (2001: 599) state that future research on the policy influence of the EP will have to take into account other variables 'like policy area of legislation, size of bills, density of amendments, political affiliation of rapporteurs of a bill', which, they claim, would involve a shift in studies from amendments to legislative acts. In contrast to research on the influence of the EP prevalent in the 1990s which assumed it to be a unitary actor (e.g. Tsebelis 1994; Moser 1996; König and Pöter 2001) the focus of recent research has shifted towards examining the internal parliamentary organisation and dynamics (studies reviewed in Chapter Three and Chapter Four). However, rarely have the intra-parliamentary structures been analysed in light of the inter-institutional context. The question posed here – under which conditions does the plenary adopt a committee report as its official position – inevitably calls for the combination of intra-parliamentary and extra-parliamentary explanatory factors.

It has already been established that the committees are on average more successful in having their reports adopted by the plenary when no informal agreement is reached between the EP and the Council of Ministers after the committee stage. The hypotheses formulated in this section aim at explaining the level of success of individual reports. How do report- and rapporteur-specific factors affect the level of success of a report in plenary? Is the effect of these factors conditional on the conclusion of a trilogue agreement? The focus of attention lies on the rapporteurs' characteristics because the rapporteurs have substantial impact on the content and fortune of committee reports owing to their strong agenda-setting powers. They are the ones responsible for drafting the committee reports, negotiating with the Council of Ministers, gathering majority support, presenting the committee reports to the plenary, and following the development of enacted legislative acts all the way until their successful implementation. Thus, the rapporteurs are able to shape content of the legislative dossiers, to which they have been assigned, even after the committee stage has passed and are likely to use that power if their draft reports were not fully accepted in the committee. Previous research has shown that the new practice of informal decision-making with the Council of Ministers has further increased their influence (Farrell and Héritier 2004). 'Rapporteurs enjoy more freedom from committees.' (Personal interview 18 with an EP administrator, DG Presidency, EXPO, 28th February 2008). Asked whether trilogue negotiations have empowered rapporteurs *vis-à-vis* their committee colleagues, one MEP responded:

> [...] *vis-à-vis* the overall committee but also *vis-à-vis* the group. Because often, you know, the more times a specific report is discussed in the group, the more times potentially a rapporteur has to modify his or her position. Now, if we make a first reading agreement, then chances are that this would only probably have been on the agenda in the group one time or something like that. And there you might have found a compromise that was pretty close to what you

would decide yourself. Or, you get a mandate, which is pretty broad, and then you make a compromise. And then, it is within the mandate but some people might have given you that compromise because they thought it was a first reading and you can always make it better in the second. (Personal interview 1 with a PSE member, 27th February 2008)

Thus, although rapporteurs are expected to represent the majority of members in their committee and, potentially, their party groups rather than to further their own policy interests, it is not necessarily the case. While it was shown in Chapter Four that members with special interests are not given systematic access to codecision reports, this does not mean that such members are excluded from writing reports altogether. In fact, this would be surprising given the staffing of some committees with members with homogenous interest group ties demonstrated in Chapter Three. Kaeding (2004, 2005) even holds that rapporteurs in the Committee on Environment, Public Health and Safety tend to be homogenous high demanders with relevant interest group affiliations. While this does not necessarily mean that such rapporteurs would be proposing legislation outlying from the median preferences on the floor, the possibility cannot be excluded without further analysis. Thus, following the distributive congressional rationale (Shepsle and Weingast 1987; Weingast and Marshall 1988), which suggests that committees serve the interests of homogeneous preference outliers, it can be expected that reports drafted by rapporteurs with special interests will be received less favourably by the plenary due to their potentially biased content. Given the lack of any EP restrictive rules safeguarding committee proposals from amendments in plenary, outlying committee reports may be largely discarded on the floor.

*H2: A committee report is less successful in plenary if it has been drafted by a rapporteur with relevant special interests.*

Similarly, while in Chapter Four no significant impact of expertise on codecision report allocation was unveiled either, in Chapter Three it was shown that committees are staffed with members with relevant expertise (see also Bowler and Farrell 1995; McElroy 2006; Whitaker 2011). According to the predictions of the informational rationale (Krehbiel 1991) legislative committees serve the informational needs of a legislature in a setting characterised by uncertainty about the link between policy output and policy outcome. If the EP committees do serve the plenary, it is reasonable to expect that the latter will readily adopt committee reports drafted by expert rapporteurs fulfilling its informational needs. This leads to the following hypothesis:

*H3: A committee report is more successful in plenary if it has been drafted by a rapporteur with relevant expertise.*

Finally, the partisan rationale (Cox and McCubbins 1993, 2007) states that committees serve the need of the majority party to control, or discipline, its members via the assignment of office and resources and, thus, to enhance party cohesion. As argued in Chapter Four, although there is neither a majority party group nor a stable majority party group coalition in the EP, the party groups most often needed to form the necessary parliamentary majorities in passing legislation can still be expected to dominate the committee work as well as the plenary. Hence, if the rapporteur comes from a party group forming the EP's working majority, committee reports are likely to be more successful on the floor. Farrell and Héritier (2004: 1200) argue that 'rapporteurs are particularly powerful, when they are closely linked to the large political groups', while 'smaller political groups in the Parliament find themselves increasingly excluded from the decision-making' (2004: 1201). The three biggest party groups in the EP in the time period are EPP-ED, PSE and ALDE. Although the Liberal group is substantially smaller than the other two, it is included in the hypothesis since it serves as a convenient coalition partner and usually sides with one of the two bigger party groups in adopting the EP position. Also, in Chapter Four it has been shown that both the EPP-ED and ALDE are over-represented in the allocation of codecision reports. Thus:

**H4:** *A committee report is more successful in plenary if it has been drafted by a rapporteur affiliated to one of the three biggest party groups – EPP-ED, PSE or ALDE.*

In the case of an early agreement, referring to EPP-ED and PSE, Héritier (2007: 100) has argued that 'the power of the rapporteurs and shadow-rapporteurs of large political groups is greatly increased while the chairs of committees and the MEPs from small political groups suffer from a relative loss of influence'. The latter have traditionally used the parliamentary committees as arenas to propose amendments and exert influence on legislation. However, the bigger party groups, being the ones to generally lead the informal negotiations with the Council of Ministers, have the means to marginalise smaller groups from the pre-floor stage of the decision-making.

## Research design

The sample used to examine Hypotheses 2, 3 and 4 is similar to the one utilised in the analysis above. Again, reports on which an agreement was reached with the Council of Ministers before the committee stage are excluded. However, the codecision reports of all and not just the most prolific legislative committees are considered. There are 334 individual codecision reports fulfilling these conditions, which are used as the units of analysis in the models below.

### Measures

The codebook of the dependent and independent variables in the models is provided in Appendix H. Their measurement is discussed below.

#### Dependent variable measurement

In order to overcome the inherent limitations of any single measure, the success of a committee report on the floor is measured in two ways. Firstly, the variable used in the aggregate analysis above is utilised, namely the proportion of amendments in the adopted EP opinion derived from a committee report:

$$Y_1 = \frac{\text{number of adopted committee amendments}}{\text{number of total adopted amendments}}$$

This variable was useful in the aggregate analysis as its values are directly comparable across reports. However, because it is a ratio, it treats equally, for instance, 2 out of 10 and 20 out of 100 committee amendments on a report adopted in plenary, concealing the size and controversy of the proposal.

Rectifying this, the alternative dependent variable takes into account the total number of changes to a committee report adopted in the final plenary position by summing up the number of rejected committee amendments and the number of accepted non-committee amendments, i.e. amendments by party groups and groups of legislators proposed at the plenary stage.

$$Y2 = \text{number of rejected committee amendments} + \\ \text{number of accepted non-committee amendments}$$

While this measure overcomes the limitations associated with the proportional dependent variable, it is not normalised, which makes comparisons across observations difficult. Specifically, it assigns one and the same value to reports to which 10 changes were made, irrespectively of whether they originally contained 10 or 100 committee amendments. This is addressed by controlling for the number of proposed committee amendments as a proxy for the complexity of the proposal.

Overall, these two dependent variables capture differently the level of success of committee reports on the floor and both have their assets and drawbacks. Finding similar results after modelling them would enhance the validity of the results. Therefore, both variants of the variable operationalisation will be used in the analyses below.

#### Independent variables

To test Hypotheses 2 and 3, the measures of committee-specific special interest and expertise of the rapporteurs are constructed in the same fashion as in the analysis of report allocation in Chapter Four. This is done in accordance with the findings in Chapter Three regarding the determinants of committee assignments. Thus, rapporteurs are considered to have committee-specific special interest if they sit on the Environment committee and are linked to green groups; sit on the Employment and Social Affairs Committee and have trade union ties; sit on the Industry Committee or the Committee on Economic and Monetary Affairs and have business/industry ties; sit on the Civil Liberties Committee and have ties to social groups; or sit on the Agriculture Committees and have ties to farming groups. As previously argued, while these special interests inevitably imply a certain level of expertise, they are also associated with clear policy preferences outlying in a certain direction and, hence, deviating from the preferences of the median MEP in the plenary in the respective field.

The operationalisation of the committee-specific expertise derived from educational and professional experience rather than interest group ties is constructed in a similar fashion. Rapporteurs are considered experts in a committee field if they: sit on the Committee of Environment, Public Health and Safety and have been educated in medicine or natural sciences/engineering; sit on the Industry Committee and have an education in natural sciences/engineering; sit on the Economic and Monetary Affairs, the Budget or the Budgetary Control Committee and have educational and professional knowledge in economics; sit on the Transport Committee and have worked in the transport sector; sit on the Legal Affairs or the Institutional Affairs Committee and have a legal education, or sit on the Foreign Affairs Committee and have experience in international relations politics.

Dummy variables for party group membership in the EPP-ED, PSE and ALDE are added to test Hypothesis 4. Furthermore, the size of the national party delegation of the rapporteur is controlled for.

The conditioning variable is a dummy for early agreement with the Council of Ministers after the committee stage, the reference category being no early agreement in the first reading of the codecision procedure. Including this dummy not only measures the effect of early agreement on the individual level but also allows evaluating the unique impact of the other potentially influential factors. Due to its strong conditioning effect portrayed in the preliminary analysis, the early agreement variable is interacted with the variables testing Hypotheses 2, 3 and 4.

In modelling the proportional dependent variable Y1, the size of the initial Commission proposal (measured in 1,000s of words) is controlled for because larger acts are expected to attract more changes. In modelling the second dependent variable Y2, this control variable is replaced with a variable measuring the number of proposed committee amendments on the Commission proposal, which is necessary because Y2 does not account for the controversy of the report, thus making comparison across observations difficult. A variable representing the number of consulted opinion-giving committees is also added because the more parties are involved in the decision-making process, the more complex a report is likely to be and, hence, the more changes to it are expected in plenary. A variable is also added to distinguish between regulations and directives on the one hand and decisions and recommendations on the other hand, where fewer changes are expected in legislative proposals of the latter type due to their limited scope.

Finally, all models include fixed effects for committees since the results of the aggregate analysis revealed huge differences between committees.

## Methods

The character and distribution of the dependent variables call for different models (see Figure 5.2 for the distributions of the dependant variables), namely a fractional logistic regression model and a count model. The two techniques are described below.

The first dependent variable Y1, measuring the proportion of adopted amendments in an EP opinion stemming from a committee report, takes values between 0 and 1 only and is not normally distributed. Instead, it contains a disproportionately high number of extreme values (0s and/or 1s depending on whether all reports are considered, or the samples of early and non-early agreements are split). Besides the violations of its assumptions, an ordinary least squares regression model poorly fits the data, making predictions beyond the observable 0–1 range. Designed specifically for modelling proportional responses, a fractional logistic regression model is suitable for estimating this dependent variable (Papke and Wooldridge 1996). It restricts predictions to the observable range of the dependent variable and does not need to meet the strict assumptions that ordinary least squares regression requires and the data violates. The fractional binomial model can be thought of as a weighted binary response model, where proportional responses represent the $n$ number of successes for $k$ trials (Hardin and Hilbe 2007: 119). In our case, an amendment adopted in plenary is a 'success' if it is derived from a committee report. The proportional dependent variable $Y_i = \frac{n_i}{k_i}$ represents the $n_i$ number of adopted committee amendments in plenary for $k_i$ overall adopted amendments in plenary to a given report $i$.

The second dependant variable, representing the number of changes to a committee report (the sum of rejected committee amendments and adopted non-committee amendments), is a typical count variable and accordingly calls for a count model. Due to the overdispersion in the dependent variable, i.e. the substantively higher conditional variance than the conditional mean (Long and Freese 2003: 266–7), a negative binomial model is more appropriate than a simple poisson count model.

## Results

The results of the fractional logistic regression and count models are presented in Table 5.2 and Table 5.4, respectively (for better readability, the fixed committee effects of both sets of models are displayed only in Appendix I and Appendix J). Each dependent variable is explored in eight different model specifications. The marginal effects of the independent variables in the best fitting Models 5 and 7 of both the fractional and count models are displayed, respectively, in Table 5.3 and Table 5.5.

With the exception of one control variable, all eight model specifications are the same for both dependent variables. Models 1 and 2 include only main effects. Models 3–6 include the interaction effects of the main independent variables with the early agreement variable one at a time. Finally, Models 7 and 8 present the main effects on the split samples of reports depending on whether they underwent an early agreement or not. This is done to verify the result of the preceding models given the exceptionally strong effect of the early agreement independent variable on the dependent variables. The results of the fractional logistic regression models and the negative binomial count models are presented below.

*Figure 5.2: Distribution of the dependent variables measuring the level of success of committee reports in plenary*

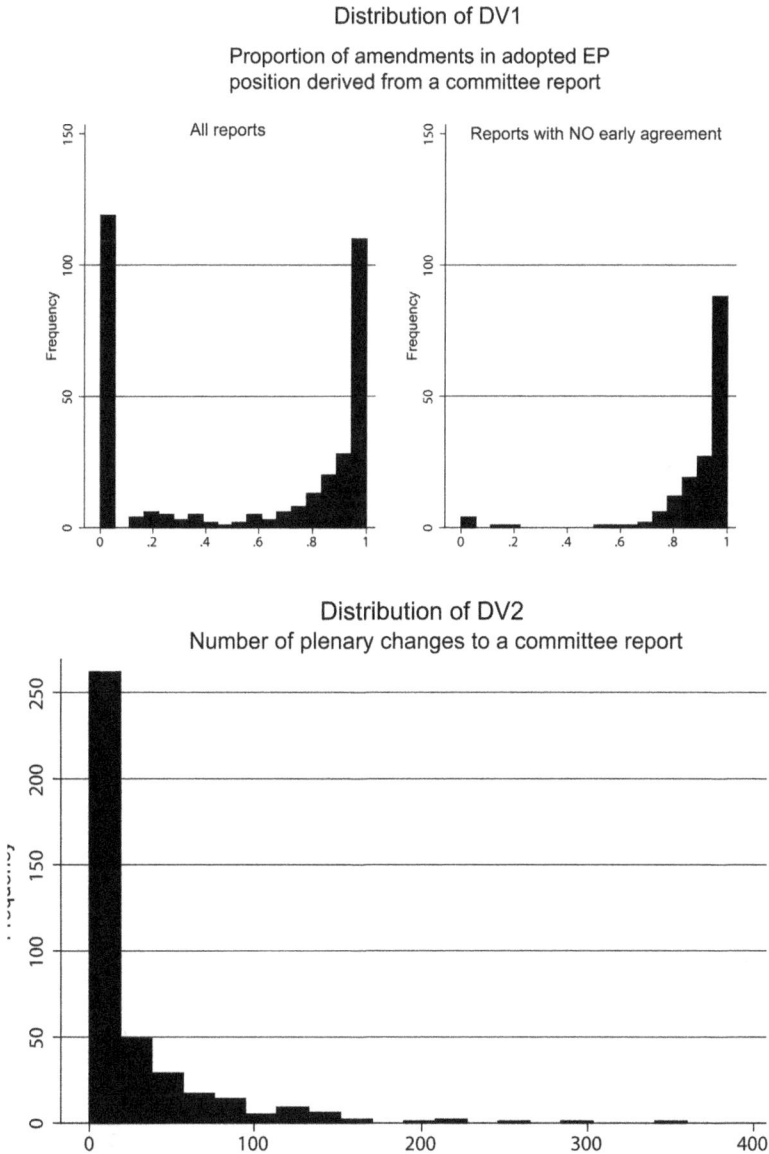

Distribution of DV1

Proportion of amendments in adopted EP position derived from a committee report

Distribution of DV2
Number of plenary changes to a committee report

102 | organising the european parliament

Table 5.2: Fractional logistic regression of the proportion of adopted amendments in the first reading EP opinion derived from a committee report

| | M1 | M2 | M3 | M4 | M5 | M6 | M7_not early | M8_early |
|---|---|---|---|---|---|---|---|---|
| Early | -3.670** | -3.666** | -3.553** | -3.408** | -3.341** | -3.791** | | |
| | (0.255) | (0.254) | (0.271) | (0.297) | (0.335) | (0.293) | | |
| Related interest | -0.030 | -0.007 | 0.533 | 0.046 | 0.092 | 0.041 | 0.319 | 0.185 |
| | (0.413) | (0.397) | (0.577) | (0.403) | (0.386) | (0.392) | (0.595) | (0.734) |
| Early*Related interest | | | -0.852 | | | | | |
| | | | (0.732) | | | | | |
| Related expertise | 0.117 | 0.106 | 0.126 | 0.575 | 0.080 | 0.094 | 1.074* | -0.922 |
| | (0.359) | (0.355) | (0.360) | (0.446) | (0.347) | (0.348) | (0.533) | (0.604) |
| Early*Related expertise | | | | -0.836 | | | | |
| | | | | (0.558) | | | | |
| National party delegation size | -0.019 | -0.020 | -0.020 | -0.020 | -0.021 | -0.019 | -0.050** | -0.003 |
| | (0.013) | (0.013) | (0.013) | (0.013) | (0.014) | (0.013) | (0.017) | (0.022) |
| EPP-ED | 0.231 | 0.331 | 0.361 | 0.357 | 0.823* | 0.324 | 1.569*** | -0.488 |
| | (0.471) | (0.373) | (0.373) | (0.370) | (0.418) | (0.384) | (0.491) | (0.595) |
| Early*EPP-ED | | | | | -0.772 | | | |
| | | | | | (0.442) | | | |
| PSE | 0.336 | 0.435 | 0.428 | 0.465 | 0.447 | 0.132 | 1.152* | 0.188 |
| | (0.468) | (0.370) | (0.371) | (0.364) | (0.348) | (0.476) | (0.518) | (0.504) |
| Early*PSE | | | | | | 0.484 | | |
| | | | | | | (0.528) | | |
| ALDE | -0.186 | | | | | | | |
| | (0.559) | | | | | | | |

| | M1 | M2 | M3 | M4 | M5 | M6 | M7_not early | M8_early |
|---|---|---|---|---|---|---|---|---|
| Size (1,000s words) | -0.008 | -0.009 | -0.009 | -0.006 | -0.007 | -0.008 | 0.011 | -0.026 |
| | (0.007) | (0.007) | (0.007) | (0.007) | (0.007) | (0.007) | (0.011) | (0.019) |
| Num. consul. committees | -0.041 | -0.038 | -0.039 | -0.034 | -0.033 | -0.028 | -0.134 | 0.064 |
| | (0.052) | (0.052) | (0.052) | (0.054) | (0.053) | (0.054) | (0.069) | (0.092) |
| Regulation/ Directive | -0.204 | -0.197 | -0.220 | -0.191 | -0.229 | -0.215 | -0.506 | -0.139 |
| | (0.534) | (0.533) | (0.539) | (0.525) | (0.533) | (0.533) | (0.544) | (0.710) |
| Committee fixed effects | Yes | Yes | Yes | Yes | Yes | Yes | Yes | Yes |
| Constant | 2.826** | 2.720** | 2.649** | 2.517** | 2.444** | 2.733** | 2.965** | -1.006 |
| | (0.724) | (0.640) | (0.618) | (0.610) | (0.713) | (0.659) | (0.553) | (1.096) |
| Pseudo LL | -109.1 | -109.2 | -108.8 | -108.6 | -108.6 | -109.0 | -37.9 | -62.7 |
| Deviance | 142.0 | 142.1 | 141.4 | 141.0 | 141.0 | 141.7 | 30.5 | 94.3 |
| N | 333 | 333 | 333 | 333 | 333 | 333 | 160 | 173 |

*Note:* Dependent variable: proportion of adopted amendments in the first reading EP opinion derived from a committee report on a codecision proposal in the period 2004–2009. Robust standard errors displayed in brackets, * significance at 5%, ** significance at 1%. Full models with the committee fixed effects shown in Appendix I.

*Analysis of the proportion of adopted amendments derived from committee reports*

Focusing first on the fractional logistic regression models presented in Table 5.2, in all models on the full sample (Models 1–6) the most pronounced effect is that of early agreement. This is portrayed in its significant negative impact on the expected proportion of adopted amendments in the EP's first reading positions derived from committee reports. As the marginal effects in Model 5 portray (displayed in Table 5.3), early agreements decrease this proportion by 0.65, where the mean proportion in the sample is 0.55. These findings corroborate the results of the aggregate analysis.

Model 1 includes all the main effects. The effect of being a member of ALDE is not significant and has the opposite direction from the one expected by Hypothesis 4. Therefore, it is dropped from the remaining models. In Models 3–6, the main effects of the rapporteur's special interests, expertise, EPP-ED or PSE affiliation are interacted one at a time with the effect of early agreement to check whether these effects are conditional on the bicameral decision-making mode. The results show no evidence for Hypotheses 2 and 3 with the exception of the positive effect of expertise, which reaches statistical significance only in Model 7 on the split sample of legislative proposals that underwent no early agreement. However, Hypothesis 4 is partially confirmed. As Model 5 shows, there is a positive impact of affiliation to the working majority party group EPP-ED on the proportion of amendments in the adopted EP position derived from a committee report when no trilogue agreement is reached. In such cases, affiliation to EPP-ED increases this proportion by 0.19 (see Model 5 in Table 5.3). The positive effect of affiliation to the working majority party group is confirmed by Model 7, which analyses only the sample of reports that underwent no early agreement. It is accompanied by a significant positive effect of affiliation to PSE, which, however, failed to reach statistical significance in the models including the overall sample. Therefore, the latter result has to be treated with caution, especially given the potential over-specification problems in the models on the small split sample.

On the whole, the results are not surprising. As an EP staffer and ex-member of the EPP secretariat commented, the differences in the legislative influence of rapporteurs depend on their party groups (Personal interview 15 with an EP administrator, Codecision and Conciliation Unit, DG IPOL, 27th February 2008). In her words, even shadow rapporteurs from the EPP-ED or PSE may be more influential than rapporteurs from, for instance, the Green/EFA group.

Besides an unexpected negative but close to zero effect of national party delegation size in Model 7 (see Table 5.2), no variable reached significance in any of the models but the committee dummies (see Appendix I). For instance, reaffirming the results of the aggregate analysis, the reports of the Employment and Social Affairs committee and the Industry committee are significantly more successful on the floor than those of other committees (see Model 5).

Notably, Model 8 fails to find any statistically significant explanation for the level of success of committee reports in plenary when an early agreement is reached with the Council of Ministers after the committee stage (see Table 5.2). Such an explanation has to be sought in different factors altogether.

*Table 5.3: Marginal effect/discrete change effects on the proportion of adopted amendments in an EP opinion derived from a committee report (Models 5 and 7)*

|  | M5 | M7_ not early |
|---|---|---|
| Early | -0.65 | |
| Related interest | 0.02 | 0.02 |
| Related expertise | 0.02 | 0.05 |
| National party delegation size | 0.00 | 0.00 |
| EPP-ED | 0.19 | 0.09 |
| Early*EPP-ED | -0.19 | |
| PSE | 0.10 | 0.05 |
| Size (1,000s words) | 0.00 | 0.00 |
| Num. consul. committees | -0.01 | -0.01 |
| Regulation/Directive | -0.05 | -0.02 |
| AFET | -0.07 | 0.04 |
| DEVE | 0.35 | 0.06 |
| INTA | -0.08 | -0.10 |
| BUDG | -0.11 | 0.07 |
| CONT | 0.38 | -0.03 |
| ECON | -0.12 | -0.02 |
| EMPL | 0.31 | -0.09 |
| ENVI | -0.22 | 0.00 |
| ITRE | 0.30 | -0.02 |
| IMCO | 0.01 | 0.00 |
| TRAN | 0.00 | 0.04 |
| REGI | 0.20 | -0.05 |
| AGRI | -0.34 | -0.18 |
| JURI | 0.02 | 0.02 |
| LIBE | 0.21 | 0.04 |
| AFCO | 0.15 | 0.06 |
| FEMM | -0.22 | -0.17 |

*Note*: For dummy variables, the effects of their discrete change from 0 to 1 on the dependent variable while holding all other variables constant at their mean are displayed. For continuous variables (national party delegation size, size (1,000s words) and number of consultative committees) their marginal effects on the dependent variable at the mean of all independent variables in the respective model are displayed. Abbreviations: AFET: Foreign Affairs; DEVE: Development; INTA: International Trade; BUDG: Budgets; CONT: Budgetary Control; ECON: Economic and Monetary Affairs; EMPL: Employment and Social Affairs; ENVI: Environment, Public Health and Food Safety; ITRE: Industry, Research and Energy; IMCO: Internal Market and Consumer Protection; TRAN: Transport and Tourism; REGI: Regional Development; AGRI: Agriculture; PECH: Fisheries; CULT: Culture and Education; JURI: Legal Affairs; LIBE: Civil Liberties, Justice and Home Affairs; AFCO: Constitutional Affairs; FEMM: Women's Rights and Gender Equality; PETI: Petitions.

*Analysis of the number of changes to committee reports in plenary*

Table 5.4 presents the result of the negative binomial models using the second dependent variable. It is important to note that in these models negative coefficients signify success for committee reports, meaning that they are likely to sustain fewer changes on the floor.

Once again, the early agreement variable has a pronounced significant effect, portraying a positive impact of an early agreement on the number of changes to a committee report in plenary. The size of the discrete change effect displayed in Table 5.5 shows that early agreement increases this number by 23.6 (see Model 5), where the mean number of changes to a report in the sample is 30.5.

Analogically to the findings of the fractional logistic regression models, the effect of affiliation to ALDE is insignificant and, therefore, dropped in the others models. Membership in EPP-ED has a significant negative effect on the number of changes to a committee report in plenary in all Models 2–7. The discrete changes displayed in Table 5.5 show that, holding other factors constant, on average 13 changes less are made to reports in plenary if they are drafted by EPP-ED rapporteurs (based on Model 5). The significant interaction effect between the variables for EPP-ED affiliation and early agreement in Model 5 shows that there are significant differences in the effect of EPP-ED affiliation depending on the existence of a trilogue agreement. Yet, additional calculations show that whenever an early agreement is struck with the Council of Ministers this effect is not only very small (-0.965 + 0.746 = -0.219) but also insignificant. Thus, the impact of EPP-ED membership predicted in Hypothesis 4 holds only for reports on legislative proposals, on which no early inter-institutional agreement is reached. Additional partial evidence for Hypothesis 4 is offered by Model 7 on the sample of non-early agreement reports, in which the negative effect of PSE membership also reaches statistical significance, although this effect is negligible (2 changes less are made to a committee report in plenary if the rapporteur is affiliated to PSE) (see Table 5.5). Furthermore, again this effect has to be treated with caution due to the potential over-specification problems in the model with 23 variables on a sample of 161 cases only.

Among the control variables, in all models the number of proposed committee amendments has, as expected, a positive marginal effect on the number of changes to a committee report in plenary (0.22), and so does the number of opinion-giving committees (1.41) (see Model 5 in Table 5.5). Predictably, if no early agreement is reached, regulations and directives sustain more changes in plenary than decisions and recommendations (2.99) (*see* Model 7 in Table 5.5). The effects of the committee fixed effects in these models conform to the results of the aggregate analysis in Table 5.1, too (see Appendix J).

Judging from the log likelihood, Model 5 seems to fit the data best. Thus, Figure 5.3 plots the observed and predicted probabilities for a given number of changes to a committee report in plenary, respectively for Model 5 and Model 7 (on the split sample of non-early agreements). The figure demonstrates that the models indeed fit the data well.

Overall, the results of the fractional logistic regression and the negative binomial models, although modelling different dependent variables, lead to comparable results. As far as membership in the working majority party group EPP-ED is concerned, there is strong evidence for Hypothesis 4 under the condition that no early agreement is reached with the Council of Ministers between the committee and plenary stages. A similar effect of PSE membership is only found when examining the sub-sample of dossiers with no early agreement. It is, thus, less clear and has to be treated with caution. There is no significant effect of ALDE membership. There is also no evidence for Hypotheses 2 and 3, save for the positive significant impact of relevant expertise on the first dependent variable in Model 7 of the split sample (no early agreements).

To summarise, only membership in the biggest party group (and potentially also in the second biggest one) has an impact on the success of committee reports on the floor, provided that no early agreement is reached with the Council of Ministers after the committee stage but the EP position is formed in the intraparliamentary decision-making process.

## Discussion

While it is generally claimed that the EP's legislative positions are *de facto* drafted in its committees (Ringe 2009), this chapter has shown that increasingly often this is not the case. The extent to which committees are successful in having the plenary adopt their reports as the official parliamentary positions is heavily influenced by extra-parliamentary developments, and, in particular, by the ever more common informal early agreements on codecision legislation with the Council of Ministers. The aggregate analysis showed that when legislative acts are adopted in the EP plenary following the traditional decision-making mode, they indeed are largely based on the committee reports. However, the legislative influence of committees is significantly diminished when an informal legislative agreement is reached with the Council of Ministers after the committee stage. In these cases, it is not uncommon to see all the committee amendments rejected or lapsed in plenary and instead an alternative set of amendments adopted in its entirety. Thus, the committees' legislative role has been significantly compromised as a result of the new mode of informal bicameral decision-making. These findings demonstrate that the legislative influence of the parliamentary committees is not unconditional.

Arguably, the new procedure of 'fast track legislation' has brought gains in efficiency and sped up the EU legislative process. However, it has also weakened some intra-parliamentary structures and actors, and has led to a decrease of transparency, deterioration of open democratic debate in committees, and severe information asymmetry between legislators. The legitimacy of the democratically elected EP is threatened by the secluded decision-making that leaves it unclear in view of whose interests the parliamentary position is negotiated at trilogue meetings. Upon an early agreement, deliberation in plenary serves only as a means of advertising actors' positions rather than making any real changes or reaching political consensus. Additionally, collusive inter-institutional decision-making

Table 5.4: Negative binomial regression of the number of adopted changes to committee reports in plenary

| | M1 | M2 | M3 | M4 | M5 | M6 | M7_not early | M8_early |
|---|---|---|---|---|---|---|---|---|
| Early | 1.942** | 1.938** | 1.910** | 1.907** | 1.600** | 1.971** | | |
| | (0.129) | (0.128) | (0.140) | (0.154) | (0.180) | (0.148) | | |
| Related interest | -0.065 | -0.095 | -0.203 | -0.103 | -0.143 | -0.111 | -0.285 | 0.013 |
| | (0.194) | (0.192) | (0.324) | (0.191) | (0.192) | (0.190) | (0.380) | (0.190) |
| Early*Related interest | | | 0.188 | | | | | |
| | | | (0.355) | | | | | |
| Related expertise | -0.270 | -0.281 | -0.287 | -0.329 | -0.273 | -0.272 | -0.496 | 0.132 |
| | (0.196) | (0.197) | (0.198) | (0.294) | (0.191) | (0.188) | (0.264) | (0.170) |
| Early*Related expertise | | | | 0.094 | | | | |
| | | | | (0.322) | | | | |
| National party delegation size | 0.003 | 0.004 | 0.004 | 0.004 | 0.003 | 0.003 | 0.005 | 0.005 |
| | (0.005) | (0.005) | (0.005) | (0.005) | (0.005) | (0.005) | (0.009) | (0.006) |
| EPP-ED | -0.388 | -0.551** | -0.555** | -0.557** | -0.965** | -0.554** | -1.083** | -0.173 |
| | (0.245) | (0.166) | (0.166) | (0.164) | (0.234) | (0.165) | (0.279) | (0.170) |
| Early*EPP-ED | | | | | 0.746** | | | |
| | | | | | (0.240) | | | |
| PSE | -0.186 | -0.355 | -0.352 | -0.361 | -0.348 | -0.287 | -0.669* | -0.137 |
| | (0.259) | (0.192) | (0.192) | (0.187) | (0.181) | (0.322) | (0.313) | (0.130) |
| Early*PSE | | | | | | -0.130 | | |
| | | | | | | (0.320) | | |
| ALDE | 0.299 | | | | | | | |

| | M1 | M2 | M3 | M4 | M5 | M6 | M7_not early | M8_early |
|---|---|---|---|---|---|---|---|---|
| | (0.276) | | | | | | | |
| Num. valid comm amendments | 0.016** | 0.016** | 0.016** | 0.016** | 0.016** | 0.016** | 0.012** | 0.019** |
| | (0.002) | (0.002) | (0.002) | (0.002) | (0.002) | (0.002) | (0.002) | (0.002) |
| Num. consul. committees | 0.105** | 0.099** | 0.100** | 0.099** | 0.103** | 0.098** | 0.136* | 0.107* |
| | (0.035) | (0.034) | (0.035) | (0.035) | (0.037) | (0.035) | (0.064) | (0.054) |
| Regulation/Directive | 0.216 | 0.217 | 0.215 | 0.217 | 0.227 | 0.220 | 1.173** | -0.173 |
| | (0.180) | (0.182) | (0.183) | (0.181) | (0.178) | (0.183) | (0.320) | (0.194) |
| Committee fixed effects | Yes | Yes | Yes | Yes | Yes | Yes | Yes | Yes |
| Constant | 0.988** | 1.159** | 1.163** | 1.184** | 1.450** | 1.162** | 1.282* | 3.009** |
| | (0.360) | (0.318) | (0.319) | (0.322) | (0.348) | (0.319) | (0.515) | (0.352) |
| Pseudo LL | -1259.7 | -1260.5 | -1260.3 | -1260.4 | -1256.0 | -1260.4 | -452.7 | -755.0 |
| Pseudo R2 | 0.101 | 0.101 | 0.101 | 0.101 | 0.104 | 0.101 | 0.109 | 0.103 |
| Alpha | 0.992 | 0.997 | 0.996 | 0.997 | 0.97 | 0.996 | 1.372 | 0.479 |
| Inalpha | -0.008 | -0.003 | -0.004 | -0.003 | -0.03 | -0.004 | 0.316 | -0.737 |
| N | 334 | 334 | 334 | 334 | 334 | 334 | 161 | 173 |

*Note*: Dependent variable: number of changes to a committee report in the first reading EP opinion on a codecision proposal in the period 2004–2009 (rejected committee amendments plus adopted non-committee amendments). Robust standard errors displayed in brackets, * significance at 5%, ** significance at 1%. Full models with the committee fixed effects shown in Appendix J.

*Table 5.5: Marginal/ discrete changes effects on the number of changes to a committee report in plenary (Models 5 and 7)*

|  | **M5** | **M7_ not early** |
|---|---|---|
| Early | 23.62 | |
| Related interest | -1.87 | -0.97 |
| Related expertise | -3.54 | -1.69 |
| National party delegation size | 0.04 | 0.02 |
| EPP-ED | -12.99 | -4.10 |
| Early*EPP-ED | 12.86 | |
| PSE | -4.43 | -2.24 |
| Num. valid comm. amendments | 0.22 | 0.04 |
| Num. consult. committees | 1.41 | 0.51 |
| Regulation/Directive | 2.87 | 2.99 |
| AFET | -0.57 | |
| DEVE | -11.11 | -4.05 |
| INTA | -2.54 | -4.39 |
| BUDG | 7.58 | -0.62 |
| CONT | -15.25 | -5.05 |
| ECON | -6.60 | -2.65 |
| EMPL | -7.07 | -3.26 |
| ENVI | -1.28 | -0.80 |
| ITRE | -8.46 | -2.65 |
| IMCO | -3.92 | -0.68 |
| TRAN | -2.81 | -3.09 |
| REGI | -8.88 | -3.08 |
| AGRI | -1.74 | -1.17 |
| JURI | -0.48 | -0.54 |
| LIBE | -8.19 | -2.94 |
| AFCO | -6.17 | 1.89 |
| FEMM | 13.74 | -4.05 |

*Note:* For dummy variables, the effects of their discrete change from 0 to 1 on the dependent variable while holding all other variables at their mean are displayed. For continuous independent variables (national party delegation size, number of valid committee amendments, and number of consultative committees), their marginal effects on the dependent variable at the mean of all independent variables in the respective model are displayed. Abbreviations: AFET: Foreign Affairs; DEVE: Development; INTA: International Trade; BUDG: Budgets; CONT: Budgetary Control; ECON: Economic and Monetary Affairs; EMPL: Employment and Social Affairs; ENVI: Environment, Public Health and Food Safety; ITRE: Industry, Research and Energy; IMCO: Internal Market and Consumer Protection; TRAN: Transport and Tourism; REGI: Regional Development; AGRI: Agriculture; JURI: Legal Affairs; LIBE: Civil Liberties, Justice and Home Affairs; AFCO: Constitutional Affairs; FEMM: Women's Rights and Gender Equality.

*Figure 5.3: Fit to the data of the negative binomial regression Models 5 and 7*

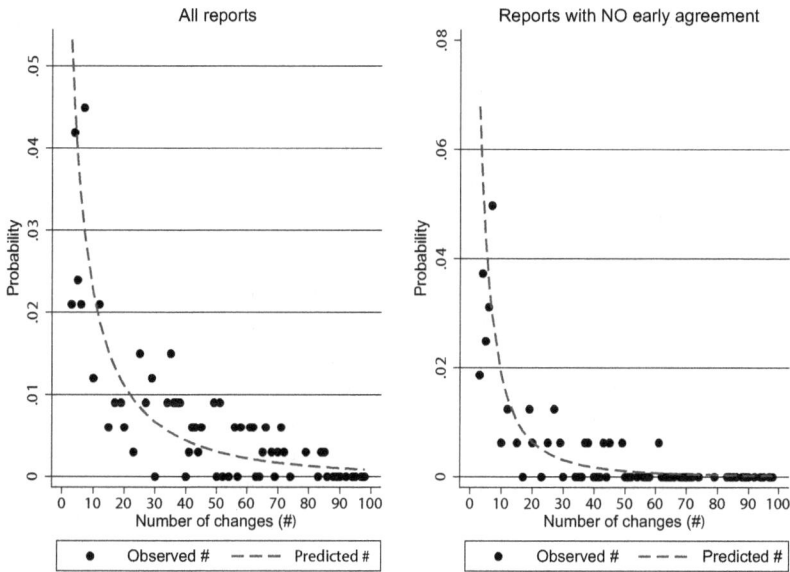

making between the EP and the Council of Ministers has challenged the very idea behind bicameralism and division of legislative power in the EU. In summary, as Héritier (2007: 103) has concluded: 'The Parliament, faced with the choice between gaining power in insulated trilogues and informal agreements on the one hand and a loss in its function as a democratic arena of debate on the other, decided in favour of the first'. As a partial remedy to the problem of transparency loss associated with early agreements, the new EP Rules of Procedure (European Parliament 2009b) include 'ANNEX XX: Code of conduct for negotiating in the context of the ordinary legislative procedures'. It provides formal rules on when an informal meeting between representatives of the EP and the Council can take place, the composition of the parliamentary representation, the mandate the rapporteur needs in order to negotiate, and the way in which meeting outcomes have to be communicated back to the committee. This formalisation of the early agreements reflects the grave problems of transparency loss and exclusion inherent in the hitherto informal decision-making mode. Whether they will be a successful remedy remains to be seen. In any case, it is a step in the right direction towards solving the transparency deficit of the EU legislative process. As a member of the EPP-ED secretariat commented:

[The question is] how you organise yourself. If you have an early second agreement, even if conciliation – a third reading – it does not say, it does not guarantee you have a transparent process. A transparent process takes two things – one is that the other members take interest and not only complain afterwards, and the second is that you have a process where you say – all right, we inform regularly in writing in prep meetings, we ask for a mandate for certain cases, so before we go for the first informal trilogue meeting we need to know what our group, what our committee stands for. You don't need the final vote in committee but you need a position, you need to have the key points. Otherwise you would be very much weaker towards the Council when you are with no clear mandate. And also when you come back it would be quite difficult to sell it. (Personal interview 11 with a member of the EPP-ED secretariat, 27th February 2008)

Taking the normative implications of early agreements aside, the special interests and expertise of rapporteurs do not appear to have a significant impact on the way committee reports are received in the plenary, providing no evidence for the distributive and informational rationales. These results largely hold irrespective of the existence of early inter-institutional agreements. In contrast, membership of the rapporteur in the biggest party group EPP-ED has a strong positive impact on the success of committee reports on the floor but only if no early agreement is reached with the Council of Ministers before the plenary stage. Thus, the explanatory power of the partisan rationale is conditional. PSE membership of the rapporteurs has similar, although not so clear, impact on the level of committees' legislative influence to that of EPP-ED membership. However, there is no effect of affiliation to ALDE – the likely coalition partner of EPP-ED and PSE in forming the EP majority. It appears that in the formal decision-making process, in accordance with the partisan rationale, the working majority party group 'gets what it wants' in committee and is able to pass it through in plenary.

Future research is needed to explore the relationship between rapporteurs and their committees. For instance, qualitative research is necessary to examine the extent to which the parliamentary committees influence early agreements reached before the committee stage. The observed strong variation in legislative influence between committees also calls for further explanation.

# chapter six | main findings and empirical implications

The substantive empirical contributions of the book are evaluated in this chapter. First, a summary of the main findings of the empirical analyses is provided. Thereafter, the research questions posed in the introductory chapter are addressed. The final section discusses the broader implications of the empirical results for European Union policies, interest representation, the EU legislative process, and, ultimately, the democratic deficit of the EU.

## Summary of the main findings

The primary goal of this book has been to evaluate the legislative role and impact of the European Parliament committees. Specifically, it analysed the rationale behind their organisation (distributive, informational or partisan) and how that affects their legislative output and influence *vis-à-vis* the parliamentary plenary. For the purpose, both the organisation of the parliamentary committees and their impact on the legislation the EP adopts were examined.

Turning first to committee assignments, in Chapter Three it was shown that the distributive and informational rationales account for the assignment of legislators to different types of committee (depending on the character of their legislative output). Purely information-driven committees with predominantly regulatory legislative output attract MEPs with relevant expertise. In contrast, members with homogeneous special interests systematically accrue on interest-driven and mixed committees that draft policies with distributive implications for certain societal groups, turning them into potential preference outlying committees. However, the strict proportionality rules on committee composition in the EP constrain the manoeuvre of party groups, which do not appear to strategically use individual committee assignments. The rules ensure that the working majority party group (coalition) is not over-represented in the composition of any committee. Therefore, the explanatory power of the partisan rationale in accounting for committee assignments is limited. Since the assignment system is conducive to legislators' self-selection, the distributive and informational rationales are better equipped to explain its consequences.

In contrast, the partisan rationale accounts for the pattern of allocation of legislative tasks, or reports, to party groups and committee members (Chapter Four). The allocation process is left completely to the discretion of party group leaders in committees and is not regulated by the formal EP Rules of Procedure. Instead, an informal code of practice guides it, which allows for disproportional representation of party groups and national party delegations in the distribution of legislative tasks. The incentive structure provided by the inter-institutional legislative procedures of the EU, which make certain reports more attractive than others, further stimulates disproportional allocation. Specifically, the stronger legislative power of the Parliament *vis-à-vis* the Council of Ministers under the codecision rather than under the consultation legislative procedure leads to keener inter- and intra-party group competition for codecision reports, from which clear winners and losers emerge. Often constituting the parliamentary working majority, the predominant centre-right party group coalition (EPP-ED and ALDE) is systematically privileged in the allocation of codecision reports. Furthermore, party group coordinators appear to have utilised report allocations as a means of disciplining their members. Thus, members loyal to the group are rewarded in the allocation of legislative tasks, while disloyal members are punished by depriving them from holding influential legislative positions. Legislators with outlying special interests and pure experts are given systematic access to drafting consultation reports only because party group coordinators are constrained by the need to enhance their groups' cohesion, which would be compromised by allocating important reports to members with outlying interests who may drive policies away from those preferred by their groups' median members. Thus, the distributive and informational rationales are limited in accounting for the distribution of legislative tasks in committees, which can be better explained by the partisan rationale. The allocation of legislative tasks within committees serves as a tool for promoting party cohesion and consolidation.

The final empirical analysis examined the extent to which the plenary has been drawing its legislative positions on the basis of committee proposals (Chapter Five). It showed that the increasingly popular informal mode of negotiating with the Council of Ministers in secluded meetings outside committees, which often result in early inter-institutional agreements, has significantly undermined committees' legislative influence. This regularity holds regardless of the party group affiliation, expertise or special interests of the rapporteurs drafting committee reports. Hence, the fate of the committees' legislative output in plenary cannot be predicted by looking solely at the committee organisation and the committee-plenary relations. Instead, the effect of the EU's inter-institutional set-up on the intra-parliamentary competition dynamics (among legislators, party groups or institutional structures) has to be considered. When the Council of Ministers does not interfere with the internal decision-making process in the EP and no early inter-institutional legislative agreement is concluded, the congressional theories are better able to explain the parliamentary legislative positions. In such cases, the partisan rationale accounts best for the level of success of committee proposals on the floor as a consequence of the open amendment rule. The committee reports drafted by members of the EPP-ED, i.e. the working majority party group in the EP, are more successful in plenary than those drafted by rapporteurs from other party groups. This suggests that the working majority party group obtains the policies it prefers irrespective of committee work – it accepts a committee report if one of its members has drafted it and amends the report on the floor if it has been prepared by a rapporteur from another party group. Beyond rapporteurs' party group affiliation, their special interests and expertise have no effect on the success of committee reports in plenary, even when no early bicameral agreements are struck. This is not surprising given that also the report allocation analysis (Chapter Four) unveiled no significant effect of such factors on the distribution of codecision reports.

To summarise, while committee assignments are driven by distributive and informational but not partisan concerns due to the formal EP proportionality rule on committee composition, mainly partisan interests shape the report allocation – a process guided only by an informal proportionality rule. The committee reports drafted by the working majority party group are also more successful in plenary than the reports by other party groups as a consequence of the open amendment rule – a regularity that holds, however, only when no early inter-institutional agreement is concluded between the EP and the Council of Ministers. Such agreements render the distributive, informational and partisan rationales unable to account for committee-plenary legislative dynamics.

## Whom do the European Parliament committees serve?

*Do the EP committees serve special interests outside the Parliament, the interests of the overall plenary or those of the working majority party group (coalition)?* While there is some evidence to support each of the three potential answers, the findings provide most support for the partisan rationale. Indeed, in the committee assignment, self-selection of members with special interests and expertise is predominant, while party group proportionality is fully observed and group affiliation and loyalty give no unwarranted advantage to any members. However, in the actual legislative assignments it is the working majority party group coalition of the European People's Party and the Liberals, as well as loyal party group members, who are privileged in the allocation of influential committee reports, while potential policy outliers and experts are marginalised. Even more indicative is the significantly better treatment of committee reports on the floor if drafted by rapporteurs from the biggest party group EPP-ED rather than by members of any other party group. So, while all MEPs are given fair access to committee membership, clearly committee work and output are dominated by the working majority party group, and, potentially, its coalition partner. It is fair to say that, on the whole, the EP committees systematically serve the interests of the working majority party group rather than special interests outside the EP or the plenary at large.[1]

Notably, while overall the organisation, work and legislative output of the parliamentary committees is largely dominated by the working majority party group (coalition), the complete answer to the research question is rather multi-faceted. As expected from the outset, no single theoretical approach was able to fully grasp

---

1. Naturally, the median policy position of the working majority party group (coalition) and that of the plenary may coincide, in which case one and the same observed outcome would provide evidence for both the partisan and informational rationales. Nevertheless, the two theoretical approaches prescribe quite different underlying processes by which this outcome is arrived at.

the complexity of the EP committees' legislative organisation and influence. In anticipation of such an outcome, the research question was qualified in search of regularities or conditions under which different rationales are better able to account for the committees' organisational aspects and their consequences: When and why are legislative committees dominated by legislators with special interests (distributive rationale), by specialists producing outcomes favouring the plenary median (informational rationale), or by loyal members of the working majority party group (coalition) (partisan rationale)? It was complemented with a question on the ability of the EP committees to actually shape the EP legislation: under which conditions are the EP committees successful in determining the parliamentary legislative positions?

Four explanatory factors emerged from the empirical analyses in the preceding chapters, indicating that which actors control the committee organisation and determine the content of the parliamentary legislation is conditional on: 1) *the type of committee and its policy areas*; 2) *the type of formal and informal parliamentary rules regulating committee-party and committee-plenary relationships*; 3) *the incentives provided by the inter-institutional legislative rules (inter-institutional legislative procedures)*; and 4) *the decision-making mode between the EP and the Council of Ministers – formal or informal negotiations.* In what follows, I discuss how each of these factors was derived.

First, in Chapter Three it was shown that there are important *differences between committees operating in different policy areas.* It classified committees: first, into interest-driven, information-driven or mixed, based on whether their legislative output is regulatory and technical or distributive and targets homogeneous organised groups outside the EP; and, second, into more and less powerful ones depending on how many codecision reports they draft and whether they influence the EU budget. The analysis of seat assignment showed that the legislative power of committees does not disproportionately affect their party group composition. However, if the policy areas in which certain committees operate systematically target the interests of organised homogeneous societal groups, they attract significantly more MEPs with relevant special interests linked to those groups. Such committees are, thus, staffed with homogeneous preference outliers. Additionally, committees that deal with highly technical issues attract legislators with relevant expertise. Overall, the committees' membership is conditional on the policy areas they deal with and the distributive and informational rationales can account for that regularity.

Second, based on the findings of all three empirical chapters, it can be deduced that *when formal rules constrain political parties the EP committees serve either legislators' special interests, or the plenary median.* Such a rule is, for example, the proportional committee composition required by the EP Rules of Procedure. This does not imply that formal rules as such always disadvantage party groups. It depends on the type of formal rule. Thus, for instance, the open amendment rule in the EP Rules of Procedure, which allows any party group to make changes to committee reports on the floor, significantly empowers party groups *vis-à-vis* committees. Whenever no formal rules apply, though, party groups do seize the opportunity of using committee organisation to their benefit. For instance, the informal report allocation system privileges the working majority party group coalition and, in general, empowers party groups to control their members in committees. Overall, the level of dominance of preference outliers, experts and party group leaders over committees depends on the character of the parliamentary rules defining committee-party group and committee-plenary relationships. Party groups are empowered by formal and informal rules that limit committee influence over the plenary or increase the party groups' power *vis-à-vis* the parliamentary committees. Preference outliers and experts have better chances of influencing committees' work and legislative output when formal rules constrain party group leaders and safeguard committee output on the floor.

Third, the explanatory power of the distributive, informational and partisan rationales is shaped by the *EU's inter-institutional legislative procedures.* The EP does not operate in a unicameral legislature but co-legislates with the Council of Ministers. Thus, its internal organisation and work are inevitably affected by the inter-institutional rules determining its standing *vis-à-vis* the other legislative chamber. A number of intricate procedures govern the balance of power between the two EU chambers. While under the co-decision (the ordinary) procedure the two institutions have equal legislative powers, under consultation the final decision lies with the Council. This asymmetric legislative power between the two legislative branches inevitably has left a mark on the internal organisation of the EP. This is best captured in the analysis of report allocation (Chapter Four). Distinguishing between the allocation of codecision and consultation legislative reports, this analysis has shown that the former is driven solely by partisan concerns, while only in the latter do distributive and informational factors play a role. Thus, it can be deduced that the working majority party group (coalition) dominates over the EP committees when 'more is at stake', i.e. when the EP has full legislative powers to shape the EU legislation. Conversely, the distributive and informational rationales are only able to account for organisational aspects of the EP committees, which are of little consequence to the adopted EU policies and, hence, of low salience for the working majority party group (coalition).

Finally, the ability of the congressional rationales to explain the committee work and legislative output is conditional upon *the decision-making mode between the EP and the Council of Ministers – formal or informal.* In particular, should the committees' legislative work be fully delegated to extra-parliamentary arenas, the congressional approaches are limited in accounting for the character of adopted legislation. This is largely because in a setting such as the secluded inter-institutional trilogue meetings it is difficult, if not impossible, to detect on a given legislative proposal what the pursued common committee line is, assuming that such a line is pursued. After all, it is just a limited number of parliamentary representatives – mainly the rapporteur and the shadow rapporteurs – who are supposed to represent the overall committee position. If they have homogeneous special interests they may pursue common particularistic policies irrespective of their party group affiliation; if they have no strong policy interests and are simply experts in the given field they may only aspire to adopt 'good' European policies and represent the median parliamentary position; and, if they are loyal representatives of their EP party groups they may be pursuing party groups' policies. But irrespective of the incentives of committee representatives in informal meetings with the Council of Ministers, they are there to look for a compromise. So, the agreements they bring back to committee are based on both their policy positions and the concession they had to make to the Council of Ministers. Hence, it is no longer the combination of committee members' goals and parliamentary rules that can predict the policies the legislature pursues as the congressional theoretical approaches prescribe. This leaves these approaches unable to account for the legislative output of committees and the plenary at large following informal bicameral decision-making.

## Empirical implications

The main questions examined in this book include: how are committees organised; how does their organisation affect their legislative output; to what extent do they shape the final parliamentary legislative positions; and, indeed, are they the main decision-making units in the EP and, if so, how do committees and parties interact and reconcile? Related to these questions, the aim of this book has been to unveil more substantively how well-informed or ideologically biased the legislation the committees produce is, when the EP acts along consensual or majoritarian lines, and how effective the legislative organisation of the EP is in allowing the Parliament to fulfil its legislative tasks and uphold its position *vis-à-vis* the Council of Ministers.

The results provide important insights to answer all these questions. They contribute to our understanding of the legislative organisation of the EP and its implications for interest representation, the parliamentary institutionalisation, the EU legislative process, European integration, and, more broadly, the democratic deficit in the EU. These implications are discussed in greater detail below.

### *Limited scope for pursuing particularistic policies in the EP*

As discussed in Chapter One, a multitude of actors are affected by the policies the EP adopts and have incentives to influence MEPs. They will only be able to directly shape the EP's legislative output if they have means of systematically targeting its members, or if they have a substantial support base within the Parliament. The EP committees and their members are the most accessible and primary targets of external pressure. They serve as channels for direct representation of societal groups beyond the representation offered by national party delegations. In this way, they can enhance the input legitimacy of the EP.

Perhaps it is easiest for societal actors and groups to shape the legislative output of a committee if that committee is simply staffed with members that are sympathetic to their policy demands. As an MEP commented in an interview:

Sometimes I go to visit lobbyists and stakeholders and they ask me 'how can I make sure that this point of view will be well represented in the next parliament.' And I just tell them: go to see the leaders of the party and make sure that you get someone in the delegation, or that will be elected on the basis of this party, that can take on board this issue. (Personal interview 14 with a PSE member, 12th February 2008)

Members with homogenous special interests have indeed accrued in certain EP committees, bringing along more than informational benefits, as previous research suggested (Ringe 2009). Links to green groups reflect more than expertise in environmental issues; links to trade unions reveal more than knowledge of employment issues; industry ties are not associated solely with knowledge in business; ties to farming groups come with certain demands; and MEPs with links to social groups tend to be more devoted to particular societal problems and would go further to solve them than their fellow parliamentarians. Committees staffed with such members may be more prone to propose policies that are substantially different from those preferred by the median legislator on the EP floor. That would not have been possible if committees had heterogeneous membership, i.e. if their members had and pursued contrasting or heterogeneous interests. However, it was demonstrated in Chapter Three that some committees are staffed with homogeneous preference outliers. Hence, the EP does provide in its committees at least the organisational structures for pursuing particularistic policies.

This has important implications not only for the internal organisation and decision-making in the EP, but more broadly for interest representation in the EU. It suggests that those actors and groups of actors who manage to organise at the European level and target committee members in the EP can potentially affect the direction of adopted EU policies. This matters most in the policy areas falling under the codecision procedure where the EP's stance counts.

However, there is a limit to the extent to which preference-outliers can shape adopted EP policies. As demonstrated in the analysis of report allocation (Chapter Four), members with special interests are given by party group coordinators systematic access to the writing of consultation but not codecision reports. It is therefore not surprising that on the whole rapporteurs' interests have no significant influence on the extent to which the EP plenary adopts committee reports under codecision. Notwithstanding these constraints, the prevalent mode of informal decision-making with the Council of Ministers and early agreements on codecision dossiers appear to have empowered the negotiating actors on behalf of the EP, i.e. the rapporteur, the shadow rapporteurs, and potentially the committee chairs. As the EP representatives in the negotiations, they benefit from asymmetric information about the Council members' positions *vis-à-vis* their committee and party group colleagues. Even the recent formalisation of the informal negotiations in the EP Rules of Procedure (European Parliament 2009b) is unlikely to completely eliminate this asymmetry. The committee representatives in trilogue meetings can, thus, advance policy positions different from those preferred by their colleagues. The shift of decision-making to informal inter-institutional meetings challenges the assertions that policy positions are endogenously created in the responsible EP committees and party positions are 'the endogenous outcome of deliberation and negotiations in committees' (Ringe 2009: 43–4).[2] Whose position do the parliamentary representatives advance in trilogue negotiations? The delegation of bargaining power from the overall committees to a limited number of representatives can lead to: 1) a shift of decision-making from committees to party groups if rapporteurs act as loyal party group members pursuing group policies; or 2) an increase in the potential for drafting outlying committee policy should the rapporteur and shadow rapporteurs have homogeneous special interests in the area of the negotiated policy (e.g. agriculture, fisheries, industry, environment) shared with their committee colleagues and collude to collectively pursue those interests irrespective of their party group affiliation. This also brings to the fore the question whether the EP is dominated by party-government or committee-government. Only the latter allows for distributive outcomes owing to gains from trade between committees with heterogeneous policy positions.

The potential for this latter scenario, however, is limited. Firstly, the analysis of the adoption of committee reports in plenary (Chapter Five) shows that when an early agreement is reached with the Council of Ministers after the committee stage, committee reports are largely, if not completely, discarded on the floor. This suggests that it is not the common committee line that committee representatives agree on in trilogues, although admittedly inter-institutional agreements reflect also the concessions they make to the Council. Instead, trilogues agreements rather appear to serve as a means for the rapporteurs to by-pass the changes made to their reports in committee. Secondly, committees' success in affecting the parliamentary positions is indeed significantly higher when their reports are not subjected to an early agreement with the Council. Yet, committees' legislative influence is not unconditional in such cases, either. It depends on the will of the working majority party group (and potentially the second biggest party group), which accepts committee proposals if it has sponsored them (i.e. if its rapporteurs drafted them) and amends them in plenary otherwise.

In summary, committee reports sustain amendments if early inter-institutional agreements are reached and whenever it is not rapporteurs from the working majority party group that draft them. Thus, overall the committees do not control the legislative output of the EP. This counteracts the effect of the staffing of some committees with homogeneous preference-outliers by limiting the chances of adopting outlying EP policies favouring certain societal groups at the expense of others. Despite the committees' informational advantage, party group control has prevented the EP committees from turning into independent high-demanding units pursuing skewed distributive policy agendas.

---

2.  Ringe (2005, 2009) argues that owing to their expertise committee members are able to provide non-committee members with 'focal point', i.e. short cut devices linking complex policy proposals with the dominant outcome preference dimensions, thus shaping legislators' decisions by affecting their perceptions of the relevant and salient proposal aspects. He holds that this is how MEPs develop their policy positions on individual legislative proposals.

Normatively speaking, this is a positive conclusion. Indeed, the accrual of members with special interests on some parliamentary committees can promote the direct participation of societal groups in formulating the EU legislation, thus increasing the input legitimacy of the Union defined as the 'consent to govern through support for participative and procedural mechanisms' (Greenwood 2007: 177–8). However, input and information provided by such societal groups are bound to be biased and promote narrow interests rather than the aggregate interests of the EU citizens. Thus, instead of improving the 'output legitimacy of EU public policy, concerned with the supply of information, ideas and expert resources for the technical quality of such policies' (Greenwood 2007: 1), policy-outlying committees can jeopardise the EP's responsiveness to the policy demands of the broader public. Indisputably, drafting particularistic policies reduces aggregate welfare. In contrast, 'parties can be better advocates in parliaments of what are called 'general public goods' as opposed to 'local public goods' (Schattschneider 1960)' (cited in Hix *et al.* 2007: 42). Hence, promoting party politics and reducing the possibility for distributional politics in the EP can increase the popular legitimacy and representativeness of the Parliament.

### *Institutionalisation of the European Parliament*

The way in which the EP chooses to organise its work and relations with the Council of Ministers has profound implications not only for the type of legislation it adopts and whom this legislation favours, but also for the institutionalisation of the EP and its ability to perform its legislative functions effectively. The efficiency demands placed on the EP have increased with its ever growing legislative workload culminating in the ratification of the Lisbon Treaty (2009) that turned the codecision procedure into the 'ordinary legislative procedure' of the EU and more than doubled the amount of policy areas in which substantive powers are conferred on the EP. The internal parliamentary organisation affects the ability of the EP to deal with this workload. Formal and informal rules have facilitated its institutionalisation and enhanced its bargaining powers in its negotiations with the Council of Ministers. In particular, they have stimulated the development of specialisation in the EP and facilitated effective majority-formation, or more precisely coalition-building between party groups, which is crucial to avoiding policy gridlock in the EU.

### *Increased specialisation*

While parliamentary seniority did not play a significant role in the internal EP organisation in the past (Bowler and Farrell 1995), it has now become one of the most important factors shaping both committee assignments and report allocation, as shown in Chapters 3 and 4. The growing importance of seniority in the organisation of the EP reflects the steady institutionalisation of the legislature.

An increasing number of legislators choose serving in the EP as their long-term career. During the 6th EP (2004–2009), 45 per cent of all legislators were incumbents (of which almost half have been in the parliament for more than one term). If the new member states, who joined the EU in 2004, are excluded, this number rises to 57 per cent. In the most recent EP Elections in 2009, half of all the elected MEPs (50.14 per cent) were incumbents (European Parliament 2009a).

The high level of continuity in committee membership has been conducive to growing specialisation in the EP. The legislature can now rely on long-serving, experienced legislators and staff members to draft well-informed policies. Moreover, the combination of committee assignment rules favouring policy specialisation and open amendment rules in plenary reducing incentives to draft particularistic policies have promoted the building of unbiased expertise in the EP. This is a significant parliamentary achievement given the limited bureaucratic staff supporting its work and the fact that it does not elect and, in turn, rely on a government for policy expertise as most national parliaments in the EU do. The growing specialisation of the EP has a positive effect on the quality of policies it adopts.

*High party group cohesion and increased frequency of ideological coalitions*

Not only has the level of specialisation in the EP increased, but also the parliamentary ability to effectively adopt legislation. The EP seems to be moving away from consensual decision-making driven by the grand coalition of the European People's Party and the European Socialists to more competitive left-right politics led by either centre-left or centre-right coalitions.

Flexible parliamentary rules encouraging coalition-driven behaviour in the distribution of parliamentary rights and resources, such as the informal report allocation system, have facilitated this development. The over-representation of EPP-ED and ALDE in the allocation of codecision reports reflects an underlying logroll between these party groups. The EPP-ED and ALDE can form together a minimum-winning party group coalition and pass legislation in the early stage of the legislative process. The ideological proximity of these two groups suggests that their collusion in obtaining parliamentary resources and legislative tasks is not the result of mere cartel behaviour but rather reflects their close policy goals.

Ideology-driven coalition formation and party cohesion improve the potential for broad political representation. In the past, consensual grand coalitions between EPP-ED and PSE prevailed, which were associated with the two party groups controlling the organisation and work of the EP and the isolation of smaller party groups from the decision-making process (Kreppel 2002a). Until the last legislative term, smaller party groups had to be satisfied with the proportional partisan composition of committees and occasionally obtaining important committee reports, which could anyway be amended in plenary. The new trend of building minimal-winning left-right coalitions can now improve the representation of smaller party groups in the adoption of the parliamentary legislation as the EPP-ED and the PSE take their policy concerns on board in order to avoid making bigger concessions to each other.

An essential prerequisite for the formation of parliamentary majorities, and, in particular, strong and credible party group coalitions, is the existence of cohesive party groups. It was demonstrated how party group leaders enhance their groups' cohesion by using the allocation of parliamentary resources as a means of disciplining their members, i.e. by using the 'carrots and sticks' approach. Promoting party group cohesion appeared to be the main mechanism driving the distribution of legislative reports in committees. As the partisan rationale suggests, the EP committees serve as an arena, which party groups use to control their members by rewarding and punishing group members for their level of group loyalty. In this way, the parliamentary organisation can explain, at least partially, the observed cohesive party voting in the EP – a phenomenon which could not be accounted for with party groups' strategic agenda control (see Hix *et al.* 2007: 105–31). It may also provide an answer to the puzzling lack of a negative effect of the 2004 and 2007 enlargements on party group cohesion (Schmitt and Thomassen 2009: 39). Party groups are no longer entirely dependent on the good will of their constituent national parties but can rely on procedural tools and structures that the parliamentary committees offer to institute discipline among their members and promote group cohesion.

Party group cohesion is important for assuring stability of decision-making in the EP. '[P]arties can increase efficiency of decision-making by internalising broad and stable categories of interests' (Schattschneider 1960: 45). In other words, they can reduce the dimensionality of the policy space by 'creating correlations between the different dimensions of politics.' (Hix *et al.* 2007: 9) and '[t]his reduction in dimensionality enhances the predictability of democratic decision-making and hence increases efficiency' (Hix *et al.* 2007: 46). Additionally, according to the model of party government, one of the preconditions for elections to function as an instrument of linkage between citizens' preferences and government policy is the internal cohesion of parliamentary parties necessary for them to implement their policies (Tsebelis 1994; Thomassen and Schmitt 1999a; Thomassen 2009). While the European party groups do not run for office in the European elections or form an EU government, voters' policy preferences are communicated to them via national party delegations, and party groups do shape the EU policies. Hence, cohesive party groups have the potential to improve representation in the EU by offering clear policy positions, which voters can identify with, and forming ideologically driven coalitions to fulfil their policy goals.

### European integration driven by left-right ideology

The influence of party groups over the EP reaches beyond majority formation on the floor. This book has shown that the European party groups largely dominate the organisation of the EP and, consequently, the content of adopted parliamentary legislation. Party groups act as agenda-setters in shaping the legislative output of the parliamentary committees by selecting rapporteurs and directing their work in party group meetings. More importantly, though, they possess veto power over committees' legislative output and can heavily amend it in plenary. In particular, the successful passage of committee reports on the floor depends on the support of the largest party groups in the EP, and mainly the EPP-ED. This finding demonstrates for the first time that party groups, and in particular the working majority party group, heavily affect the legislative output of the EP not only at the voting stage but also at the stage of legislation preparation. It complements previous studies, which have reached a consensus that decision-making in the EP is largely orchestrated by European party groups and is, thus, structured not along national but along ideological lines (see Chapter One).

The dominance in the organisation of the EP committees of the European People's Party and, to a lesser extent, the centrist Liberal Group facilitates ideology-driven politics in the EP rather than politics guided by particularistic national interests. The switch to more centre-right rather than grand party group coalitions in the EP is not an isolated parliamentary process. Instead, it is stimulated by the unprecedented concurrent dominance of centre-right majorities since 2005 in all three EU legislative institutions (the EP, the Council of Ministers and the European Commission), the so called 'unified government' in the EU (Hix *et al.* 2007: 8). The literature has shown some evidence that decision-making is structured along left-right conflicts in the Council of Ministers, too (Mattila and Lane 2001; Mattila 2004; Aspinwall 2006; Hagemann and Høyland 2008, 2010). As a result, the EU is turning into a regular political system, in which political parties deliberate and decide on policies. Article 10 TEU specifies that the Parliament is there to represent directly the EU citizens, while the Council of Ministers represents the member states. In reality, though, the collective decision-making between the two institutions is increasingly driven by left-right party politics rather than national dynamics or pro-/anti-EU integration sentiments.

The rise of left-right politics in the EU has important implications for the observed European integration in general – one driven from within the EU by ideological rather than national divisions. Indisputably, the overall institutional structure of the EU, its enlargement and the transfer of sovereignty from the national to the European level remain the prerogative of national governments and are delineated in intergovernmental conferences (Mair and Thomassen 2010: 28). However, it has become difficult to subscribe to Moravcsik's long-standing claim (1998a) that the EU is largely an intergovernmental organisation based simply on the cooperation of sovereign states. There are more subtle ways in which the European integration deepens, namely via the proliferation of European legislation in policy areas which have been already delegated to the EU level, left unconstrained by narrow national interest. The ability of national governments to block European legislation is curtailed by the application of the qualified majority rule and the codecision powers of the EP in many policy areas. While in the examined period (2004–2009) the codecision procedure applied to only certain types of policy, following the recent adoption of the Lisbon Treaty (2009) it has become the 'ordinary legislative procedure' and now applies to the majority of community policies. Given the partisan, left-right politics in the EP, this is expected to lead to even more ideologically driven EU policies rather than ones based on national divisions. Thus, national interests are further constrained in shaping most

EU policies. This is a positive step in the direction of a truly European system of representation, which can be made possible only if policy preferences are shared across borders (Thomassen and Schmitt 1999b: 188).

Notably, this also comes at the expense of a somewhat compromised national system of representation. It is difficult to imagine that the citizens of all member states in the EU share exactly the same concerns and that no territory- or nation-specific issues exist. Thus, the stronger influence of transnational party groups over EU legislation after the adoption of the Lisbon Treaty (2009) may be accompanied by heightened pressure on MEPs by their national parties and parliaments, and increased mobilisation of organised national societal interests at the European level. Should the hitherto disinterest of national parties in the work of MEPs and the lack of mobilisation of national parliaments in scrutinising EU legislation continue, the traditionally national prerogative of legislating would be inadvertently lost to the EU level. Exemplifying this process, already 50 per cent of the member states' national laws stem from the need to incorporate adopted EU policies into national legislation (Greenwood 2007: 6).[3]

### *The European Parliament – a solution to the democratic deficit in the European Union?*

Knowing more about the internal organisation and work of the EP facilitates assessing its role in the political system of the EU. The EP owes much of its perpetual empowerment to the hopes vested in it to solve the problems of legitimacy and responsiveness deficit in the Union. The extent to which it manages to aggregate public opinion and policy preferences as well as translate those into the European legislation is debatable.

#### *Increasing output legitimacy*

The EP has now become so powerful that it is no longer possible to maintain the argument that the national channel for representation and accountability is sufficient, as claimed by Moravcsik (1998a). Being the only directly elected institution of the EU, the EP is seen as the Union's legitimating institution. It has the potential to directly represent the voice of the European citizens. The 'second order' character of the EP elections (Reif and Schmitt 1980; Van der Eijk and Franklin 1996; Marsh 1998; Hix and Marsh 2007; Van der Brug and Van der Eijk 2007), however, cast doubts on whether the EP can fulfil this function. Among others, this has lead Farrell and Scully (2007: i) to the gloomy conclusion that 'while considerable efforts have been made to increase the status of the EP, it is in crucial respects a failure as a representative body.'

---

3.    'A frequently cited guesstimate (somewhat lacking in transparent justification) is that 50 per cent of all legislation (and 75–80 per cent of economic and environmental legislation) passing though member state parliaments bears a "made in Brussels" stamp, although no one doubts the general point about the significance of EU activity'. (Greenwood 2007: 6)

Competition in the EP elections is mainly criticised for being based on national rather than European issues, where parties compete on the left-right rather than on the pro-/anti- European integration dimension. This criticism seems misconceived. Both Bartolini (2005) and Thomassen (2009) rightfully point out that the constitutive European issue, i.e. issues related to constitutional EU matters, lie in the domain of national governments' jurisdiction and are not tackled at the EU level. Bartolini (2005: 35) even warns that there is a certain danger in politicising constitutive issues the same way as left-right issues. Referring to this as the 'sleeping giant', Van der Eijk and Franklin (2004) claim that the potential for politicisation of the pro-/anti-European integration dimension is in fact rising with the number of people with extreme positions. This can shift the debate from 'what kind of EU' to 'if EU'. Since the EU legislates in policy areas that have traditionally belonged to the national domain, such as economic, social and legal regulation, the EP elections should be fought on left-right issues instead. Luckily, the current organisation of the EP is not conducive to extreme anti-EU sentiments but, instead, channels left-right politics. Since the European party groups are coalitions of national parties with similar policy positions and operate in the same policy space as national parties, 'party and policy competition in the EP is an extension of national politics by other means' (McElroy and Benoit 2010: 396). Consequently, the positions of party groups in the EP and the preferences of voters happen to be closely aligned on the left-right ideological dimension (Thomassen 2009: 234; Schmitt and Thomassen 1999; Mair and Thomassen 2010). While this is more of a 'lucky' development rather than the outcome of a deliberate process, as a result the European party groups function effectively as representatives of the people in terms of policy outcomes. (Mair and Thomassen 2010: 30). This led Mair and Thomassen (2010: 30) to conclude that for the time being 'the deficit is not as pronounced as is commonly believed to be the case'.

The second main criticism of the EP elections is that national parties and not the transnational European parties compete in them, although the latter are the ones to orchestrate the EP work and shape EU policies. It is argued that this limits the input legitimacy of the European party groups as well as their ability to represent the interests of the EU citizens and be held accountable for that. Such a critique overlooks the fact that the European party groups are in fact cohesive ideological coalitions of national parties promoting the policy goals of national parties. Their numerical strength can decrease if their constituent national parties are punished in the EP elections, in which case they are indirectly held accountable.

This book has shown that although the EP elections may fail to directly aggregate the preferences of the EU citizens, the legislative organisation of the EP helps it to represent these preferences by promoting left-right party-driven policy making. This meets Scharpf's (1999: 10: 10) criterion for democracy in the EU. According to him, 'a more modest form of legitimisation must have to uphold the Union, that is, an output-oriented legitimisation brought about by government for the people.' In the next subsection, I turn to examining the potential for input legitimisation of the EP's work besides the European elections.

*Efficient policy-making at the expense of transparency*

How does the EP facilitate the effective participation of EU citizens in the legislative process and the consideration of their policy interests in shaping policy? The EP's input legitimacy depends not only on accommodating the policy preferences of national political parties that received people's votes, but also on having the necessary institutional structures to obtain direct input from the EU citizens as well as organised national and European groups in shaping EU policies.

This is one of the main roles of the parliamentary committees. They have traditionally served as open to the public arenas for democratic debate between committee members, representatives of the other EU institutions, experts and societal lobby groups. However, the ability of committees to fulfil this important role has been compromised by the rising tide of decision-making in informal inter-institutional settings. The lack of transparency of this decision-making mode jeopardises the representative function of the EP. It limits the input legitimacy of the EP by curtailing the possibility for direct participation of societal actors in the legislative process. Arguably, it also places the output legitimacy of the EP in question as it is not clear whose interests the parliamentary representatives represent when striking agreements with members of the Council of Ministers, what concessions they make and why. This makes it difficult to hold legislators accountable by not voting them back to office, as national parties and voters cannot monitor their actions.

The ability of the EP committees to include societal groups in the decision-making process and represent their policy stances is also compromised by the decreasing legislative influence of committees. Their role in the legislative process is diminished not only by the shift of the deliberation process away from the committee arenas, but also by the trend of altogether dismissing committees' legislative reports when early inter-institutional agreements are reached with the Council of Ministers. As shown in Chapter Five, such early agreements are generally not disputed on the EP floor and, if they are struck, it is not uncommon to find all the proposed committee amendments dropped in plenary and an alternative set of amendments adopted instead. Thus, it has become difficult to claim that committee proposals are rarely modified in plenary (Bowler and Farrell 1995: 234) as early agreements were made on more than 60 per cent of the codecision legislative proposals in the 6th EP. Committee influence on the EP positions has become conditional on intermediary negotiations with the Council of Ministers, which render deliberations on committee reports in plenary largely futile.

From a more positive perspective, early legislative agreements with the Council improve the efficiency of the EU legislative process. Indeed, Reh *et al.* (2010: 36) show that the ever more frequent decision to 'go informal' can be explained with the need to gather information and reduce the transaction costs of internal coordination, especially after the increase in the number of legislative participants following the big EU Eastern enlargement. This decision-making mode thus brings into question the forecasts that the growing powers of the EP in drafting the European legislation would lead to a gridlock in the legislative process by increasing the number of veto players. Rasmussen (2011) demonstrated that decreased uncertainty in the negotiations between the EP and the Council of Ministers as well as their increasingly closer working relationship are the main drivers of early legislative agreements under codecision, alongside legislators' impatience and high workload. Thus, the EP empowerment has not led to a slowdown of the European integration, and might have in fact stimulated it. Nevertheless, it is doubtful whether lack of transparency, undermined open democratic debate in committees and severe informational asymmetry between legislators are a justified price to pay for increased efficiency.

Collusive decision-making between the EP and the Council of Ministers also casts a shadow on the EU political system. Moravcsik (1998b: 605) holds that '[c]onstitutional checks and balances, indirect democratic control via national governments, and the increasing powers of the EP are sufficient to ensure that EU policy-making is, in nearly all cases, clean, transparent, effective and politically responsive to the demands of European citizens.' Checks and balances in the EU, however, seem to have been compromised. The division of legislative power between the EP and the Council of Ministers has become unclear, undermining the very idea of a bicameral legislative system in the EU. The parliamentary committees fail to serve as internal institutional hurdles strengthening the legislative power of the EP *vis-à-vis* the Council of Ministers in the bicameral legislative structure of the EU by enhancing the bargaining position of the EP (following Diemeier and Myerson's (1999) account of the role of legislative committees). Upon an early agreement, deliberation on the parliamentary floor serves only as a means of advertising actors' positions to voters rather than discussing committee proposals, making real legislative changes or reaching political consensus. If the EP takes its decisions in collusion with the Council before even having adopted its own position (in committee and plenary) or without ever having even a draft position, then why have a democratically elected parliament?

It is not argued here that coalitions across the EU institutions should not be formed. Indeed, overcoming inter-institutional checks and balances is the key to avoiding policy gridlock.[4] However, the processes that bring about these coalitions and the policies they adopt need to be transparent for democracy in the EU to function well. 'A basic precondition for a system of pluralist design and a system in quest of democratic legitimacy, is transparency' (Greenwood 2007: 3). It is also an essential precondition for 'bringing Europe closer to the citizens' as a formula for the EU democratic legitimisation. As the 'Declaration on the right of access to information' annexed to the Treaty of the European Union (1992) states: 'transparency of the decision-making process strengthens the democratic nature of the institutions and the public's confidence in the administration' (European Commission 1992).

---

4. Generally, 'bicameralism promotes stability by making changes to the status quo more difficult.' (Tsebelis 1997: 229)

# chapter seven | towards a combined theoretical framework

This book contributes to the theoretical literature on legislative organisation in two ways, elaborated upon in this chapter. Firstly, it demonstrates how the congressional theoretical approaches can be applied to the study of legislatures other than the US Congress after an informed modification of their underlying assumptions without a loss of generalisability. Secondly, and more importantly, the book identifies conditions under which the alternative congressional rationales are better able to account for organisational design. Thus, it contributes to consolidating the congressional theoretical framework.

## General application of the congressional theoretical approaches

The book has shown how the congressional theoretical approaches can be used to inform the study of a legislature in many substantive respects different from the US Congress. Their application to the case of the European Parliament was not straightforward because the underlying assumptions of congressional approaches, mainly regarding legislators' electoral motivations, do not hold so clearly in the case of the EP. Yet, their partly conflicting, partly complementary predictions could be tested here. This was only possible after the informed modification of their assumptions, preserving the underlying logic of the alternative rationales. The two main assumptions of these theories are related to: 1) the individual goals of legislators and the type of policy they pursue to fulfil these goals: particularistic policy, 'good' policy, or party policy; and 2) the dimensionality of the policy space. I discuss here what made their adaptation to the case of the EP possible and what minimal prerequisites have to be met to replicate that in the study of other legislatures.

The distributive rationale can be tested in a legislative setting, in which two conditions are met. Firstly, heterogeneity of policy interests should exist in the legislature, which naturally entails a multi-dimensional policy space. Secondly, the number of legislators with homogeneous interests on single policy dimensions must be sizeable enough to form committees that pursue collective policy goals. This is necessary to facilitate trade between committees across policy dimensions, which is needed to get majority support for committee proposals in the chamber. Provided that these conditions are met, it is possible to test the predictions of the distributive rationale irrespective of the source of legislators' policy interests. Failure to acknowledge this has discouraged scholars from applying the congressional theories in new contexts. For instance, in the study of the EP, the distributive rationale has been discarded owing to the weak electoral connection of MEPs to strictly defined theoretical constituencies, which would induce them to pursue particularistic policies favouring those constituencies in the same way it induces congressmen. However, legislators need not have territorial interests to systematically pursue policies in a given area that differ from those preferred by the majority of their colleagues. There may be another source of their particularistic policy preferences, such as their interest group ties, as assumed here. The latter can also promote legislators' electoral chances and career prospects. In another legislative setting, the special policy interests of legislators may derive from yet another source. The nature of this source, however, is not important. As far as testing the distributive rationale is concerned, legislators' preferences and motivations may even be genuinely intrinsic. As long as the specified above preconditions of the rationale are met it can inform the study of any legislature.

Alternatively, the informational congressional rationale assumes that legislators pursue 'good' policies, i.e. well-informed policies, which closely represent the ideal policy preferences of the median voter in the House of Representatives. Thus, committees can fulfil the informational needs of the chamber in a context of uncertainty. The assumption that legislators pursue 'good' policies is not difficult to make in any legislative context. It is particularly uncontroversial in the case of the EP – a legislature with limited resources, which, unlike national legislatures, cannot rely on a government for policy expertise. Thus, in this study it was assumed that MEPs pursue 'good' European policies – not ideologically biased but well-informed, median policies aimed at improving policy outcomes. Uni-dimensionality of the policy space is the more restrictive second assumption that needs to be met to test the informational rationale. While complete uni-dimensionality is probably unrealistic, this assumption was justifiable here due to the overarching scholarly agreement that a single left-right dimension explains most votes and party positions in the EP. Further theoretical adjustments are necessary to test the informational rationale if one embarks on testing its predictions in the study of a legislature in which the assumption of uni-dimensionality of the policy space is unrealistic.

Finally, the partisan congressional rationale assumes that legislators pursue re-election, which their congressional party can facilitate by presenting a good image to the electorate. Hence, legislators delegate the power to assign office within the Congress to party leaders as a means the latter can use to discipline members and enhance the party cohesion. At first sight, it may seem that this rationale is most applicable to the study of the EP. Its uni-dimensionality assumption is easily justifiable, as discussed above. More importantly, national parties do not shape the electoral fortunes of MEPs only indirectly, but largely determine them. However, it is not the national parties but the European party groups that control office allocation within the EP. Hence, the European party groups are a closer equivalent to the congressional parties. They unite national political parties with close ideological positions and owe their powers to their ability to advance national party policy. It is the latter that MEPs are assumed to pursue because they depend on their national parties for their re-election to the EP or for any further political career. Party groups facilitate members' goals when they act cohesively and, therefore, they are granted control over the parliamentary organisation to discipline members and, thus, achieve group cohesion. Finally, given the lack of a majority party in the

Parliament, it was argued here that the working majority party group (coalition) could fulfil that role. For it to be able to serve members' policy goals, it is important that this coalition is based on ideological proximity rather than on the pursuit of parliamentary rights only. All these adaptations depart significantly from the original partisan theory. Yet, the main causal mechanism is preserved – party groups use the parliamentary legislative organisation to discipline group members, which ultimately serves the individual goals of the latter. Thus, even these substantial modifications of the partisan rationale did not preclude its application.

In conclusion, the lack of a perfect fit of the assumptions of the congressional rationales to a new legislative setting does not eliminate the value of relying on these highly sophisticated rationales to understand legislative organisation.

## Factors explaining variation in organisational choice

In this section, I turn to presenting the contributions of the present study to the body of research consolidating the congressional rationales. The study of different aspects of the EP's internal legislative organisation has been conducted on the presumption that the three main congressional rationales are not exclusive but are rather complementary. While this is acknowledged in the theoretical literature (Shepsle and Weingast 1995), little has been done to consolidate the existing approaches or to explain variation in their explanatory power (however, see Maltzman 1997).

The committees of the EP offered a convenient laboratory for the study of legislative organisation and the role of committees in bicameral legislatures (operating in separated-power systems). Notwithstanding the numerous similarities between the EP and the US Congress, the findings in this book diverged from what we know about the US Congress. What can we learn from the observed differences? Undoubtedly, they are linked to the different types of rule shaping the EP committees' organisation and legislative power as compared to the congressional committees and the different principals controlling MEPs as compared to congressmen. By varying features of the institutional context it is possible to identify conditions under which the congressional rationales can explain organisational design. The following section develops preliminary theoretical propositions about these conditions, combining the findings of this book with hitherto knowledge about the US Congress.

As mentioned above, the congressional literature itself is limited in accounting for variation in the explanatory power of different theoretical rationales. Shepsle and Weingast (1995: 3) admit that '[d]ifferent theories are associated with different "epochs of congressional history,"' and Gilligan and Krehbiel (1995: 67) forecast that '[f]uture research will empirically explain variation in the way legislators choose to organise their collective activities.' Still, Maltzman and Smith (1995) and Maltzman (1997) offer the only contributions in this direction. They hypothesise that 'the relative importance [for legislators] of various principals – home constituencies, party, the parent chamber – is likely to differ across committees and vary over time' (Maltzman and Smith 1995: 257). Based on this presumption,

Maltzman (1997) shows that variation in the explanatory power of alternative congressional theories can be explained with three factors: procedural innovations, strength of majority-party caucus and the salience of a committee's agenda over time. In particular, members of committees dealing with issues of high salience are more likely to act with regard to the preferences of their parties and the overall chamber; committee members of cohesive parties are more responsive to their parties, as are members working under procedures increasing parties' control over the legislative process; and finally, committee independence is decreased by monitoring procedures that distribute policy information to non-committee members (1997: 30–40).

The theoretical developments in this book follow Maltzman's work, although they are not driven by the principal-agent approach that he employed. Variation was found in the degree to which the alternative theoretical approaches can explain different organisational aspects of the legislative committees and their work, which can be accounted for with three main factors: 1) the types of committee and their policy areas; 2) the types of rule applied to regulate the relationship between committees, the floor, and political groups; and 3) the policy-specific rules regulating the distribution of power between the two legislative chambers in the bicameral system. All three are institutional factors that affect individual and party behaviour in shaping the legislative committees, their work and legislative output. On the basis of the observed regularities in the findings in this book and our knowledge on the congressional committees so far, three theoretical propositions are developed below regarding the conditions under which the predictions of the distributive, informational and partisan rationales are expected to hold. They are discussed in turn below.

*Type of committee*

Not all committees are created equal. Some have strong legislative powers; others deal with the European Union budget; still others are constrained to consultative work. Alongside their jurisdictions, the policy areas which committees cover further affect the degree to which they are subject to internal pressure from party groups and the plenary as a whole, or external pressure from interest groups, national parties, and other EU institutions. Furthermore, some committees operate in highly specialised policy areas requiring a certain level of expertise from their members to fully participate in the decision-making process, while others deal with rather general issues. Given these differences between committees, it is inconceivable, perhaps even naïve, to expect the organisation of all of them to be guided by the same logic, be it distributive, informational or partisan. Acknowledging this, some congressional studies have distinguished between different types of committee (see Chapter Three). These studies have focused their classifications primarily on differences between committees based on how targeted their policies are to specific territorial constituencies (e.g. Cox and McCubbins 1993, 2007; Adler and Lapinski 1997). The categorisation offered in Chapter Three more broadly distinguishes between committees that do and that do not draft policies affecting certain organised homogeneous societal groups outside the legislature, irrespectively of whether those are situated on the sub-national, national or European level. The findings in the analysis of committee assignments (Chapter Three) demonstrated significant differences between such committees in terms of their staffing. They have shown that committees drafting policies with distributive implications for homogeneous organised groups outside the Parliament are staffed with members with special interests (as the distributive rationale predicts), while committees drafting predominantly regulatory legislation are staffed with experts. Partisan factors have no effect on committee assignments, as a result of the restrictive parliamentary rules on committee composition (discussed in the next subsection). In light of these findings, the first proposition made in this book for future studies is:

*Proposition 1a:*  *Given that party proportionality in committee composition is formally enforced, distributive or informational rationales can account for committee assignments depending on whether a committee drafts policies that respectively:*

- *affect homogeneous organised societal groups*
- *have a regulatory character and do not affect specific organised societal groups*

## *Type of parliamentary rule*

The types of rule regulating the relationship between committees, the plenary and party groups are the second factor that can explain variation in the extent to which the distributive, informational and partisan rationales can account for legislative organisation and committee power. So far, extensive testing of these three approaches has been limited to the US Congress, which by itself does not present sufficient variation, even over time, to test the relationship between different types of parliamentary rule and organisational outcomes. Therefore, this book offers important new insights by not only comparing the impact of different types of rule on organisational aspects and the legislative power of the committees but also by allowing for a comparison between the US Congress and the EP, and as a result, further theoretical development.

There are significant differences in the formal rules of the US Congress and the EP pertaining to committee composition and amendments on the floor (see Table 7.1). Firstly, while a strict proportionality rule regulates committee composition in the EP, the distribution of seats in the US Congress is left unconstrained by the formal rules, leading to an advantage of the majority party in the composition of the most important committees (Schneider 2008). Secondly, the committees of the EP do not enjoy similar gate-keeping powers and restrictive amendment rules as the committees of the US House of Representatives (Saturno 2006).[1] Owing to

---

1.   Committees' gate-keeping powers give them the option of not bringing a bill to the floor. These powers can be over-ruled with a discharge petition (Beth 2010). The prescription of a closed rule to a legislative committee proposal by the Rules Committee safeguards it from amendments in the

these substantial differences, it is possible to observe how alternative legislative rules affect organisational choice.

Table 7.1 gives an overview of the congressional and EP rules as pertaining to committee assignments, report allocation (where applicable) and amendments on the floor. It further specifies the expected outcomes of these rules and the ensuing theoretical predictions. These predictions are informed by the theoretical literature surveyed in Chapter Two and the results demonstrated in this book.

First, turning to the rules shaping the committee-party relationship, it was demonstrated that since a formal proportionality rule guides the composition of the EP committees, committee seats are indeed distributed proportionally to party groups. In contrast, the majority party is over-represented on the most powerful congressional committees due to the lack of a similar formal rule in the US House of Representatives. Analogically, since only informal proportionality rules guide the allocation of legislative reports to party groups in the EP committees, the working majority party group coalition is over-represented in the allocation of the most important reports, i.e. the codecision reports. These observations are a natural consequence of the respective rules. It is less clear, though, why the European party group leaders do not use the assignments to important committees strategically to discipline group members, i.e. reward loyal members with competitive seats and prevent disloyal ones from obtaining them, as they do with the allocation of legislative reports. It is argued here that this is due to the higher pressure that national party delegations can exert on the committee assignments, which are supposed to 'as far as possible, reflect the composition of Parliament' (European Parliament 2009b, Rule 186, ex Rule 177). In contrast, report allocations are not regulated by formal parliamentary rules, and they are done on a rolling basis and decentralised to committees, making an overall under-representation of a certain national party delegation less visible. Thus, while party group leaders are limited in their ability to use committee assignments strategically to promote group goals, in the report allocation they can exert pressure on individual members independently of national parties. This provides an additional explanation as to why party groups have not formalised the rules on report allocation, besides the fact that the current system advantages the majority group (coalition). Party group leaders are better able to control group members if they are not constrained by the need to accommodate the wishes of national party delegations within their ranks. This sheds more light on the relationship between party groups and national party delegation in the EP and its impact on committee organisation. While it is difficult to generalise from this observation of the particular multi-level party organisation within the EP, it is still possible to draw abstract propositions about the link between parliamentary rules, internal party organisation and committee organisation. Thus, the following proposition may apply to legislatures characterised by internally divided political parties:

---

Committee of the Whole and on the floor (Saturno 2006).

*Table 7.1: Impact of formal and informal organisational rules in the US House of Representatives and the European Parliament*

| | House of Representatives of the US Congress | | | European Parliament | | |
|---|---|---|---|---|---|---|
| | Rules | Expected effect | Theoretical predictions | Rules | Expected effect | Theoretical predictions |
| Committee assignments | *No proportionality rule* | Members of majority party advantaged. Preference outliers and specialists can self-select. | +Partisan<br>+/- Distributive<br>+/- Informational | *Formal proportionality rule* | No advantage to members of the bigger party groups. Committee assignments distributed proportionally to national party delegations within party groups. Preference outliers and specialists can self-select. | -Partisan<br>+Distributive<br>+Informational |
| Report allocation | *n/a* | n/a | n/a | *Informal proportionality rule* | Members of the working majority party group (coalition) advantaged. Reports are not allocated proportionally to national party delegations within party groups. Party group members rewarded/punished for level of group loyalty. Preference-outliers and specialists disadvantaged. | +Partisan<br>-Distributive<br>-Informational |
| Amendments in plenary | *Formal closed or open amendment rule* | Limited party power. Facilitated 'trade' between committees. Incentive for specialisation in committees. | -Partisan<br>+Distributive<br>+Informational | *Formal open amendment rule* | Parties empowered. No 'trade' between committees. Limited incentives for committees to specialise. | +Partisan<br>-Distributive<br>-Informational |

Propositions 2a:

> *The partisan rationale accounts better for internal committee organisation if no formal rules assure the proportional allocation of parliamentary positions and tasks to factions within parties, be those ideological or territorial.*
>
> *Conversely, distributive and informational rationales account better for internal committee organisation if formal rules assure the proportional allocation of parliamentary positions and tasks to factions within parties, be those ideological or territorial.*

Second, if the rules shaping committee-plenary legislative relations are considered, formal closed amendment rules protecting committees' legislative proposals limit the explanatory power of the partisan rationale when it comes to decision-making on the floor. Instead, they enhance the explanatory power of distributive and informational accounts. The opposite holds for formal rules subjecting committees' work to full review in plenary. Maltzman (1997) argues that committee independence is decreased by monitoring procedures that distribute policy information to non-committee members (1997: 30–40). One could see the open amendment rule in plenary as such a procedure, compelling committee members to seek the approval of non-committee members already at the committee stage in order to facilitate the adoption of committee reports on the floor. In the EP, this is generally done by party group contingents in their working group meetings, which take place every month after the committee and before the plenary debates. In this way, the open amendment rule increases party group control over committee members not only at the voting stage but also at the stage of preparing legislative reports. These observations lead to the following theoretical propositions for future research:

Propositions 2b:

> *Distributive and informational rationales account better for the level of committees' legislative power if a closed amendment rule governs committee-plenary legislative relations.*
>
> *Conversely, partisan factors account better for the level of committees' legislative power if an open amendment rule governs committee-plenary legislative relations.*

### *Policy-specific rules regulating the bicameral balance of power*

The final factor suggested here, which can explain variation in the extent to which the different congressional rationales account for committee organisation, is the institutional context. In particular, the institutional rules of a political system define the jurisdictions and powers of a legislature in different fields, which consequently affect its priorities and the internal organisation of its work. For instance, in the EU, the balance of power between the EP and the Council of Ministers is symmetric under the codecision and asymmetric under the consultation legislative procedure.

This allows considering whether and, if so, how the legislative organisation of the EP has adjusted in response to the stimuli these different inter-institutional rules provide. As Shackleton and Raunio (2003: 172) argue: 'the codecision procedure, as well as affording an arena for measuring relative influence, also raises major issues of institutional design. It offers a laboratory for examining how institutions respond to a relationship of interdependence.'

In Chapter Four, it was demonstrated that the distributive and informational rationales can only account for the allocation of committee reports falling under the consultation procedure, under which the EP, as the name suggests, has only very limited, consultative powers. In contrast, the partisan rationale is better able to account for the distribution of codecision reports among party groups and group members, for which competition is much higher due to the substantively stronger legislative powers of the Parliament under the codecision procedure. It appears that the inter-institutional rules that shape the parliamentary legislative influence affect also the intra-parliamentary organisation. Thus, the findings regarding the effect of the inter-chamber balance of power on report allocation in the EP can increase our general knowledge of the link between legislative organisation and bicameralism. On the basis of the results in Chapter Five, the following propositions are derived:

Proposition 3a:

> *In policy areas in which a legislative chamber has comparatively weak power, the distributive and informational rationales can better account for internal committee organisation.*

Proposition 3b:

> *In policy areas in which a legislative chamber has comparatively strong power, the partisan rationale can better account for internal committee organisation.*

These propositions are quite broad and can also be tested in the study of a unicameral legislature, the legislative influence of which *vis-à-vis* the government varies in different policy areas.

Studies of the US Congress may also benefit from explicitly modelling the potentially varying incentives and constraints that the inter-institutional relations between the House of Representatives, the Senate and the Presidency provide. '[W]ithout taking into account bicameral interactions, we are likely to be misled in our study of bicameral institutions' (Tsebelis 1997: 230)

Overall, the book adds to the theoretical literature on legislative organisation, having demonstrated the broad applicability of the congressional theoretical approaches to a new context upon an informed adaptation. It has further contributed to the consolidation of the congressional rationales by offering explanations for the variation in their explanatory power and formulating testable theoretical propositions for future research. These propositions could be tested either in a future comparative legislative study, or in a time-series study of a single legislature.

# chapter eight | concluding remarks

This book brings a number of contributions to the theoretical and empirical literature on legislative organisation and the European Parliament. Yet, it has also its limitations. Acknowledging this, in this concluding chapter a number of suggestions for future research on the EP's legislative organisation are outlined. The final lines are dedicated to recapitulating the main achievements of the book.

## Suggestions for future research

This book has contributed to our knowledge about the EP committees. Full understanding of the rationale behind the EP organisation and its consequences, however, requires further scholarly attention. Since analytical studies on the topic are relatively recent, unexplored aspects are numerous. Two directions for future research are suggested below. The first one entails explaining variation in organisational design over time. The second one involves a shift of focus from organisational aspects to their consequences for policy-making in the EP and European Union policies more broadly.[1]

### *Explaining variation over time*

In this book factors explaining various organisational aspects of the EP's committees and their legislative output in a single parliamentary term (2004–2009) have been examined. Analytical research on the explanatory power of such factors over time is still limited (for a recent study in that direction, see Whitaker 2011; see also Kreppel 2002a). The progressive empowerment of the EP with each EU treaty revision and the consecutive enlargements of the EU could have hardly left its legislative organisation intact. This raises important questions regarding the impact of the changes in the EU's external environment on the internal EP set-up.

Thus, extensive research covering a longer span of time is necessary to evaluate how the gradual empowerment of the Parliament has affected its committees and their work through time. Only thus can we fully understand how and why the EP set-up has evolved to its present state. As Maltzman and Smith (1995: 257) have hypothesised, 'the relative importance [for legislators] of various principals – home constituencies, party, the parent chamber – is likely to differ across committees and vary over time'. Why do party groups dominate the EP's committee organisation today and did they always dominate over it? Alternatively, was in-

---

1.  For a more exhaustive discussion of the gaps in our knowledge on the EP organisation and suggestions for future research, refer to Yordanova (2011b).

formational or distributive behaviour prevalent in the past when the Parliament was still a weak legislature? According to the predictions of Maltzman (1997), increased salience causes a shift from distributive to party-driven behaviour. Yet, in the EP case, why would distributive concerns be important at all at a time when the committees served as purely consultative bodies and could not determine legislative output?

Similarly, little is known about the impact of changes in the external environment on the links between MEPs and their national parties and governments. How were these links affected by the change of the MEPs' selection mechanism from appointment by national parliaments to direct elections in 1979? Have national parties been strengthening their control over MEPs as the parliamentary powers increased with each treaty revision? For instance, Whitaker (2005: 25) asks whether the committee contingents of national party delegations have become more representative of their delegations as the EP gained greater influence. In a later study on voting in the 6th EP he found evidence that this is indeed the case (Whitaker 2011: 106–24). Yet, the more general question, regarding the channels national parties have used over time to maintain control over their MEPs, remains open. Have they systematically exercised their electoral control over legislators as generally assumed in the literature? Or, have they relied on other reward and punishment mechanisms?

Little is known about how EU enlargements have affected the parliamentary internal organisation and decision-making. With the almost doubled number of EU member states following the 2004 and 2007 enlargements, the pressure to reform the EP's internal set-up and operation to accommodate new members in the office allocation and policy formation process undoubtedly increased. For instance, the ever more frequent resort to informal trilogues and inter-institutional agreements at the early stage of the codecision procedure could have served as a solution to the decreased bargaining success of the EP *vis-à-vis* the Council of Ministers following the big Eastern enlargement (Costello and Thomson 2011). Not only is the Parliament generally more successful in advancing its position in the first reading of the codecision procedure than in the conciliation committee in third reading (Häge and Kaeding 2007; Costello and Thomson 2011), but also informal negotiations outside the traditional parliamentary arenas, i.e. outside its committees and plenary sittings, *de facto* limit the number of legislative participants (Reh *et al.* 2010). It seems, therefore, that the resulting decreased legislative influence of the EP committees was the price paid to circumvent prolonged bargaining within the EP and between the EP and the Council of Ministers that the enlargements could trigger. We know little of the myriad of other institutional adaptations the Parliament has undergone in the period.

Finally, the collection of longitudinal data would for the first time allow studying some hitherto unexplored phenomena. An example is the career advancement of incumbent legislators within the EP, and, linked to it, the institutionalisation of the EP. Are senior parliamentary members more active and productive legislators? For instance, Cox and Terry (2008: 603) examine the determinants of 'legislative success' in the Congress by analysing the causal effect of becoming a chair or part of the majority party caucus/conference on a legislator's productivity. Upon the collection of panel data, analyses like that could be easily conducted in the study of MEPs' parliamentary work. Automated data collection repositories, such as the one Høyland *et al.* (2009) offer, now greatly facilitate such research.

## *Consequences of organisational design for policies and policy-making*

Our knowledge of the substantive consequences of the EP's legislative organisation is fairly limited. In order to explain, for instance, the level of inclusion and influence of different actors in the policy-making process as well as policy outcomes and their responsiveness to voters' preferences, the hitherto dependent variables like committee assignment, report allocation, etc., have to become independent ones.

For instance, how does the choice of a rapporteur affect the procedural development and content of legislation? In his model on legislative bargaining in the EU, Tsebelis (1995: 84–8) argues that rapporteurs enable co-operative decision-making in the EP. However, Kaeding (2005: 100–01) justly points out that the importance of rapporteurs in EU policy making should not be just assumed or modelled in theoretical accounts but also empirically demonstrated. Initial steps in this direction are offered in Chapter Five. Yet, it leaves it unclear why committees allow rapporteurs to negotiate with the Council of Ministers outside the committee arena. The analysis showed that agreements reached in informal inter-institutional negotiations tend to pass unamended through committee and plenary. Why do committees accept the deals negotiated by rapporteurs in these arenas? Does that mean that rapporteurs are acting as honest brokers of committees rather than furthering their individual policy goals or the policy goals of their national parties or party groups? There is mixed evidence on this question in the recent literature. On the one hand, Rasmussen (2011) shows that rapporteurs with biased views are unlikely to even strike early agreements. On the other hand, Costello and Thomson (2010) demonstrate that they manage to influence the EP's opinion in 'fast track legislation' under the codecision procedure and this influence is motivated primarily by their national interests rather than those of the EP median (or even of their party groups).[2] In contrast, if the EP position is formed following the formal decision-making process, it generally reflects the preferences of the median MEP rather than those of the rapporteur (Costello and Thomson 2010) and there is no evidence that the rapporteurs defect in second reading from the adopted EP

---

2. The impact of the rapporteur's nationality is not stronger if the rapporteur comes from a governing party represented in the Council of Ministers rather than an opposition party (Costello and Thomson 2010). More generally, the governing status of the rapporteur's national party does not affect the bargaining success of the EP in bicameral negotiations (Costello and Thomson 2011). According to a recent study (Rasmussen 2011) and contrary to previous expectations (Høyland 2006b), it also does not affect the likelihood of an early agreement with the Council under codecision.

position when the latter does not fit with their preferences (Costello and Thomson 2011). Are the rapporteurs then serving as better agents of the plenary when they do not strike inter-institutional deals outside the parliamentary committees but base their reports solely on committee deliberations? Or, are they simply not able to exert such a strong influence over the parliamentary positions as to bias them in their favour whenever they do not manage to conclude a bicameral agreement?

The final parliamentary position, of course, depends also on the extent to which committee members other than the rapporteur shape the formulation of committee reports by means of making amendments, participating in the committee debate, and following the rapporteur's negotiations with the Council of Ministers. Perhaps more research in this direction will explain why bigger party groups accept the reports and inter-institutional deals of rapporteurs from smaller party groups. Whom do such deals favour and how do they affect the character of adopted EU policies? Case studies can be instructive in answering such questions, though only a limited number of such studies exist (Judge 1992; Judge and Earnshaw 1994; Roederer-Rynning 2003; Benedetto 2005; Lindberg 2008; Jensen and Winzen 2012).

In any case, it is difficult to deny that committee members have a comparative advantage in influencing legislation with respect to non-committee members. This is because it is much easier to make amendments before proposals reach the floor and, of course, due to their informational advantage.[3] Ringe (2009) argues that owing to this informational advantage committee members are able to shape the voting behaviour of their non-committee party (group) colleagues, placing committees at the heart of EP decision-making instead of the party groups.[4] The proposed mechanism works only if committee party contingents are able to send a unified signal to non-committee party members, i.e. if the party (group) specialists agree on a common position. Yet, while voting in committees is rather consensual and not characterised by party divisions (Settembri and Neuhold 2009), often this is not the case at the plenary stage (Hix et al. 2007). So, while offering important insights into policy formation in the EP, Ringe's theory (2009) is unable to explain voting behaviour and the level of intra- and inter-party group conflict in these cases. When do the committee contingents of party groups support different policies than their non-committee party group colleagues? Under which conditions do committee members switch their voting position on committee amendments between the committee and the plenary stage? How heavily are they influenced by pressure coming from their national party and party group leadership? Committee members

---

3. A single committee member can propose amendments in committee while in plenary at least a group of forty members or a party group is required to exploit the open amendment rule (European Parliament 2009b, Rule 156, ex Rule 150).

4. Ringe's (2009) model underscores that due to time scarcity legislators cannot gather information on each and every policy proposal. Instead, non-experts need to rely for cues on colleagues with relevant expertise, i.e. members specialising in the respective committees, with whom they share the greatest degree of outcome preference coherence. These are the members specialising in the respective committees who sit in the same national party delegation or party group.

from smaller party groups, which do not form a part of the working majority group coalition, may be subject to lesser pressure from their group leadership and, consequently, tend to vote more in favour of committee amendments than their committee colleagues from bigger party groups. Using the NOMINATE scores a Monte Carlo permutations method, similar to the one employed by McElroy (2006), can be applied to compare the mean policy positions (in voting) of the committee contingents of a party group and of the non-committee contingents of that group. The results of such an analysis will bring more insights into how particularistic the policies pursued by the EP (committees) are and whose preferences they embody. If regardless of their party group affiliation committee members usually support their committees' reports on the floor more than non-committee members, perhaps there is a conflict between committees representing alternative policy viewpoints. If not, it would appear that lack of consensus on the floor occurs instead as a result of party conflict rather than inter-committee confrontation.

Finally, committee-plenary relations in the EP are certainly affected by the interdependence of the Parliament and the Council of Ministers in adopting EU legislation. Yet, research on the link between intra- and inter-institutional legislative politics in the EU is in its infancy (Naurin and Rasmussen 2011). How does the parliamentary organisation affect decision-making between the EP and the Council of Ministers and vice versa? Chapter Four briefly addressed the latter question by demonstrating the effect of the inter-institutional division of power on the intra-parliamentary distribution of tasks. Research on the former question is scarce, too. For instance, Hagemann and Høyland (2010) studied the relationship between coalitions in the EP and the Council and demonstrated that the level of disagreement on codecision dossiers within the two institutions is correlated. Specifically, if the division in the Council is along the traditional left-right dimension, a left-right division will also prevail in the Parliament.[5] Additionally, Costello (2010) argues that the two chambers are more likely to disagree when MEPs act as party representatives than when they act as national representatives.[6] Certain aspects of the institutions' internal set-up and work as well as the mode of bicameral decision-making they predispose to may be promoting party rather than national divisions within and between the two EU chambers. Thus, the new mode of informal and collusive bicameral decision-making could be causing a spillover of the traditionally ideological internal divisions in the Parliament to the Council of Ministers. That would mean that informal inter-institutional negotiations promote inter-chamber coalitions based on party political lines.[7] The prevalent dimension

5. Interestingly, this happens to empower the Council because when the EP is divided along party lines it is less likely to meet the majority requirement needed to amend the Council's common position in the second reading of the codecision procedure.

6. He further holds that in some policy areas, such as agriculture and structural funds, nationality plays a particularly important role, which *de facto* diminishes the impact of the recent parliamentary empowerment in these areas by the Lisbon Treaty.

7. Indeed, in recent years, the party political differences between the EP and the Council of Minis-

of bicameral contestation is likely to shape in turn the chambers' legislative organisation. Yet, our knowledge of the link between legislative organisation and bicameral decision-making in the EU is in its infancy. Only by taking into account this link can we fully understand the parliamentary set-up as well as the dimensionality of bicameral legislative negotiations, inter-chamber coalition patterns and policy outcomes.

## Final remarks

The final words are dedicated to recapitulating the main achievements of this book. First, it contributes to our knowledge of the legislative organisation of the EP. The empirical findings show that its organisation is clearly dominated by partisan considerations. It serves the needs of party group leadership to discipline members and enhance group cohesion. Further, it facilitates pre-floor coalition formation by the working majority party group and promotes that group's ability to dominate decision-making and adopted policies in committees and on the floor.

Second, the book contributes to the theoretical literature on legislative organisation. It demonstrates how the highly developed congressional rationales of legislative organisation can be adapted and successfully applied in the study of a legislature different to the US Congress. More importantly, the findings in this book informed new theoretical propositions regarding the conditions under which the alternative theoretical approaches are better equipped to explain committees' organisation and its consequences. Thus, the project has contributed to consolidating the congressional theoretical approaches by accounting for variation in their explanatory power.

Last but not least, the results in this book have substantive implications for interest representation, decision-making within the EP and between the EU legislative institutions, and the democratic deficit in the EU. They show that while the internal EP set-up stimulates specialisation, it leaves limited scope for particularistic policies pursued by homogeneous preference-outliers. Furthermore, the shift away from the consensual decision-making and grand party group coalitions towards more conflictual, left-right party politics in the EP is observable in the committee organisation, reflecting and reinforcing the overall trend of ideology-driven law making in the EU rather than one constrained by narrow national interests. This arguably positive development for the direction of European integration comes at the price of increasingly collusive, informal and non-transparent decision-making in the EU. Thus, the institutional checks and balances instituted in the EU treaties to promote democracy have been undermined – too high a price to pay for increased flexibility and, potentially, efficiency. To conclude on a more positive note, serious measures have already been taken in the Parliament to re-formalise the legislative bargaining with the Council of Ministers. The new additions to the

---

ters have decreased (Warntjen *et al.* 2008).

EP Rules of Procedure (European Parliament 2009b: Annex XX) may succeed in bringing the decision-making back to the parliamentary legislative committees where it belongs. Whether this will happen remains a question for future research.

# | references

**Primary sources: List of semi-structured interviews**

Personal interview 1:     a PSE member, 27th February 2008
Personal interview 2:     an EPP-ED member, 6th February 2008
Personal interview 3:     a PSE member, 12th February 2008
Personal interview 4:     an ALDE member, 13th February 2008
Personal interview 5:     an ALDE member, 13th February 2008
Personal interview 6:     a member of Green/EFA group, 30th January 2008
Personal interview 7:     an EPP-ED member, 11th February 2008
Personal interview 8:     a PSE member, 26th February 2008
Personal interview 9:     an EPP-ED member, 27th February 2008
Personal interview 10:    an ALDE member, 27th February 2008
Personal interview 11:    a member of the EPP-ED secretariat, 27th February 2008
Personal interview 12:    a PSE member, 13th February 2008
Personal interview 13:    an EP administrator, Codecision and Conciliation Unit, DG IPOL, 22nd February 2008
Personal interview 14:    a PSE member, 12th February 2008
Personal interview 15:    an EP administrator, Codecision and Conciliation Unit, DG IPOL, 27th February 2008
Personal interview 16:    an EP administrator, Legislative Coordination Unit, DG IPOL, 25th February 2008
Personal interview 17:    an EP administrator, Legislative Coordination Unit, DG IPOL, 22nd February 2008
Personal interview 18:    an EP administrator, DG Presidency, EXPO, 28th February 2008
Personal interview 19:    an EP administrator, Legislative Coordination, DG IPOL, 27th February 2008
Personal interview 20:    an EP administrator, Legislative Coordination, DG IPOL, 25th February 2008

## Secondary resources

Adler, S. E. and Lapinski, J.S. (1997) 'Demand-side theory and congressional committee composition: A constituency characteristics approach', *American Journal of Political Science*, 41(3): 895–918.

Alexander, D. S. (1916) *History and Procedure of the House of Representatives*, Boston: Houghton Mufflin.

Aspinwall, M. (2006) 'Government preferences on European integration: An empirical test of five theories', *British Journal of Political Science*, 37(1): 89–114.

Attina, F. (1990) 'The voting behaviour of the European Parliament members and the problem of the Europarties', *European Journal of Political Research*, 18(5): 557–79.

Austen-Smith, D. (1990) 'Information transmission in debate', *American Journal of Political Science*, 34(1): 124–52.

— (1993) 'Information and influence: Lobbying for agendas and votes', *American Journal of Political Science*, 37(3): 799–833.

Austen-Smith, D. and Riker, W. (1987) 'Asymmetric information and the coherence of legislation', *American Political Science Review*, 81(3): 897–918.

Bach, S. and Smith, S. S. (1988) *Managing Uncertainty in the House of Representatives: Adaptation and Innovation in Special Rules*, Washington: The Brookings Institution.

Bartolini, S. (2005) *Restructuring Europe. Centre formation, system building, and political structuring between the nation state and the European Union*, Oxford: Oxford University Press.

Bartus, T. (2005) 'Estimation of marginal effects using margeff', *Stata Journal*, 5(3): 309–29.

Benedetto, G. (2005) 'Rapporteurs as legislative entrepreneurs: The dynamics of codecision procedure in Europe's Parliament', *Journal of European Public Policy*, 12(1): 67–88.

Beth, R. S. (2010) 'CRS report for Congress, order code 97–552 GOV. The discharge rule in the House: Principal features and uses', Online. Available /http://www.rules.house.gov/archives/97–552.pdf (accessed 15 January 2010).

Binder, S. A. (1996) 'The partisan basis of procedural choice: Allocating parliamentary rights in the House, 1789–1990', *American Political Science Review*, 90(1): 8–20.

Bouwen, P. (2004) 'The logic of access to the European Parliament: Business lobbying in the Committee on Economic and Monetary Affairs', *Journal of Common Market Studies*, 42(3): 473–95.

Bowler, S. and Farrell, D. M. (1995) 'The organizing of the European Parliament: Committees, specialization and co-ordination', *British Journal of Political Science*, 25(2): 219–43.

Brady, D. (1973) *Congressional Voting in a Partisan Era: A study of the McKinley Houses and a comparison to the modern House of Representatives*, Lawrence: University of Kansas Press.

Brzinski, J. B. (1995) 'Political group cohesion in the European Parliament, 1989–1994', in C. Rhodes and S. Mazey (eds) *The State of the European Union: Building a European polity?*, London: Longman, pp. 135–58.

Burns, C. (2006) 'Co-decision and inter-committee conflict in the European Parliament post-Amsterdam', *Government and Opposition*, 41(2): 230–48.

Campbell, C. C. and Davidson, R. H. (1998) 'US congressional committees: Changing legislative workshops', *Journal of Legislative Studies*, 4(1): 124–42.

Carrubba, C. J., Gabel, M., Murrah, L., Clough, R., Montgomery, E. and Rebecca, S. (2006) 'Off the record: Unrecorded legislative votes, selection bias and roll-call vote analysis', *British Journal of Political Science*, 36 (4): 691–704.

Collins, K., Burns, C. and Warleigh, A. (1998) 'Policy entrepreneurs: The role of European Parliament committees in the making of EU policy', *Stature Law Review*, 19(1): 1–11.

Coman, E. E. (2009) 'Reassessing the influence of party groups on individual members of the European Parliament', *West European Politics*, 32(6): 1099–117.

Cooper, J. (1970) *The Origins of the Standing Committees and the Development of the Modern House*, Houston, TX: Rice University Studies.

Cooper, J. and Young, C. D. (1989) 'Bill introduction in the nineteenth century: A study of institutional change', *Legislative Studies Quarterly*, 14(1): 67–105.

Copeland, G. and Patterson, S. (1994) *Parliaments in the Modern World*, Ann Arbor: University of Michigan Press.

Corbett, R. (2001) 'Academic modelling of the codecision procedure: A practitioner's puzzled reaction', *European Union Politics*, 1(3): 373–81.

Corbett, R., Jacobs, F. and Shackleton, M. (1990) *The European Parliament*, Harlow: Longman.

—— (1992) The European Parliament, 2nd edn, Harlow: Longman Current Affairs.

—— (1995) *The European Parliament*, 3rd edn, London, : Cartermill Pub.

—— (2000) *The European Parliament*, 4th edn, London: John Harper Publishing.

—— (2003a) *The European Parliament*, 5th edn, London: John Harper Publishing.

—— (2003b) 'The European Parliament at fifty: A view from the inside', *Journal of Common Market Studies*, 41(2): 353–73.

—— (2005) *The European Parliament*, 6th edn, London: John Harper Publishing.

—— (2007) *The European Parliament*, 7th edn, London: John Harper.

Costello, R. (2010) 'A people's house and a senate's house? Understanding conflict between the European Union's legislative institutions', paper presented at ECPR Pan-European Conference on EU Politics in Porto, June 24–26

2010. Online. Available /www.jhubc.it/ecpr–porto/virtualpaperroom/109. pdf (accessed 10 December 2011).

Costello, R. and Thomson, R. (2010) 'The policy impact of leadership in committees: Rapporteurs' influence on the European Parliament's opinions', *European Union Politics,* 11(2): 219–40.

— (2011) 'The nexus of bicameralism: Rapporteurs' impact on decision outcomes in the European Union', *European Union Politics,* 12(3): 337–57.

Cox, G. W. and McCubbins, M. D. (1993) *Legislative Leviathan: Party government in the House,* Berkeley: University of California Press.

— (1997) 'Toward a theory of legislative rules changes: Assessing Schickler and Rich's evidence', *American Journal of Political Science,* 41(4): 1376–86.

— (2007) *Legislative Leviathan: Party government in the House,* 2nd edn, New York: Cambridge University Press.

Cox, G. W. and Terry, W. C. (2008) 'Legislative productivity in the 93d-105th Congresses', *Legislative Studies Quarterly,* 33(4): 603–18.

Crombez, C. (2000) 'Institutional reform and co-decision in the European Union', *Constitutional Political Economy,* 11(1): 41–57.

Crombez, C., Steunenberg, B. and Corbett, R. (2000) 'Understanding the EU legislative process', *European Union Politics,* 1(3): 363–81.

Diermeier, D. and Myerson, R. B. (1999) 'Bicameralism and its consequences for the internal organization of legislatures', *The American Economic Review,* 89 (5): 1182–96.

Eurlex (2006) '2006/512/EC: Council Decision of 17 July 2006 amending Decision 1999/468/EC laying down the procedures for the exercise of implementing powers conferred on the Commission', Online Available /http://eur–lex.europa.eu/LexUriServ/LexUriServ. do?uri=CELEX:32006D0512:EN:NOT (accessed 10 January 2012).

European Commission (1992) 'Treaty on the European Union', Online. Available /http://eur–lex.europa.eu/en/treaties/dat/11992M/htm/11992M. html#0101000037 (accessed 23 January 2010).

European Parliament (2004) 'Activity Report 1 May 1999 to 30 April 2004', Online. Available /http://www.europarl.europa.eu/code/information/ activity_reports/activity_report_2004_en.pdf (accessed 11 May 2007).

— (2007a) 'Conciliation and codecision activity report: July 2004 to December 2006', Online. Available /www.statewatch.org/news/2007/ jun/ep–co–decision–rep.pdf (accessed 3 December 2009).

— (2007b) 'Rules of Procedure of the European Parliament', Online. Available /http://www.europarl.europa.eu/sides/getLastRules. do;jsessionid=3193B6C48F3E2C35F538B75E34C9FF8C. node2?language=EN&reference=TOC (accessed 3 March 2008).

— (2009a) 'Briefing special edition – European Parliament constituent plenary sitting – Strasbourg 14 – 16 July 2009', Online. Available /http:// www.europarl.europa.eu/pdfs/news/expert/briefing/20090629BRI57511

/20090629BRI57511_en.pdf (accessed 2 December 2009).

— (2009b) 'Rules of Procedure of the European Parliament', Online. Available /http://www.europarl.europa.eu/sides/getLastRules.do?language=EN&reference=TOC (accessed 1 November 2009).

European Parliament, Council and Commission (2007) 'Joint declaration on practical arrangements for the codecision procedure (Article 251 of the EC Treaty) (2007/C 145/02)', *Official Journal of the European Union*, 145(C): 5–9.

Eurosource (2005) *Eurosource*, London: Dod's Parliamentary Communications, Publications Professionnelles Parlementaires.

Faas, T. (2003) 'To defect or not to defect? National, institutional and party group pressures on MEPs and their consequences for party group cohesion in the European Parliament', *European Journal of Political Research*, 42(6): 841–66.

Farrell, D. (2006a) 'EPRG 2000 and 2006 MEP surveys dataset', Online. Available /http://www.lse.ac.uk/collections/EPRG (accessed 13 October 2006).

Farrell, D. M., Hix, S., Johnson, M. and Scully, R. (2006b) 'A Survey of MEPs in the 2004–09 European Parliament', paper presented at the Annual Conference of the American Political Science Association in Philadelphia, 18 August 2006. Online. Available /www.esds.ac.uk/doc/6086/mrdoc/pdf/6086userguide.pdf (accessed 27 March 2007).

Farrell, H. and Héritier, A. (2003) 'Formal and informal institutions under codecision: Continuous constitution-building in Europe', *Governance*, 16(4): 577–600.

— (2004) 'Interorganizational negotiation and intraorganizational power in shared decision making: Early agreements under codecision and their impact on the European Parliament and Council', *Comparative Political Studies*, 37(10): 1184–212.

Farrell, H. and Scully, R. (2007) *Representing Europe's Citizens? Electoral institutions and the failure of parliamentary representation*, Oxford; New York: Oxford University Press.

Fenno, R., Jr. (1966) *Power of the Purse*, Boston: Little, Brown.

— (1973) *Congressmen in Committees*, Boston: Little, Brown.

Ferejohn, J. A. (1974) *Pork Barrel Politics: Rivers and harbors legislation, 1947–1968*, Stanford, CA: Stanford University Press.

Ferrara, F. and Weishaupt, J. T. (2004) 'Get your act together: Party performance in European Parliament elections', *European Union Politics*, 5(3): 283–306.

Fitzmaurice, J. (1978) *The European Parliament*, Farnborough, Hants: Saxon House.

Gabel, M. and Hix, S. (2002) 'The European Parliament and executive politics in the EU: Voting behaviour and the commission president investiture procedure', in M. O. Hosli, A. van Deemen and M. Widgrén (eds) *Institutional Challenges in the European Union*, London and New York: Routledge, pp. 22–47.

Gamm, G. and Shepsle, K. (1989) 'Emergence of legislative institutions: Standing committees in the House and Senate, 1810–1825', *Legislative Studies Quarterly,* 14(1): 39–66.

Garman, J. and Hilditch, L. (1998) 'Behind the scenes: An examination of the importance of the informal processes at work in conciliation', *Journal of European Public Policy,* 5(2): 271–84

Gilligan, T. W. and Krehbiel, K. (1987) 'Collective decision-making and standing committees: An informational rationale for restrictive amendment procedures', *Journal of Law, Economics, and Organization,* 3(2): 287–335.

—      (1989a) 'Asymmetric information and legislative rules with a heterogeneous committee', *American Journal of Political Science,* 33(2): 459–90.

—      (1989b) 'Collective choice without procedural commitment', in P. C. Ordeshook (ed.) *Models of Strategic Choice in Politics,* Ann Arbor: The University of Michigan Press, pp. 295–314.

—      (1990) 'Organization of informative committees by a rational legislature', *American Journal of Political Science,* 34(2): 531–64.

—      'The gains from exchange hypothesis of legislative organization', in K. A. Shepsle and B. R. Weingast (eds) *Positive Theories of Congressional Institutions,* Ann Arbor: The University of Michigan Press, pp. 37–70.

Goodwin, G. J. (1970) *The Little Legislatures: Committees in Congress,* Amherst: University of Massachusetts Press.

Greenwood, J. (2007) *Interest Representation in the European Union,* 2nd edn, Basingstoke: Palgrave Macmillan.

Häge, F. M. and Kaeding, M. (2007) 'Reconsidering the European Parliament's legislative influence: Formal vs. informal procedures', *Journal of European Integration,* 29(3): 341–61.

Hagemann, S. and Høyland, B. (2008) 'Parties in the Council?', *Journal of European Public Policy,* 15(8): 1205–21.

—      (2010) 'Bicameral politics in the European Union', *Journal of Common Market Studies,* 48(4): 811–33.

Han, J. (2007) 'Analysing roll calls of the European Parliament: A Bayesian application', *European Union Politics,* 8(4): 479–507.

Hasbrouck, P. (1927) *Party Government in the House of Representatives,* New York: Macmillan Company.

Hardin, J. W. and Hilbe, J. (2007) *Generalized Linear Models and Extensions,* 2nd edn, College Station, Texas: Stata Press

Hausemer, P. (2006) 'Participation and political competition in committee report allocation: Under what conditions do MEPs represent their constituents?', *European Union Politics,* 7(4): 505–30.

Héritier, A. (1999) *Policy-Making and Diversity in Europe: Escaping deadlock,* New York: Cambridge University Press.

—      (2007) *Explaining Institutional Change in Europe,* New York: Oxford University Press.

Hix, S. (2001) 'Legislative behaviour and party competition in the European Parliament: An application of Nominate to the EU', *Journal of Common Market Studies,* 39(4): 663–88.

— (2002a) 'Constitutional agenda-setting through discretion in rule interpretation: Why the European Parliament won at Amsterdam', *British Journal of Political Science*, 32(2): 259–80.

— (2002b) 'Parliamentary behaviour with two principals: Preferences, parties, and voting in the European Parliament', *American Journal of Political Science*, 46(3): 688–98.

— (2004) 'Electoral institutions and legislative behaviour: Explaining voting defection in the European Parliament', W*orld Politics*, 56 (2): 194–223.

Hix, S., Amie, K. and Abdul, N. (2003a) 'The party system in the European Parliament: Collusive or competitive?', *Journal of Common Market Studies,* 41(2): 309–31.

Hix, S. and Lord, C. (1997) *Political Parties in the European Union*, New York: St. Martin's Press.

Hix, S. and Marsh, M. (2007) 'Punishment or protest? Understanding European Parliament elections', *Journal of Politics,* 69(2): 495–510.

Hix, S. and Noury, A. (2009) 'After Enlargement: Voting patterns in the sixth European Parliament', *Legislative Studies Quarterly,* 34(2): 159–74.

Hix, S., Noury, A. and Roland, G. (2004) 'How to choose the European executive: A counterfactual analysis, 1979–1999', in C. B Blankart. and D. C. Mueller (eds) *A Constitution for the European Union*, Cambridge, Mass.: MIT Press, pp. 168–202.

— (2005) 'Power to the parties: Cohesion and competition in the European Parliament, 1979–2001', *British Journal of Political Science,* 35(2): 209–34.

— (2006a) 'Dimensions of politics in the European Parliament', *American Journal of Political Science,* 50(2): 494–511.

— (2006b) 'Investiture and censure of the Santer Commission', in S. Hix, A. Noury and G. Roland (eds) *Democratic Politics in the European Parliament*, New York: Cambridge University Press, pp. 182–99.

— (2007) *Democratic Politics in the European Parliament*, Cambridge: Cambridge University Press.

Hix, S., Raunio, T. and Scully, R. (1999) 'An Institutional Theory of Behaviour in the European Parliament', paper presented at the Joint Sessions of the European Consortium for Political Research in Mannheim, March 1999. Online. Available /http://www.lse.ac.uk/collections/EPRG/pdf/Working%20Paper%201.pdf (accessed 28 March 2007).

— (2003b) 'Fifty years on: Research on the European Parliament', *Journal of Common Market Studies,* 41(2): 191–202.

Hobolt, S. and Høyland, B. (2011) 'Selection and sanctioning in European Parliamentary elections', *British Journal of Political Science,* 41(3): 477 – 98.

Hosmer, D. W. and Lemeshow, S. (2000) *Applied Logistic Regression*, 2nd edn, New York: John Wiley & Sons.

Høyland, B. (2006a) 'Allocation of codecision reports in the fifth European Parliament', *European Union Politics*, 7(1): 30–50.

— (2006b) 'A second look at roll call voting in the European Parliament', Online. Available /http://folk.uio.no/bjornkho/Hoyland–Itemresponse. pdf.(accessed 10 December 2006).

Høyland, B., Sircar, I. and Hix, S. (2009) 'Forum section: An automated database of the European Parliament', *European Union Politics*, 10(1): 143–52.

Huber, J. (1996) 'The vote of confidence in parliamentary democracies', *American Political Science Review*, 90(2): 269–82.

Jensen, T. and Winzen, T. (2012) 'Legislative negotiations in the European Parliament', *European Union Politics*, 13(1): 118-49.

Judge, D. (1992) '"Predestined to save the Earth": The Environment committee of the European Parliament', *Environmental Politics*, 1(4): 186–212.

Judge, D. and Earnshaw, D. (1994) 'Weak European Parliament influence? A study of the Environment committee of the EP', *Government and Opposition*, 29(2): 262–76.

— (2003) *The European Parliament*, New York: Palgrave Macmillan.

— (2008) *The European Parliament*, 2nd edn, Basingstoke, New York: Palgrave Macmillan.

Kaeding, M. (2004) 'Rapporteurship allocation in the European Parliament', *European Union Politics*, 5(3): 353–71.

— (2005) 'The world of committee reports: Rapporteurship assignment in the European Parliament', *The Journal of Legislative Studies*, 11(1): 82–104.

Kaeding, M. and Hardacre, A. (2010) 'The execution of delegated powers after Lisbon. A timely analysis of the regulatory procedure with scrutiny and its lessons for delegated acts', Mimeo, Online. Available http://cadmus. eui.eu/handle/1814/14956 (accessed 12 December 2011).

Kardasheva, R. (2009) 'The power of delay: The European Parliament's influence in the consultation procedure', *Journal of Common Market Studies*, 47(2): 385–409.

Kasack, C. (2004) 'The legislative impact of the European Parliament under the revised co-decision procedure: Environmental, public health and consumer protection policies', *European Union Politics*, 5(2): 241–60.

Katz, R. S. (1999) 'Role orientations in parliaments', in R.Katz and B. Wessels (eds) *The European Parliament, the National Parliaments and European Integration*, Oxford: Oxford University Press, pp. 61–86.

Kiewiet, D. R. and McCubbins, M. D. (1991) *The Logic of Delegation*, Chicago: University of Chicago Press.

Kirchner, E. J. (1984) *The European Parliament: Performance and prospects*, Aldershot: Gower.

König, T., Lindberg, B., Lechner, S. and Pohlmeier, W. (2007) 'Bicameral conflict resolution in the European Union: An empirical analysis of conciliation committee bargains', *British Journal of Political Science*, 37(2): 281–312.

König, T. and Pöter, M. (2001) 'Examining the EU legislative process: The relative importance of agenda and veto power', *European Union Politics*, 2(3): 329–51.

Krehbiel, K. (1991) *Information and Legislative Organization*, Ann Arbor: University of Michigan Press.

— (2004) 'Legislative organization', *Journal of Economic Perspectives*, 18(1): 113–28.

Kreppel, A. (1999) 'What affects the European Parliament's legislative influence? An analysis of the success of EP amendments', *Journal of Common Market Studies*, 37(3): 521–37.

— (2000) 'Rules, ideology and coalition formation in the European Parliament: Past, present and future', *European Union Politics*, 1(3): 340–62.

— (2002a) The European Parliament and Supranational Party System: A study of institutional development, New York: Cambridge University Press.

— (2002b) 'Moving beyond procedure: An empirical analysis of European Parliament legislative influence', *Comparative Political Studies*, 35(7): 784–813.

— (2003) 'Necessary but not sufficient: Understanding the impact of treaty reform on the internal development of the European Parliament', *Journal of European Public Policy*, 10(6): 844–911.

Kreppel, A. and Hix, S. (2003) 'From grand coalition to left–right confrontation: Explaining the shifting structure of party competition in the European Parliament', *Comparative Political Studies*, 36(1/2): 75–96.

Kreppel, A. and Tsebelis, G. (1999) 'Coalition formation in the European Parliament', *Comparative Political Studies*, 32(8): 933–66.

Lijphart, A. (1991) 'Foreword: "Cameral change" and institutional conservatism', in L. D. Longley and D. M. Olson (eds) *Two Into One: The Politics and Processes of National Legislative Cameral Change*, Boulder, Colorado: Westview Press, pp. ix-xii.

Lindberg, B. (2008) 'Are political parties controlling legislative decision-making in the European Parliament? The case of the Services directive', *Journal of European Public Policy*, 15(8): 1184–204.

Long, S. J. (1997) *Regression Models for Categorical and Limited Dependent Variables*, Thousand Oaks: Sage.

Long, S. J. and Freese, J. (2003) *Regression Models for Categorical Dependent Variables Using Stata*, Texas: Stata Press.

Longley, L. D. and Davidson, R. H. (1998) 'Parliamentary committees: Changing perspectives on changing institutions', *Journal of Legislative Studies*, 4(1): 1–20.

Lowi, T. (1969) *The End of Liberalism: The Second Republic of the United States*, New York: W. W. Norton.

Mahoney, C. (2008) *Brussels Versus the Beltway: Advocacy in the United States and the European Union*, Washington DC: Georgetown University Press.

Mair, P. and Thomassen, J. (2010) 'Political representation and government in the European Union', *Journal of European Public Policy,* 17(1): 20–35.

Majone, G. (1996) *Regulating Europe*, London: Routledge.

Maltzman, F. (1997) *Competing Principals: Committees, parties and the organization of Congress*, Ann Arbor: University of Michigan Press.

Maltzman, F. and Smith, S. S. (1995) 'Principals, goals, dimensionality, and congressional committees', in K. A. Shepsle and B. R. Weingast (eds) *Positive Theories of Congressional Institutions*, Ann Arbor: The University of Michigan Press, pp. 253–72.

Mamadouh, V. and Raunio, T. (2002) 'Allocating reports in the European Parliament: How parties influence committee work', European Parliament Research Group. Online. Available /http://www2.lse.ac.uk/government/research/resgroups/EPRG/pdf/workingPaper7.pdf (accessed 27 December 2005).

Mamadouh, V. and Raunio, T. (2003) 'The committee system: Powers, appointment and report allocation', *Journal of Common Market Studies,* 41(2): 333–51.

Marsh, M. (1998) 'Testing the second-order election model after four European elections', *British Journal of Political Science,* 28(4): 591–607.

Marshall, D. (2010) 'Who to lobby and when: Institutional determinants of interest group strategies in European Parliament committees', *European Union Politics,* 11(4): 553–75.

Mattila, M. (2004) 'Contested decisions: Empirical analysis of voting in the EU Council of Ministers', *European Journal of Political Research,* 43(1): 29–50.

Mattila, M. and Lane, J. (2001) 'Why unanimity in the Council? A roll call analysis of Council voting', *European Union Politics,* 2(1): 31–52.

Mattson, I. and Strøm, K. (1996) 'Parliamentary committees', in H. Doering (ed.) *Parliaments and Majority Rule*, Frankfurt: Campus Verlag, pp. 249–307.

Mayhew, D. (1974) *The Electoral Connection*, New Haven, CT: Yale University Press.

McElroy, G. (2001) 'Committees and party cohesion in the European Parliament', European Parliament Research Group. Online. Available /http://www2.lse.ac.uk/government/research/resgroups/EPRG/pdf/workingPaper8.pdf (accessed 17 March 2006).

— (2006) 'Committee representation in the European Parliament', *European Union Politics*, 7(1): 5–29.

— (2007a) 'Legislative politics', in B. J. Rosamond, K. E. Jorgensen and M. Pollack (eds) *Handbook of European Union Politics*, London: Sage, pp. 175–94.

— (2007b) 'Legislative politics as normal? Voting behaviour and beyond in the European Parliament', *European Union Politics*, 8(3): 433–48.

McElroy, G. and Benoit, K. (2007) 'Party groups and policy positions in the European Parliament', *Party Politics*, 13(1): 5–28.

—      (2010) 'Party policy and group affiliation in the European Parliament', *British Journal of Political Science*, 40(2): 377–98.

Mezey, M. L. (1979) *Comparative Legislatures*, Durham, NC: Duke University Press.

Moravcsik, A. (1998a) *The Choice for Europe: Social purpose and state power from Messina to Maastricht*, Ithaca: Cornell University Press.

—      (1998b) 'In defence of the 'democratic deficit': Reassessing legitimacy in the European Union', *Journal of Common Market Studies*, 40(4): 603–24.

Moser, P. (1996) 'The European Parliament as a conditional agenda setter: What are the conditions? A critique of Tsebelis (1994)', *American Political Science Review*, 90(4): 834–8.

Naurin, D. and Rasmussen, A. (2011) 'Special Issue: Linking inter- and intra-institutional change in the European Union', *West European Politics*, 34(1): v–179

Neuhold, C. (2001) 'The "legislative backbone" of keeping the institution upright? The role of European Parliament committees in the EU policy-making process', Online. Available /http://eiop.or.at/eiop/texte/2001–010a.htm (accessed 1 December 2005).

North, D. C. (1990) *Institutions, Institutional Change, and Economic Performance*, New York: Cambridge University Press.

Norton, P. (1998) 'Nascent institutionalization: Committees in the British Parliament', *Journal of Legislative Studies*, 4(1): 143–61.

Noury, A. (2002) 'Ideology, nationality, and Euro-Parliamentarians', *European Union Politics*, 3(1): 33–58.

Papke, L. E. and Wooldridge, J. M. (1996) 'Econometric methods for fractional response variables with an application to 401(k) plan participation rates', *Journal of Applied Econometrics*, 11(6): 619–32.

Polsby, N. W. (1968) 'The institutionalization of the U.S. House of Representatives', *American Political Science Review*, 62(1): 144–68.

Poole, K. and Rosenthal,H. (1997) *Congress: A political-economic history of roll call voting*, Oxford: Oxford University Press.

Proksch, S. and Slapin, J. B. (2010) 'Position-taking in European Parliament speeches', *British Journal of Political Science*, 40(3): 587–611.

—      (2011) 'Parliamentary questions and oversight in the European Union', *European Journal of Political Research*, 50(1): 53–79.

Rasmussen, A. (2008) 'The EU conciliation committee: One or several principals?', *European Union Politics*, 9(1): 87–113.

—      (2011) 'Early conclusion in bicameral bargaining: Evidence from the co-decision legislative procedure of the European Union', *European Union Politics*, 12(1): 41–64.

Rasmussen, A. and Toshkov, D. (2010) 'The interinstitutional division of power and time allocation in the European Parliament', *West European Politics*, 34(1): 71–96.

Raunio, T. (1997) *The European Perspective: Transnational party groups in the 1989–1994 European Parliament*, Ashgate: Aldershot.

Reh, C., Héritier, A., Bressanelli, E. and Koop, C. (2010) 'The informal politics of legislation: Explaining secluded decision-making in the European Union', paper presented at the American Political Science Association in Washington, 2–5 September 2010. Online. Available /http://www.ucl.ac.uk/spp/research/esrc–project/Paper_APSA_2010_Reh_et_al.pdf (accessed 5 May 2011).

Reif, K. and Schmitt, H. (1980) 'Nine second-order elections: A conceptual framework for the analysis of European Election results', *European Journal of Political Research*, 8(1): 3–45.

Ringe, N. (2005) 'Policy preference formation in legislative politcs: Structure, actors, and focal points', *American Journal of Political Science*, 49(4): 731–45.

— (2009) *Who Decides, and How? Preferences, uncertainty, and policy choice in the European Parliament*, Oxford: Oxford University Press.

Rittberger, B. (2000) 'Impatient legislators and new issue-dimensions: A critique of the Garrett–Tsebelis "standard version" of legislative politics', *Journal of European Public Policy*, 7(4): 554–75.

— (2005) *Building Europe's Parliament. Democratic Representation Beyond the Nation State*, Oxford: Oxford University Press.

Robinson, J. (1963) *The House Rules Committee*, Indianapolis: Bobbs-Merrill.

Roederer-Rynning, C. (2003) 'From 'talking shop' to 'working Parliament'? The European Parliament and agricultural change', *Journal of Common Market Studies*, 41(1): 113–35.

Rohde, D. (1991) *Parties and Leaders in the Post-Reform House*, Chicago: University of Chicago Press.

Saturno, J. V. (2006) 'CRS report for Congress, order code 98–612 GOV: Special rules and options for regulating the amending process', Online. Available /http://www.rules.house.gov/archives/98–612.pdf (accessed 15 January 2010).

Scarrow, S. E. (1997) 'Political career paths and the European Parliament', *Legislative Studies Quarterly*, 22(2): 253–62.

Scharpf, F. W. (1999) *Governing Europe: Effective and Democratic?*, Oxford: Oxford University Press.

Schattschneider, E. E. (1960) *The Semi Sovereign People: A realist's view of democracy in America*, New York, NY: Hold, Rinehart and Winston.

Schmitt, H. and Thomassen, J. (1999) *Political Representation and Legitimacy in the European Union*, Oxford: Oxford University Press.

— (2009) 'The European party system after Enlargement', in J. Thomassen (ed.) *The Legitimacy of the European Union after Enlargement*, Oxford: Oxford University Press, pp. 23–43.

Schneider, J. (2008) 'Congressional research service, report 98–367: House committees: assignment process', Online. Available /http://stuff.mit.edu/afs/sipb/contrib/wikileaks–crs/wikileaks–crs–reports/98–367.pdf (accessed 14 January 2010).

Scully, R. (1997) 'The European Parliament and codecision: A reassessment', *The Journal of Legislative Studies*, 3(3): 58–73.

— (2000) 'Democracy, legitimacy and the European Parliament', in M. G. Cowles and M. Smith (eds) 7th edn. *The State of the European Union*, Oxford: Oxford University Press, pp. 228–45.

— (2001) 'National parties and European Parliamentarians: Developing and testing an institutional theory', Mimeo, Online. Available /http://www2. lse.ac.uk/government/research/resgroups/EPRG/pdf/workingPaper6.pdf (accessed 1 September 2010).

Selck, T. J. (2004) 'The European Parliament's legislative powers reconsidered: Assessing the current state of the procedural models literature', *Politics*, 24(2): 79–87.

Selck, T. J. and Steunenberg, B. (2004) 'Between power and luck: The European Parliament in the EU legislative process', *European Union Politics*, 5(1): 25–46.

Settembri, P. and Neuhold, C. (2009) 'Achieving consensus through committees: Does the European Parliament manage?', *Journal of Common Market Studies*, 47(1): 127–51.

Shackleton, M. and Raunio, T. (2003) 'Codecision since Amsterdam: A laboratory for institutional innovation and change', *Journal of European Public Policy*, 10(2): 171–87.

Shaw, M. (1998) 'Parliamentary committees: A global perspective', *Journal of Legislative Studies*, 4(1): 225–51.

Shepsle, K. (1978) *The Giant Jigsaw Puzzle*, Chicago: University of Chicago Press.

Shepsle, K. and Weingast, B. (1987) 'The institutional foundation of committee power', *American Political Science Review*, 81(1): 85–104.

— (1995) *Positive Theories of Congressional Institutions*, Ann Arbor: The University of Michigan Press.

Silbey, J. (1967) *The Shrine of Party: Congressional voting behavior, 1841–1852*, Pittsburgh: University of Pittsburgh Press.

Sinclair, B. (1989) *The Transformation of the U.S. Senate*, Baltimore: John Hopkins University Press.

Slapin, J. B. and Proksch, S. (2010) 'Look who's talking: Parliamentary debate in the European Union', *European Union Politics*, 11(3): 333–57.

Strøm, K. (1998) 'Parliamentary committees in European democracies', *Journal of Legislative Studies*, 4(1): 21–59.

Thomassen, J. (ed.) (2009) *The Legitimacy of the European Union after Enlargement*. Oxford: Oxford University Press.

Thomassen, J., Noury, A. and Voeten, E. (2004) 'Political competition in the European Parliament: Evidence from roll call and survey analyses', in G. Marks and M. Steunbergen (eds) *European Integration and Political Conflict*, Cambridge: Cambridge University Press, pp. 141–61.

Thomassen, J. and Schmitt, H. (1999a) 'Introduction: Political representation and legitimacy in the European Union', in H. Schmitt and J. Thomassen (eds) *Political Representation and Legitimacy in the European Union*, Oxford: Oxford University Press, pp. 1–22.

Thomassen, J. and Schmitt, H. (1999b) 'Issue congruence', in H. Schmitt and J. Thomassen (eds) *Political Representation and Legitimacy in the European Union*, Oxford: Oxford University Press, pp. 186–208.

Tsebelis, G. (1994) 'The power of the European Parliament as a conditional agenda setter', *American Political Science Review*, 88(1): 128–42.

— (1995) 'Conditional agenda-setting and decision-making inside the European Parliament', *Journal of Legislative Studies*, 1(1): 65–93.

— (1997) *Bicameralism*, Cambridge, U.K; New York: Cambridge University Press.

Tsebelis, G. and Garrett, G. (2000) 'Legislative politics in the European Union', *European Union Politics*, 1(1): 9–36.

Tsebelis, G., Jensen, C. B., Kalandrakis, A. and Kreppel, A. (2001) 'Legislative procedures in the European Union: An empirical analysis', *British Journal of Political Science*, 31(4): 573–99.

Van der Brug, W. and Van der Eijk, C. (2007) *European Elections and Domestic Politics: Lessons from the past and scenarios for the future*, Notre Dame, IN: Notre Dame University Press.

Van der Eijk, C. and Franklin, M. (eds) (1996) *Choosing Europe? The European electorate and national politics in the face of Union*. Ann Arbor: University of Michigan Press.

— (2004) 'Potential for contestation on European matters at national elections in Europe', in G. Marks and M. Steenbergen (eds) *European Integration and Political Conflict*, Cambridge: Cambridge University Press, pp. 33–50.

Voeten, E. (2009) 'Enlargement and the "normal" European Parliament', in J. Thomassen (ed.) *The Legitimacy of the European Union After Enlargement*, Oxford: Oxford University Press, pp. 93–113.

Warntjen, A., Crombez C. and Hix, S. (2008) 'The party political make-up of EU institutions', *Journal of European Public Policy*, 15(8): 1243–53.

Weingast, B. R. and Marshall, W. (1988) 'The industrial organization of Congress', *Journal of Political Economy*, 96(1): 132–63.

Westlake, M. (1994) *A Modern Guide to the European Parliament*, London and New York: Pinter Publishers.

Whitaker, R. (2001) 'Party control in a committee-based legislature? The case of the European Parliament', *Journal of Legislative Studies*, 7(4): 63–88.

— (2005) 'National parties in the European Parliament', *European Union Politics*, 6(1): 5–28.

— (2011) *The European Parliament's Committees: National party influence and legislative empowerment*, London: Routledge.

Wilson, W. (1885) *Congressional Government: A study in American politics*, Boston: Houghton Mufflin Company.

Yordanova, N. (2009) 'Rationale behind committee assignments in the European Parliament: Distributive, informational and partisan perspectives', *European Union Politics,* 10(2): 263–90.

— (2011a) 'The effect of inter-institutional rules on the division of power in the European Parliament: Allocation of consultation versus codecision reports', *West European Politics*, 34(1): 1501–25.

— (2011b) 'The European Parliament: In need of a theory', *European Union Politics*, 12(4): 597–617.

Yoshinaka, A., McElroy G. and Bowler, S. (2006) 'Rapporteurs in the European Parliament: Distributional, informational or partisan?', paper presented at Midwest Political Science Association in Chicago, 20–3 April 2006. Online. Available /http://www.allacademic.com/meta/p_mla_apa_research_citation/1/3/7/2/8/pages137282/p137282–5.php (accessed 29 February 2008).

— (2010) 'The appointment of rapporteurs in the European Parliament', *Legislative Studies Quarterly,* 35(4): 457–86.

# | appendices

## Appendix A Chapter 3: Codebook of the data set on the MEPs' profiles in the 6th European Parliament

| VARIABLES | CODING |
|---|---|
| Dependent variable: membership in a named committee | 1 = yes, 0 = no |
| *Special interests* | |
| Business and industry | 1 = yes, 0 = no |
| Trade union | 1 = yes, 0 = no |
| Green | 1 = yes, 0 = no |
| Farming | 1 = yes, 0 = no |
| Social groups | 1 = yes, 0 = no |
| *Educational and professional experience* | |
| International relations experience | 1 = yes, 0 = no |
| Ex-Head of national executive | 1 = yes, 0 = no |
| Economics and finance | 1 = yes, 0 = no |
| Medicine | 1 = yes, 0 = no |
| Natural sciences and engineering | 1 = yes, 0 = no |
| Transport and telecommunications | 1 = yes, 0 = no |
| Local government experience | 1 = yes, 0 = no |
| Legal | 1 = yes, 0 = no |
| *EP seniority* | |
| EP experience within party group (Years served in the EP relative to party group mean) | 1 = more than group mean, 0 = less than group mean |
| Continuing committee member from the last EP term | 1 = yes, 0 = no |
| *Partisan Measures* | |
| EPP-ED membership | 1 = yes, 0 = no |
| PSE membership | 1 = yes, 0 = no |
| Party group disloyalty in voting | Absolute distance from party group median on 1 dimension NOMINATE |
| Holds a high party group office (group chairmen or vice chairman) | 1 = yes, 0 = no |
| Size of national party delegation relative to party group size | Size of national party delegation divided by size of party group |
| Held an official national party office | 1 = yes, 0 = no |
| *Demographics* | |
| New member state nationality | 1 = yes, 0 = no |
| Gender | 1 = male, 0 = female |
| Age relative to party group 75th percentile | 1 = older than 75th percentile, 0 = younger than 75th percentile |

*Note:* See the List of Abbreviations at the beginning of the book.

**Descriptive statistics on the profiles of MEPs in each European party group**

| | EPP-ED | PSE | ALDE | G/EFA | EUL/NGL | IND/DEM | UEN | na | Plenary |
|---|---|---|---|---|---|---|---|---|---|
| *Special Interests* | | | | | | | | | |
| Industry (%) | 47 (17.5) | 24 (12.0) | 18 (20.5) | 2 (4.8) | 4 (9.8) | 10 (27.8) | 5 (18.5) | 5 (16.7) | 115 (15.7) |
| Trade Union Ties (%) | 9 (3.4) | 29 (14.5) | 4 (4.5) | 1 (2.4) | 5 (12.2) | 0 (0.0) | 2 (7.4) | 1 (3.3) | 51 (7.0) |
| Green Ties (%) | 10 (3.5) | 7 (3.5) | 0 (0.0) | 14 (33.3) | 2 (4.9) | 1 (2.8) | 2 (7.4) | 1 (3.3) | 37 (5.1) |
| Farming (%) | 29 (10.8) | 5 (2.5) | 2 (2.3) | 1 (2.4) | 1 (2.4) | 1 (2.8) | 2 (7.4) | 3 (10.0) | 44 (6.0) |
| Social Group Ties (%) | 14 (5.2) | 29 (14.5) | 9 (10.2) | 5 (11.9) | 5 (12.2) | 1 (2.8) | 1 (3.7) | 0 (0.0) | 64 (8.7) |
| *Expertise/Seniority* | | | | | | | | | |
| International Relations (%) | 160 (59.7) | 129 (64.5) | 55 (62.5) | 25 (59.5) | 17 (41.5) | 11 (30.6) | 11 (40.7) | 9 (30.0) | 417 (57.0) |
| Ex-Head of Executive (%) | 4 (1.5) | 5 (2.5) | 2 (2.3) | 0 (0.0) | 0 (0.0) | 0 (0.0) | 1 (3.7) | 0 (0.0) | 12 (1.6) |
| Economics (%) | 54 (20.1) | 42 (21.0) | 17 (19.3) | 4 (9.5) | 8 (19.5) | 7 (19.4) | 8 (29.6) | 5 (16.7) | 145 (19.8) |
| Medicine (%) | 25 (9.3) | 8 (4.0) | 4 (4.5) | 1 (2.4) | 4 (9.8) | 4 (11.1) | 0 (0.0) | 3 (10.0) | 49 (6.7) |
| Science/ Engineering (%) | 30 (11.2) | 19 (9.5) | 4 (4.5) | 6 (14.3) | 8 (19.5) | 6 (16.7) | 3 (11.1) | 3 (10.0) | 79 (10.8) |
| Transport/ Telecom. (%) | 13 (4.9) | 9 (4.5) | 1 (1.1) | 4 (9.5) | 0 (0.0) | 2 (5.6) | 2 (7.4) | 0 (0.0) | 31 (4.2) |
| Local Government (%) | 150 (56.0) | 114 (57.0) | 42 (47.7) | 22 (52.4) | 14 (34.1) | 12 (33.3) | 17 (63.0) | 16 (53.3) | 387 (52.9) |
| Legal (%) | 80 (29.9) | 42 (21.0) | 27 (30.7) | 1 (2.4) | 3 (7.3) | 4 (11.1) | 6 (22.2) | 9 (30.0) | 172 (23.5) |
| Average Years Served (std) | 4.1 (5.4) | 4.1 (5.3) | 3.2 (4.8) | 3.5 (4.4) | 2.4 (4.8) | 2.4 (4.9) | 2.5 (4.2) | 2.5 (5.0) | 3.6 (5.2) |

| | EPP-ED | PSE | ALDE | G/EFA | EUL/NGL | IND/DEM | UEN | na | Plenary |
|---|---|---|---|---|---|---|---|---|---|
| **Partisan measures** | | | | | | | | | |
| Official party group role (%) | 11 (4.1) | 8 (4.0) | 6 (6.8) | 6 (14.3) | 4 (9.8) | 3 (8.3) | 6 (22.2) | n/a | 44 (6.0) |
| Official national party role (%) | 187 (69.8) | 134 (67.0) | 52 (59.1) | 34 (81.0) | 29 (70.7) | 24 (66.7) | 16 (59.3) | 14 (46.7) | 490 (66.9) |
| Median party group position on 1st dimension NOMINATE | 0.211 | 0.211 | 0.071 | -0.4215 | -0.755 | 0.135 | 0.166 | n/a | |
| Average distance from party group median on 1st dimension NOMINATE (std) | 0.05 (0.06) | 0.03 (0.03) | 0.02 (0.02) | 0.03 (0.07) | 0.05 (0.05) | 0.36 (0.42) | 0.03 (0.40) | n/a | |
| **Demographics** | | | | | | | | | |
| Male (%) | 204 (76.1) | 121 (60.5) | 55 (62.5) | 12 (28.6) | 29 (70.7) | 33 (91.7) | 23 (85.2) | 24 (80.0) | 501 (68.4) |
| Average age (std) | 51.8 (9.8) | 50.6 (9.4) | 52.5 (10.2) | 48.8 (7.4) | 51.2 (10.3) | 53.7 (11.3) | 50 (10.1) | 50.4 (11.4) | 51.3 (9.8) |
| Age – 75th percentile | 59 | 57 | 60.5 | 54 | 56 | 59.5 | 57 | 59 | 58 |
| Total size | 268 | 200 | 88 | 42 | 41 | 36 | 27 | 30 | 732 |

*Note*: Shown in brackets are the per cent of party group/plenary members with the respective characteristic for dummy variables and the standard deviations from the mean value of the reported characteristic within party group/plenary for continuous variables. See the List of Abbreviations at the beginning of the book.

## Appendix B Chapter 3: Committee nomenclature since 1983

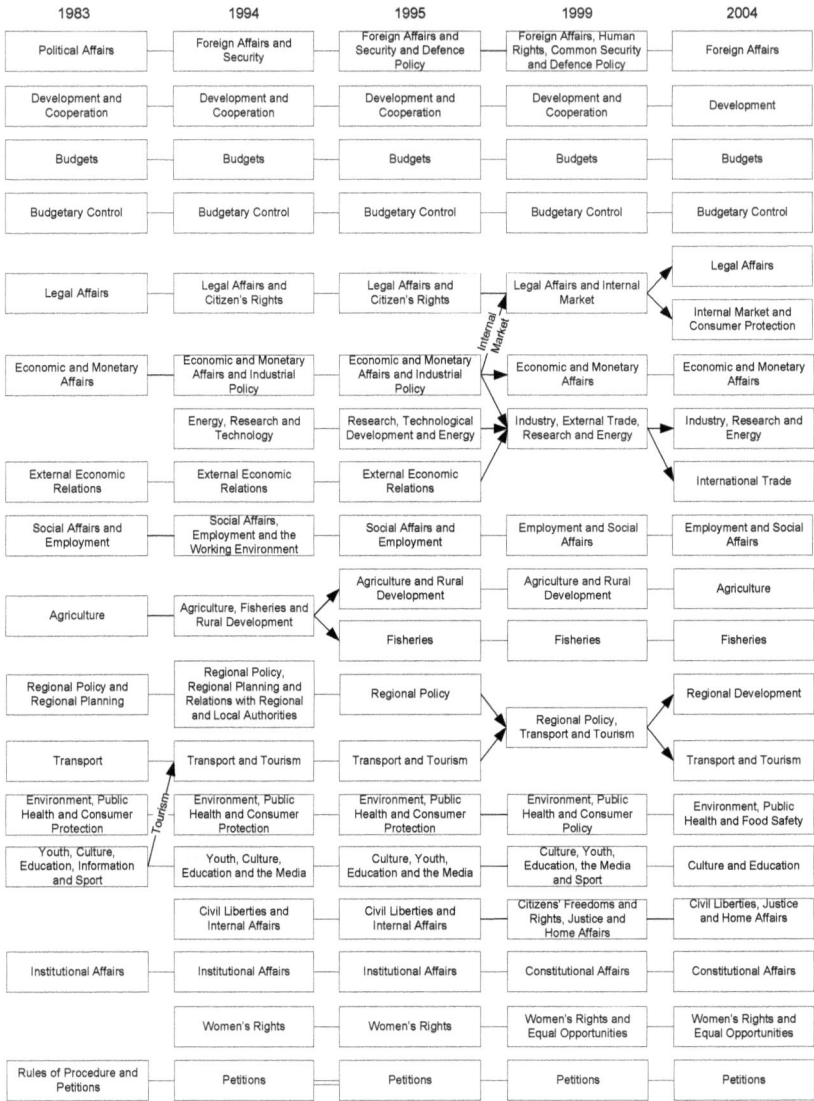

| 1983 | 1994 | 1995 | 1999 | 2004 |
|---|---|---|---|---|
| Political Affairs | Foreign Affairs and Security | Foreign Affairs and Security and Defence Policy | Foreign Affairs, Human Rights, Common Security and Defence Policy | Foreign Affairs |
| Development and Cooperation | Development and Cooperation | Development and Cooperation | Development and Cooperation | Development |
| Budgets | Budgets | Budgets | Budgets | Budgets |
| Budgetary Control | Budgetary Control | Budgetary Control | Budgetary Control | Budgetary Control |
| Legal Affairs | Legal Affairs and Citizen's Rights | Legal Affairs and Citizen's Rights | Legal Affairs and Internal Market | Legal Affairs; Internal Market and Consumer Protection |
| Economic and Monetary Affairs | Economic and Monetary Affairs and Industrial Policy | Economic and Monetary Affairs and Industrial Policy | Economic and Monetary Affairs | Economic and Monetary Affairs |
| | Energy, Research and Technology | Research, Technological Development and Energy | Industry, External Trade, Research and Energy | Industry, Research and Energy |
| External Economic Relations | External Economic Relations | External Economic Relations | | International Trade |
| Social Affairs and Employment | Social Affairs, Employment and the Working Environment | Social Affairs and Employment | Employment and Social Affairs | Employment and Social Affairs |
| Agriculture | Agriculture, Fisheries and Rural Development | Agriculture and Rural Development | Agriculture and Rural Development | Agriculture |
| | | Fisheries | Fisheries | Fisheries |
| Regional Policy and Regional Planning | Regional Policy, Regional Planning and Relations with Regional and Local Authorities | Regional Policy | Regional Policy, Transport and Tourism | Regional Development |
| Transport | Transport and Tourism | Transport and Tourism | | Transport and Tourism |
| Environment, Public Health and Consumer Protection | Environment, Public Health and Consumer Protection | Environment, Public Health and Consumer Protection | Environment, Public Health and Consumer Policy | Environment, Public Health and Food Safety |
| Youth, Culture, Education, Information and Sport | Youth, Culture, Education and the Media | Culture, Youth, Education and the Media | Culture, Youth, Education, the Media and Sport | Culture and Education |
| | Civil Liberties and Internal Affairs | Civil Liberties and Internal Affairs | Citizens' Freedoms and Rights, Justice and Home Affairs | Civil Liberties, Justice and Home Affairs |
| Institutional Affairs | Institutional Affairs | Institutional Affairs | Constitutional Affairs | Constitutional Affairs |
| | Women's Rights | Women's Rights | Women's Rights and Equal Opportunities | Women's Rights and Equal Opportunities |
| Rules of Procedure and Petitions | Petitions | Petitions | Petitions | Petitions |

*Source*: Own graph based on the Rules of Procedure of the European Parliament since 1983.

**Appendix C Chapter 3: Logistic regression of committee assignment to an MEP in the first half of the 6th EP**

| | AFET | BUDG | ECON | EMPL | ENVI | ITRE | IMCO | TRAN | AGRI | JURI | LIBE |
|---|---|---|---|---|---|---|---|---|---|---|---|
| *Special interests* | | | | | | | | | | | |
| Business/Industry | | | 1.48** | -0.49 | -0.16 | 0.91* | 0.79 | | | | |
| | | | (-0.39) | (-0.39) | (-0.39) | (-0.39) | (-0.43) | | | | |
| Trade union | | | 0.82 | 1.92** | | | | | | | |
| | | | (-0.61) | (-0.45) | | | | | | | |
| Green | | | | | 2.01** | 0.14 | | | -1.33 | | |
| | | | | | (-0.52) | (-0.64) | | | (-1.43) | | |
| Farming | | | | | -1.37 | | | | 3.22** | | |
| | | | | | (-1.19) | | | | (-0.52) | | |
| Social group | | | | | | | | | | | 1.30** |
| | | | | | | | | | | | (-0.42) |
| *Expertise/seniority* | | | | | | | | | | | |
| International relations | 1.57** | | | | | | | | | | |
| | (-0.4) | | | | | | | | | | |
| Ex-Head Executive | 1.84** | | | | | | | | | | |
| | (-0.68) | | | | | | | | | | |
| Economics/Finance | | 1.23** | 0.96* | -0.39 | | | -0.08 | | | | |
| | | (-0.37) | (-0.38) | (-0.5) | | | (-0.47) | | | | |
| Medicine | | | | | 1.57** | | | | | | |
| | | | | | (-0.53) | | | | | | |

| | AFET | BUDG | ECON | EMPL | ENVI | ITRE | IMCO | TRAN | AGRI | JURI | LIBE |
|---|---|---|---|---|---|---|---|---|---|---|---|
| Science/Engineering | | | | | 0.93* | 1.11** | | | | | |
| | | | | | (-0.47) | (-0.4) | | | | | |
| Transport/Telecommnication | | | | | | | | 2.99** | | | |
| | | | | | | | | (-0.52) | | | |
| Local government | | | | | | | | | 0.6 | | |
| | | | | | | | | | (-0.45) | | |
| Legal | | | | | | | | | | 1.61** | 0.44 |
| | | | | | | | | | | (-0.47) | (-0.35) |
| Committee incumbent | 3.45** | 3.59** | 3.62** | 3.40** | 4.66** | 2.97** | 3.51** | 3.82** | 4.07** | 2.05** | 3.17** |
| | (-0.45) | (-0.52) | (-0.57) | (-0.53) | (-0.59) | (-0.58) | (-0.62) | (-0.52) | (-1.02) | (-0.72) | (-0.52) |
| EP experience within party group | -0.51 | 0.48 | -0.54 | -1.05* | -0.38 | -1.58** | -0.34 | -0.58 | -0.019 | -0.88 | -0.64 |
| | (-0.4) | (-0.48) | (-0.51) | (-0.53) | (-0.52) | (-0.6) | (-0.47) | (-0.52) | (-0.54) | (-0.7) | (-0.48) |
| ***Partisan measures*** | | | | | | | | | | | |
| EPP-ED | -0.4 | 0.41 | 0.039 | -0.09 | -0.7 | 0.18 | 0.26 | -0.66 | -1.01 | -0.3 | -0.19 |
| | (-0.36) | (-0.47) | (-0.47) | (-0.44) | (-0.43) | (-0.43) | (-0.5) | (-0.45) | (-0.61) | (-0.58) | (-0.39) |
| PSE | -0.26 | 0.27 | 0.093 | -0.44 | -0.91 | 0.25 | 0.58 | -0.25 | 0.058 | -0.16 | -0.44 |
| | (-0.37) | (-0.48) | (-0.49) | (-0.47) | (-0.48) | (-0.43) | (-0.49) | (-0.47) | (-0.52) | (-0.61) | (-0.41) |
| Party group disloyalty | -2.41 | -0.35 | -0.58 | 1.75 | 0.88 | -6.14 | 1.6 | 0.83 | 0.24 | -1.63 | -3.34 |
| | (-2.66) | (-1.85) | (-1.41) | (-1.23) | (-1.44) | (-3.74) | (-1.14) | (-1.36) | (-1.77) | (-3.02) | (-3.76) |
| Holds group office | -0.5 | -0.39 | 0.57 | 0.36 | -1.19 | 0.083 | 0.92 | -1.45 | -2.2 | 0.46 | 0.28 |
| | (-0.61) | (-0.84) | (-0.63) | (-0.63) | (-1.04) | (-0.72) | (-0.61) | (-1.13) | (-1.59) | (-0.79) | (-0.61) |

| | AFET | BUDG | ECON | EMPL | ENVI | ITRE | IMCO | TRAN | AGRI | JURI | LIBE |
|---|---|---|---|---|---|---|---|---|---|---|---|
| National party size relative to group size | -0.005 | 2.36 | 1.39 | -4.95 | -4.19 | 2.15 | 2.05 | -2.39 | 1.26 | 2.39 | -5.31 |
| | (-2.29) | (-2.76) | (-2.84) | (-2.99) | (-2.62) | (-2.48) | (-2.76) | (-2.72) | (-2.96) | (-3.18) | (-2.92) |
| Held national party office | 0.46 | -0.33 | -0.16 | 0.97* | -0.22 | -0.51 | -0.39 | 1.39** | -0.23 | 0.78 | -0.43 |
| | (-0.32) | (-0.37) | (-0.39) | (-0.43) | (-0.37) | (-0.33) | (-0.38) | (-0.48) | (-0.44) | (-0.54) | (-0.33) |
| *Demographics* | | | | | | | | | | | |
| New member state | 0.67 | 1.15** | -0.12 | -0.28 | -0.24 | -0.04 | 0.07 | 0.45 | 0.16 | 0.72 | -0.085 |
| | (-0.35) | (-0.41) | (-0.47) | (-0.45) | (-0.45) | (-0.39) | (-0.5) | (-0.45) | (-0.55) | (-0.52) | (-0.42) |
| Male | 1.01** | -0.062 | 0.4 | 0.1 | -0.12 | -0.099 | -0.91* | 0.52 | -0.19 | 0.4 | -0.19 |
| | (-0.37) | (-0.39) | (-0.45) | (-0.39) | (-0.38) | (-0.35) | (-0.38) | (-0.43) | (-0.45) | (-0.55) | (-0.35) |
| Age in top quartile of party group | -0.39 | -0.47 | -0.097 | 0.37 | -0.91 | -0.23 | 0.21 | -0.74 | -0.66 | 0.76 | -0.066 |
| | (-0.36) | (-0.48) | (-0.43) | (-0.4) | (-0.5) | (-0.41) | (-0.41) | (-0.5) | (-0.6) | (-0.47) | (-0.39) |
| Constant | -4.42** | -3.91** | -4.03** | -3.34** | -2.05** | -2.60** | -3.03** | -4.19** | -3.32** | -5.23** | -1.90** |
| | (-0.64) | (-0.63) | (-0.66) | (-0.61) | (-0.53) | (-0.53) | (-0.59) | (-0.66) | (-0.7) | (-0.85) | (-0.51) |
| N | 695 | 695 | 695 | 695 | 695 | 695 | 695 | 695 | 695 | 695 | 695 |
| - Log likelihood | 176.7 | 131.5 | 123.9 | 132.8 | 130.6 | 151.3 | 128.1 | 125.3 | 100.6 | 88.7 | 152.5 |
| McFadden pseudo Rsq | 0.26 | 0.21 | 0.27 | 0.24 | 0.38 | 0.15 | 0.15 | 0.27 | 0.33 | .15 | 0.16 |
| Percentage classified | 91.37% | 94.10% | 94.39% | 94.39% | 93.53% | 94.24% | 94.53% | 95.68% | 95.68% | 96.55% | 92.95% |

*Note*: Dependent variable: individual member assignment to the respective committee in 2004. Standard errors in brackets, * significance at 10%; ** significance at 5%. See the List of Abbreviations in the beginning of the book.

## Appendix D Chapter 3: Association between current and previous committee membership

In this appendix the strong impact of previous committee membership on re-assignment to the same committee, i.e. committee incumbency, is explored further using conditional probabilities. Thus, in the table below, the number of people with certain previous committee experience in each current committee is represented as a proportion of the number of experienced MEPs in that committee. Fisher's exact test is used to check the statistical significance of the observed associations. This test has been chosen because of the low expected frequencies in some of the table's cells. The analysis aims to identify what the level of continuity in the committee membership is, or in other words the extent to which MEPs tend to stay in the same committees on which they have already served in the past. Committee assignment of legislators on the same committee as the one they sat on during the last legislative term or on a committee requiring similar expertise is considered as a sign of specialisation. The analysis focuses, therefore, on the long-term trend of committee membership for those MEPs who have already served in the EP before 2004. All of the committees are considered here.

The table below represents the conditional probability of having specific previous committee experience given current committee membership for an MEP who has served in the EP prior to 2004. The results provide a sound proof of the second hypothesis in Chapter 3, namely that the EP committees maintain a high degree of specialization. All the results on the diagonal in the table are statistically significant, showing that committees tend to attract MEPs who have already served on the same committee in a previous term of the EP. In analysing the table, one has to take into account that some committees have been united in the past (*see* Appendix B). This is partly explains why, for instance, previous experience in the Committee on Agriculture and Rural Development is associated with current membership on the Committee on Fisheries, and the other way round (united until 1995). The same refers to the Committee on the Internal Market and Consumer Protection and the Committee on Legal Affairs (united in 1999); and the Committee on Transport and Tourism and the Committee on Regional Development (united in 1999). A similar association exists between previous membership on the Committee on Industry, Research and Energy and current membership on the Committee on Economic and Monetary Affairs, as well as between previous membership on the Committee on International Trade and current membership on Committee on the Internal Market and Consumer Protection. However, the relationship here goes only in one direction, suggesting a movement in the committee hierarchy. The association between previous membership on the Committee on Economic and Monetary Affairs and the allocation to the Committee on Legal Affairs in 2004 can be explained by the fact that the functioning of the internal market has been an issue dealt with by both committees at different times.

More interesting here is the association between previous and current membership on the Committee on Budgets and the Committee on Budgetary Control, whose members tend to serve on both committees and thus work on closely related issues. The same trend is observed between the Committee on Foreign Affairs and the Committee on Constitutional Affairs, both of which operate in the sphere of high politics. There is a statistically significant association between previously serving on the Committee on International Trade or on the Committee on Budgets, and current membership on the Committee on Economic and Monetary Affairs, which is in line with the informational rationale as expertise in economics is relevant for the activities of all of them. As the jurisdictions of the Committee on Fisheries to a large extent fall within the realm of international economic relations, it is not surprising that a large proportion of people that were previously on this committee joined the Committee on International Trade in 2004. It appears also that MEPs tend to enrol on the Committee on Culture and Education if they have had previous experience on the Committee on Women's Rights and Gender Equality, and the other way round. None of these committees require particular expertise. Having previously been on the Committee on Women's Rights and Gender Equality is also linked to membership on the Committee on Environment, Public Health and Food Safety, as women are over–represented in the latter committee. Furthermore, people who were previously on the Committee on the Internal Market and Consumer Protection and the Committee on Legal Affairs tend to be allocated to the Committee on Petitions, likely as their second committee.

On the whole, a clear pattern of committee membership can be observed. Committees tend to attract members who have specialised in a certain field. This regularity is even stronger for committees, which operate in well-defined areas requiring particular expertise or seniority.

## Conditional probability distributions of previous committee experience given current committee membership

| Previous \ Current | AFET | DEVE | INTA | BUDG | CONT | ECON | EMPL | ENVI | ITRE | IMCO | TRAN | REGI | AGRI | PECH | CULT | JURI | LIBE | AFCO | FEMM | PETI | n |
|---|---|---|---|---|---|---|---|---|---|---|---|---|---|---|---|---|---|---|---|---|---|
| AFET | .77* | .17 | .29 | .10 | .07 | .04 | .04 | .03* | .12 | .05 | .13 | .17 | .00* | .14 | .00 | .13 | .00* | .43* | .09 | .00 | 61 |
| DEVE | .15 | .56* | .06 | .00 | .07 | .04 | .04 | .12 | .00 | .05 | .09 | .06 | .11 | .09 | .00 | .07 | .09 | .00 | .00 | .10 | 31 |
| INTA | .08 | .11 | .41* | .10 | .07 | .28* | .13 | .03 | .53* | .05 | .13 | .06 | .00 | .05 | .00 | .13 | .14 | .00 | .00 | .30 | 42 |
| BUDG | .15 | .06 | .29 | .90* | .50* | .16* | .00* | .03* | .18 | .26 | .00* | .17 | .16 | .09 | .11 | .00 | .14 | .07 | .18 | .20 | 53 |
| CONT | .10 | .06 | .18 | .35* | .50* | .00 | .04 | .09 | .12 | .16 | .09 | .00 | .11 | .05 | .00 | .07 | .05 | .07 | .00 | .10 | 31 |
| ECON | .13* | .06 | .29 | .05 | .07 | .72* | .04 | .03 | .29 | .21 | .00 | .00 | .00 | .00 | .00 | .40* | .05 | .07 | .09 | .10 | 45 |
| EMPL | .08 | .11 | .18 | .10 | .14 | .16 | .83* | .06 | .00 | .11 | .04 | .11 | .05 | .00 | .00 | .00 | .23 | .21 | .27 | .20 | 51 |
| ENVI | .03* | .06 | .12 | .00 | .00 | .04 | .13 | .85* | .06 | .16 | .04 | .06 | .05 | .05 | .00 | .07 | .09 | .00 | .09 | .10 | 45 |
| ITRE | .10 | .11 | .29 | .25 | .00 | .36* | .13 | .12 | .65* | .16 | .17 | .00 | .00 | .05 | .00 | .00 | .09 | .14 | .18 | .30 | 54 |
| IMCO | .13 | .06 | .18 | .05 | .07 | .12 | .00* | .00* | .06 | .58* | .00 | .17 | .00 | .05 | .00 | .53* | .14 | .14 | .09 | .40* | 41 |
| TRAN | .18 | .06 | .18 | .00 | .07 | .12 | .09 | .09 | .06 | .11 | .74* | .44* | .11 | .27 | .11 | .07 | .05 | .14 | .09 | .10 | 50 |
| REGI | .08 | .11 | .24 | .05 | .07 | .12 | .04 | .18 | .06 | .11 | .74* | .50* | .11 | .32 | .22 | .00 | .05 | .29 | .18 | .20 | 58 |
| AGRI | .03 | .00 | .18 | .10 | .14 | .00 | .04 | .03 | .06 | .00 | .00 | .06 | .74* | .32* | .11 | .00 | .05 | .00 | .00 | .00 | 27 |
| PECH | .04 | .00 | .29* | .10 | .00 | .04 | .04 | .03 | .12 | .05 | .09 | .22 | .32* | .68* | .00 | .00 | .05 | .00 | .00 | .00 | 27 |
| CULT | .13 | .11 | .12 | .15 | .00 | .04 | .00 | .03 | .12 | .11 | .00 | .17 | .00 | .05 | .78* | .00 | .05 | .07 | .36* | .00 | 31 |
| JURI | .08 | .06 | .12 | .00 | .14 | .04 | .00 | .03 | .06 | .53* | .00 | .17 | .00 | .09 | .00 | .53* | .14 | .00 | .09 | .40* | 33 |

**Current**

| Previous | AFET | DEVE | INTA | BUDG | CONT | ECON | EMPL | ENVI | ITRE | IMCO | TRAN | REGI | AGRI | PECH | CULT | JURI | LIBE | AFCO | FEMM | PETI | n |
|---|---|---|---|---|---|---|---|---|---|---|---|---|---|---|---|---|---|---|---|---|---|
| LIBE | .03 | .17 | .12 | .05 | .21 | .04 | .04 | .06 | .00 | .16 | .09 | .06 | .05 | .14 | .11 | .13 | **.45*** | .14 | .00 | .10 | 34 |
| AFCO | **.23*** | .00 | .24 | .05 | .07 | .08 | .00 | .09 | .00 | .05 | .13 | .06 | .00 | .05 | .11 | .13 | .18 | **.64*** | .00 | .10 | 40 |
| FEMM | .05 | .22 | .06 | .05 | .07 | .04 | .09 | **.18*** | .06 | .00 | .04 | .06 | .00 | .05 | **.44*** | .07 | .05 | .00 | **.64*** | .00 | 27 |
| PETI | .13 | .00 | .18 | .00 | .07 | .04 | .09 | .06 | .00 | .16 | .00 | .00 | .00 | .00 | .22 | .13 | **.23*** | .14 | .00 | **.40*** | 26 |
| TOTAL[1] | 2.69 | 2.06 | 4.00 | 2.45 | 2.50 | 2.48 | 1.78 | 2.15 | 2.53 | 3.05 | 2.61 | 2.50 | 1.79 | 2.68 | 2.33 | 2.47 | 2.27 | 2.57 | 2.36 | 3.10 | |
| (n)[2] | (39) | (18) | (17) | (20) | (14) | (25) | (23) | (33) | (17) | (19) | (23) | (18) | (19) | (22) | (9) | (15) | (22) | (14) | (11) | (10) | |
| Size (in 2004) | 78 | 34 | 33 | 47 | 34 | 48 | 50 | 63 | 51 | 39 | 51 | 50 | 42 | 34 | 35 | 26 | 53 | 28 | 35 | 25 | |
| %MEPs with experience | 50% | 53% | 52% | 43% | 41% | 52% | 46% | 52% | 33% | 49% | 45% | 36% | 45% | 65% | 26% | 58% | 42% | 50% | 31% | 40% | |

*Note:* Total % of MEPS in the 6th EP with previous committee experience: 44.7%. Each cell represents the number of MEPs of the column committee with previous experience on the row committee as a proportion of total number of experienced MEPs on column committee; * significance at the 5% level (2-tailed). [1] Note that the TOTAL of the conditional frequencies does not add up to 1 because MEPs can serve on more than one committee and in multiple EP terms. [2] Members with EP experience acquired prior to 2004. See the List of Abbreviations at the beginning of the book.

**Appendix E Chapter 3: Log regression of committee assignment to an MEP in the first half of the 6th EP**

| | AFET | BUDG | ECON | EMPL | ENVI | ITRE | IMCO | TRAN | AGRI | JURI | LIBE |
|---|---|---|---|---|---|---|---|---|---|---|---|
| **Special interests** | | | | | | | | | | | |
| Business/Industry | | | 0.51** (-0.16) | -0.12 (-0.19) | -0.058 (-0.19) | 0.32* (-0.15) | 0.24 (-0.16) | | | | |
| Trade union | | | 0.35 (-0.22) | 0.82** (-0.21) | | | | | | | |
| Green | | | | | 0.82** (-0.26) | 0.033 (-0.26) | | | -0.11 (-0.32) | | |
| Farming | | | | | -0.94 (-0.82) | | | | 1.34** (-0.25) | | |
| Social group | | | | | | | | | | | 0.55** (-0.18) |
| **Expertise/seniority** | | | | | | | | | | | |
| International relations | 0.55** -0.13 | | | | | | | | | | |
| Ex-Head Executive | 1.04* -0.41 | | | | | | | | | | |
| Economics/Finance | | 0.43** (-0.14) | 0.47** (-0.14) | -0.2 (-0.18) | | | -0.06 (-0.16) | | | | |
| Medicine | | | | | 0.62** (-0.24) | | | | | | |
| Science/Engineering | | | | | 0.33 (-0.2) | 0.43* (-0.18) | | | | | |

| | AFET | BUDG | ECON | EMPL | ENVI | ITRE | IMCO | TRAN | AGRI | JURI | LIBE |
|---|---|---|---|---|---|---|---|---|---|---|---|
| Transport/Telecommunication | | | | | | | | 1.25** (-0.26) | | | |
| Local government | | | | | | | | | 0.18 (-0.14) | | |
| Legal | | | | | | | | | | 0.54** (-0.16) | 0.12 (-0.13) |
| Committee incumbent | 1.96** (-0.31) | 1.72** (-0.32) | 1.90** (-0.37) | 1.79** (-0.35) | 2.67** (-0.43) | 1.30** (-0.32) | 1.76** (-0.42) | 1.78** (-0.3) | 2.34** (-0.72) | 0.84* (-0.35) | 1.62** (-0.34) |
| EP experience in party group | -0.19 (-0.16) | 0.2 (-0.16) | -0.17 (-0.19) | -0.50* (-0.2) | -0.29 (-0.21) | -0.47* (-0.18) | -0.1 (-0.16) | -0.22 (-0.19) | 0.075 (-0.17) | -0.25 (-0.21) | -0.24 (-0.17) |
| **Partisan measures** | | | | | | | | | | | |
| EPP-ED | -0.1 (-0.15) | 0.08 (-0.15) | 0.0023 (-0.17) | -0.083 (-0.16) | -0.29 (-0.16) | 0.049 (-0.15) | 0.03 (-0.16) | -0.15 (-0.16) | -0.25 (-0.19) | -0.13 (-0.18) | -0.14 (-0.14) |
| PSE | -0.11 (-0.16) | 0.014 (-0.16) | 0.021 (-0.17) | -0.21 (-0.17) | -0.29 (-0.17) | 0.085 (-0.15) | -.13 (-0.16) | -0.031 (-0.17) | 0.07 (-0.17) | -0.05 (-0.19) | -0.23 (-0.15) |
| Party group disloyalty | -1.38 (-1.26) | -0.34 (-0.71) | -0.24 (-0.51) | 0.56 (-0.5) | 0.31 (-0.49) | -1.97 (-1.35) | 0.58 (-0.44) | 0.44 (-0.5) | 0.18 (-0.51) | -0.49 (-0.85) | -1.86 (-1.52) |
| Holds group office | -0.087 (-0.24) | -0.22 (-0.29) | 0.19 (-0.26) | 0.16 (-0.24) | -0.72 (-0.53) | 0.052 (-0.25) | 0.33 (-0.22) | -0.65 (-0.47) | -0.14 (-0.31) | 0.28 (-0.25) | 0.21 (-0.22) |
| National party size relative to group size | 0.31 (-0.85) | 0.4 (-0.91) | 0.73 (-1.01) | -1.89 (-1.06) | -1.26 (-0.92) | 0.91 (-0.89) | 0.44 (-0.92) | -0.52 (-1) | 0.56 (-1.02) | 0.41 (-1.09) | -2.16* (-1.01) |
| Held national party office | 0.2 (-0.13) | -0.062 (-0.13) | -0.063 (-0.14) | 0.36* (-0.15) | -0.011 (-0.14) | -0.15 (-0.12) | -0.11 (-0.13) | 0.38* (-0.15) | -0.17 (-0.14) | 0.22 (-0.16) | -0.11 (-0.12) |

| | AFET | BUDG | ECON | EMPL | ENVI | ITRE | IMCO | TRAN | AGRI | JURI | LIBE |
|---|---|---|---|---|---|---|---|---|---|---|---|
| **Demographics** | | | | | | | | | | | |
| New member state | 0.24 | 0.36* | -0.043 | -0.13 | -0.15 | -0.037 | 0.1 | 0.2 | 0.097 | 0.25 | -0.013 |
| | (-0.14) | (-0.15) | (-0.16) | (-0.16) | (-0.17) | (-0.14) | (-0.15) | (-0.15) | (-0.18) | (-0.16) | (-0.14) |
| Male | 0.37** | -0.071 | 0.17 | -0.048 | -0.12 | -0.045 | -0.31* | 0.13 | -0.026 | 0.14 | 0.012 |
| | (-0.14) | (-0.14) | (-0.15) | (-0.14) | (-0.14) | (-0.13) | (-0.13) | (-0.14) | (-0.15) | (-0.17) | (-0.13) |
| Age in top quartile of party group | -0.22 | -0.18 | -0.022 | 0.11 | -0.34 | -0.1 | 0.06 | -0.2 | -0.22 | 0.28 | -0.05 |
| | (-0.15) | (-0.16) | (-0.16) | (-0.15) | (-0.18) | (-0.15) | (-0.14) | (-0.17) | (-0.18) | (-0.16) | (-0.14) |
| Constant | -1.63** | -1.30** | -1.52** | -1.11** | -0.71** | -0.98** | -1.05** | -1.47** | -1.27** | -1.78** | -0.71** |
| | (-0.23) | (-0.2) | (-0.22) | (-0.2) | (-0.2) | (-0.19) | (-0.2) | (-0.23) | (-0.22) | (-0.25) | (-0.19) |
| | | | | | | | | | | | |
| Observations | 695 | 695 | 695 | 695 | 695 | 695 | 695 | 695 | 695 | 695 | 695 |
| - Log likelihood | 176.6 | 132.1 | 122.3 | 131.3 | 131.0 | 152.7 | 128.2 | 126.0 | 100.7 | 87.8 | 151.8 |

*Note*: Dependent variable: individual member assignment to the respective committee in 2004. Standard errors in brackets. * significance at 10%; ** significance at 5%.

# Appendix F Chapter 4: Committee-specific special interests and expertise of members and substitutes per party group

| | EPP-ED | PSE | ALDE | GREEN/EFA | EUL/NGL | IND-DEM | UEN | na |
|---|---|---|---|---|---|---|---|---|
| *Committee-specific interests* | | | | | | | | |
| Farming ties in AGRI | 20 (32) | 5 (21) | 2 (4) | 1 (4) | 1 (3) | 1 (6) | 1 (4) | 3 (7) |
| Green ties in ENVI | 10 (44) | 4 (29) | 0 (16) | 8 (10) | 1 (8) | 0 (6) | 1 (6) | 0 (2) |
| Trade union ties in EMPL | 4 (29) | 12 (30) | 2 (12) | 0 (5) | 2 (8) | 0 (2) | 0 (2) | 0 (4) |
| Social groups in LIBE | 3 (39) | 7 (26) | 2 (16) | 2 (6) | 1 (5) | 0 (3) | 1 (4) | 0 (4) |
| Industry/business group ties in ECON | 15 (39) | 7 (26) | 7 (12) | 1 (4) | 0 (4) | 2 (3) | 2 (3) | 0 (4) |
| Industry/business group ties in ITRE | 12 (38) | 6 (29) | 4 (12) | 0 (6) | 2 (6) | 1 (1) | 0 (3) | 1 (4) |
| *Committee-specific expertise* | | | | | | | | |
| International relations experience in AFET | 47 (59) | 37 (43) | 16 (18) | 7 (9) | 6 (10) | 3 (9) | 3 (8) | 3 (5) |
| Legal expertise in JURI | 18 (21) | 5 (12) | 3 (6) | 0 (4) | 0 (2) | 1 (1) | 1 (2) | 1 (2) |
| Legal expertise in AFCO | 15 (21) | 6 (15) | 3 (6) | 0 (3) | 1 (2) | 0 (3) | 1 (2) | 2 (3) |
| Medical education in ENVI | 10 (44) | 2 (29) | 3 (16) | 0 (10) | 3 (8) | 1 (6) | 0 (6) | 1 (2) |
| Natural sciences and engineering educ. in ENVI | 7 (44) | 4 (29) | 3 (16) | 3 (10) | 3 (8) | 1 (6) | 0 (6) | 0 (2) |
| Natural sciences and engineering educ. in ITRE | 12 (38) | 8 (29) | 2 (12) | 1 (6) | 1 (6) | 0 (1) | 1 (3) | 1 (4) |
| Transport experience in TRAN | 6 (35) | 3 (27) | 1 (12) | 3 (6) | 0 (6) | 1 (6) | 1 (4) | 0 (5) |
| Economics expertise in BUDG | 15 (40) | 9 (29) | 4 (12) | 0 (4) | 1 (2) | 2 (2) | 1 (2) | 1 (4) |
| Economics expertise in CONT | 8 (25) | 4 (15) | 4 (8) | 1 (4) | 1 (4) | 2 (4) | 1 (1) | 0 (2) |
| Economics expertise in ECON | 20 (39) | 12 (26) | 5 (12) | 1 (4) | 1 (4) | 3 (3) | 1 (3) | 2 (4) |

*Note:* The total number of members in the respective column category with or without the interests or expertise in the respective row is displayed in brackets.

Abbreviations: AFET: Foreign Affairs; AFCO: Budgets; BUDG: Budgets; CONT: Budgetary Control; ECON: Economic and Monetary Affairs; EMPL: Employment and Social Affairs; ENVI: Environment, Public Health and Food Safety; ITRE: Industry, Research and Energy; TRAN: Transport and Tourism; AGRI: Agriculture; JURI: Legal Affairs; LIBE: Civil Liberties, Justice and Home Affairs; EPP-ED: Group of European People's Party (Christian Democrats) and European Democrats; PSE: Socialist Group in the European Parliament; ALDE: Group of the Alliance of Liberals and Democrats for Europe; G/EGA: Group of the Greens/European Free Alliance; EUL/NGL: Confederal Group of the European United Left – Nordic Green Left; IND/DEM: Independence/Democracy Group; UEN: Union of Europe of the Nations Group; na: Non-attached member.

**Appendix G Chapter 4: Count models of codecision and consultation report allocation during 2004-2007 (committee fixed effects displayed)**

| | COD M1 | COD M2 | COD M3 | CNS M1 | CNS M2 | CNS M3 |
|---|---|---|---|---|---|---|
| Committee-related interest group ties | 0.127 | | 0.144 | .280** | | 0.322** |
| | (0.150) | | (0.133) | (.129) | | (0.157) |
| Committee-related expertise | 0.001 | | 0.048 | .424* | | 0.405* |
| | (0.184) | | (0.157) | (.253) | | (0.232) |
| Party group disloyalty | | -3.270** | -3.378** | | -3.232** | -2.541* |
| | | (1.274) | (1.501) | | (1.480) | (1.323) |
| EPP-ED | | 0.531* | 0.641** | | 0.126 | 0.237 |
| | | (0.272) | (0.291) | | (0.383) | (0.481) |
| PSE | | 0.225 | 0.366 | | -0.233 | -0.062 |
| | | (0.286) | (0.289) | | (0.449) | (0.517) |
| ALDE | | 0.596* | 0.593** | | 0.311 | 0.219 |
| | | (0.310) | (0.283) | | (0.511) | (0.508) |
| National party delegation size | | 0.014** | -0.002 | | 0.016** | 0.011 |
| | | (0.007) | (0.008) | | (0.007) | (0.008) |
| Time in government | | 0.120 | 0.092 | | -0.164 | -0.080 |
| | | (0.169) | (0.137) | | (0.171) | (0.192) |
| No. of codecision reports | | | | | | 0.543*** |
| | | | | | | (0.180) |
| No. of consultation reports | | | 0.418*** | | | |
| | | | (0.096) | | | |
| Previously in committee | | | 0.878*** | | | -0.126 |
| | | | (0.148) | | | (0.250) |
| Chair | | | 0.156 | | | 1.189*** |
| | | | (0.526) | | | (0.396) |
| Coordinator | | | .458** | | | 0.574 |
| | | | (0.203) | | | (0.383) |
| Male | -0.480*** | -0.461*** | -0.360*** | -0.173 | -0.126 | -0.134 |
| | (0.106) | (0.097) | (0.121) | (0.171) | (0.145) | (0.144) |
| Age | 0.006 | 0.002 | -0.008 | 0.016* | 0.014 | 0.011 |
| | (0.008) | (0.008) | (0.008) | (0.009) | (0.009) | (0.010) |

|  | COD M1 | COD M2 | COD M3 | CNS M1 | CNS M2 | CNS M3 |
|---|---|---|---|---|---|---|
| Substitute | **-1.822***** | **-1.842***** | **-1.435***** | **-1.062***** | **-1.104***** | **-0.750***** |
|  | (0.292) | (0.283) | (0.262) | (0.238) | (0.240) | (0.241) |
| DEVE | **0.747***** | **0.771***** | **0.890***** | **-0.695***** | **-1.077***** | **-0.837***** |
|  | (0.154) | (0.024) | (0.141) | (0.218) | (0.044) | (0.220) |
| INTA | **0.327**** | **0.287***** | **0.425**** | **0.961***** | **0.635***** | **0.849***** |
|  | (0.159) | (0.053) | (0.174) | (0.217) | (0.058) | (0.221) |
| BUDG | -0.131 | **-0.181***** | **-0.176**** | **0.553***** | **0.401***** | **0.390***** |
|  | (0.085) | (0.038) | (0.079) | (0.094) | (0.039) | (0.098) |
| CONT | 0.043 | **0.154***** | **0.176*** | **0.439***** | **0.305***** | **0.422***** |
|  | (0.092) | (0.040) | (0.100) | (0.120) | (0.052) | (0.093) |
| ECON | **1.731***** | **1.760***** | **1.575***** | **1.339***** | **1.363***** | **1.184***** |
|  | (0.049) | (0.031) | (0.108) | (0.101) | (0.036) | (0.152) |
| EMPL | **1.548***** | **1.630***** | **1.590***** | **0.661***** | **0.456***** | **0.588**** |
|  | (0.125) | (0.016) | (0.123) | (0.229) | (0.041) | (0.235) |
| ENVI | **2.560***** | **2.553***** | **2.408***** | **0.679***** | **0.511***** | 0.096 |
|  | (0.077) | (0.031) | (0.103) | (0.130) | (0.051) | (0.333) |
| ITRE | **1.400***** | **1.367***** | **1.435***** | **1.137***** | **0.993***** | **0.999***** |
|  | (0.074) | (0.033) | (0.092) | (0.142) | (0.034) | (0.169) |
| IMCO | **1.879***** | **1.809***** | **1.975***** |  |  |  |
|  | (0.161) | (0.048) | (0.131) |  |  |  |
| TRAN | **2.459***** | **2.463***** | **2.489***** | **0.338**** | **0.158***** | 0.081 |
|  | (0.120) | (0.029) | (0.131) | (0.146) | (0.016) | (0.188) |
| REGI | 0.163 | **0.209***** | **0.385***** | **-0.632***** | **-0.920***** | **-0.627***** |
|  | (0.156) | (0.027) | (0.142) | (0.219) | (0.018) | (0.211) |
| AGRI | **-0.738***** | **-0.636***** | **-1.022***** | **2.046***** | **1.940***** | **2.048***** |
|  | (0.112) | (0.032) | (0.183) | (0.243) | (0.051) | (0.236) |
| PECH | **0.439***** | **0.379***** | -0.202 | **2.894***** | **2.537***** | **2.784***** |
|  | (0.157) | (0.026) | (0.220) | (0.218) | (0.053) | (0.210) |
| CULT | **1.949***** | **1.950***** | **2.086***** | 0.165 | **-0.176***** | -0.138 |
|  | (0.158) | (0.021) | (0.142) | (0.220) | (0.049) | (0.257) |
| JURI | **2.203***** | **2.203***** | **2.119***** | **1.152***** | **1.038***** | **0.706***** |
|  | (0.046) | (0.024) | (0.071) | (0.091) | (0.070) | (0.134) |

| | COD M1 | COD M2 | COD M3 | CNS M1 | CNS M2 | CNS M3 |
|---|---|---|---|---|---|---|
| LIBE | 2.174*** | 2.152*** | 1.752*** | 2.942*** | 2.595*** | 2.548*** |
| | (0.134) | (0.022) | (0.223) | (0.223) | (0.058) | (0.244) |
| AFCO | | | | -0.760*** | -0.917*** | -0.837*** |
| | | | | (0.087) | (0.025) | (0.103) |
| FEMM | 0.426** | 0.386*** | 0.608*** | | | |
| | (0.177) | (0.081) | (0.155) | | | |
| Constant | -3.034*** | -3.254*** | -3.178*** | -3.775*** | -3.339*** | -3.744*** |
| | (0.491) | (0.516) | (0.561) | (0.514) | (0.488) | (0.749) |
| Log-pseudo-likelihood | -243.0 | -232.2 | -217.3 | -228.2 | -221.8 | -214.5 |
| McFadden pseudo R2 | 0.22 | 0.24 | 0.29 | 0.15 | 0.16 | 0.19 |
| Alpha | | | | 1.767 | 1.479 | 1.005 |
| lnalpha | | | | 0.570 | 0.391 | 0.005 |
| N | 1547 | 1475 | 1475 | 1471 | 1399 | 1399 |

*Note:* Dependent variables: number of codecision (COD M1-3) and consultation (CNS M1-3) reports allocated to a committee member/substitute. Robust standard errors displayed in brackets, * significance at 10%, ** significance at 5%, *** significance at 1%. See the List of Abbreviations at the beginning of the book.

**Appendix H Chapter 5: Measurement of the dependent and independent variables**

| Variable | Measurement |
|---|---|
| DV1: Proportion of amendments in EP opinion derived from a committee report | Proportion of amendments in the adopted EP opinion derived from a committee report (number of adopted committee amendments/total number of adopted amendments in plenary) |
| DV2: Number of changes to a committee report | Number of rejected or lapsed committee amendments in plenary + number of adopted non-committee amendments in plenary |
| Early | Early agreement after the committee vote: 0=no; 1=yes (reference category: no early agreement) |
| Size (1,000s words) | Word count of the initial Commission legislative proposal in 1000s of words |
| Num. consul. committees | Number of opinion-giving, or consultative, committees |
| Num. valid comm. ams. | Number of proposed committee amendments |
| Regulation/Directive | A legislative proposal for : 1=a regulation or a directive; 0=a decision or a recommendation |
| Related interest | Relevant special interests of the rapporteur: 0=no; 1=yes (see Appendix F) |
| Related expertise | Relevant expertise of the rapporteur: 0=no; 1=yes (see Appendix F) |
| National party delegation size | Number of MEPs from the rapporteur's national party in 6th EP (2004-2009) |
| EPP-ED | Rapporteur is a member of EPP-ED: 0=no; 1=yes |
| PSE | Rapporteur is a member of PSE: 0=no; 1=yes |
| ALDE | Rapporteur is a member of ALDE: 0=no; 1=yes |

*Note:* See the List of Abbreviations at the beginning of the book.

**Appendix I Chapter 5: Fractional logistic regression of the proportion of adopted amendments in an EP opinion derived from a committee report (committee fixed effects displayed)**

| | M1 | M2 | M3 | M4 | M5 | M6 | M7_not early | M8_early |
|---|---|---|---|---|---|---|---|---|
| Early | -3.670** | -3.666** | -3.553** | -3.408** | -3.341** | -3.791** | | |
| | (0.255) | (0.254) | (0.271) | (0.297) | (0.335) | (0.293) | | |
| Related interest | -0.030 | -0.007 | 0.533 | 0.046 | 0.092 | 0.041 | 0.319 | 0.185 |
| | (0.413) | (0.397) | (0.577) | (0.403) | (0.386) | (0.392) | (0.595) | (0.734) |
| Early*Related interest | | | -0.852 | | | | | |
| | | | (0.732) | | | | | |
| Related expertise | 0.117 | 0.106 | 0.126 | 0.575 | 0.080 | 0.094 | 1.074* | -0.922 |
| | (0.359) | (0.355) | (0.360) | (0.446) | (0.347) | (0.348) | (0.533) | (0.604) |
| Early*Related expertise | | | | -0.836 | | | | |
| | | | | (0.558) | | | | |
| National party delegation size | -0.019 | -0.020 | -0.020 | -0.020 | -0.021 | -0.019 | -0.050** | -0.003 |
| | (0.013) | (0.013) | (0.013) | (0.013) | (0.014) | (0.013) | (0.017) | (0.022) |
| EPP-ED | 0.231 | 0.331 | 0.361 | 0.357 | 0.823* | 0.324 | 1.569** | -0.488 |
| | (0.471) | (0.373) | (0.373) | (0.370) | (0.418) | (0.384) | (0.491) | (0.595) |
| Early*EPP-ED | | | | | -0.772 | | | |
| | | | | | (0.442) | | | |
| PSE | 0.336 | 0.435 | 0.428 | 0.465 | 0.447 | 0.132 | 1.152* | 0.188 |
| | (0.468) | (0.370) | (0.371) | (0.364) | (0.348) | (0.476) | (0.518) | (0.504) |

| | M1 | M2 | M3 | M4 | M5 | M6 | M7_not early | M8_early |
|---|---|---|---|---|---|---|---|---|
| Early*PSE | | | | | | 0.484 | | |
| | | | | | | (0.528) | | |
| ALDE | -0.186 | | | | | | | |
| | (0.559) | | | | | | | |
| Size (1000s words) | -0.008 | -0.009 | -0.009 | -0.006 | -0.007 | -0.008 | 0.011 | -0.026 |
| | (0.007) | (0.007) | (0.007) | (0.007) | (0.007) | (0.007) | (0.011) | (0.019) |
| Num. consul. committees | -0.041 | -0.038 | -0.039 | -0.034 | -0.033 | -0.028 | -0.134 | 0.064 |
| | (0.052) | (0.052) | (0.052) | (0.054) | (0.053) | (0.054) | (0.069) | (0.092) |
| Regulation/Directive | -0.204 | -0.197 | -0.220 | -0.191 | -0.229 | -0.215 | -0.506 | -0.139 |
| | (0.534) | (0.533) | (0.539) | (0.525) | (0.533) | (0.533) | (0.544) | (0.710) |
| AFET | -0.367 | -0.321 | -0.349 | -0.179 | -0.274 | -0.290 | | -0.008 |
| | (1.260) | (1.269) | (1.273) | (1.284) | (1.260) | (1.279) | | (1.564) |
| DEVE | 2.868 | 2.855 | 2.838 | 2.786 | 3.063 | 2.921 | 1.121 | 16.10** |
| | (1.671) | (1.673) | (1.648) | (1.611) | (1.716) | (1.707) | (0.914) | (1.667) |
| INTA | -0.487 | -0.482 | -0.441 | -0.432 | -0.347 | -0.433 | 14.03** | -13.49** |
| | (1.097) | (1.105) | (1.101) | (1.100) | (1.141) | (1.116) | (1.206) | (1.563) |
| BUDG | -0.258 | -0.247 | -0.174 | -0.123 | -0.453 | -0.266 | -1.133 | |
| | (0.719) | (0.723) | (0.709) | (0.704) | (0.743) | (0.738) | (0.601) | |
| CONT | 12.06** | 12.06** | 12.90** | 12.19** | 12.85** | 12.17** | 13.16** | |
| | (1.018) | (1.019) | (1.008) | (1.003) | (1.050) | (1.044) | (0.994) | |

| | M1 | M2 | M3 | M4 | M5 | M6 | M7_not early | M8_early |
|---|---|---|---|---|---|---|---|---|
| ECON | -0.569 | -0.570 | -0.545 | -0.609 | -0.514 | -0.555 | -0.440 | -0.525 |
| | (0.890) | (0.891) | (0.888) | (0.876) | (0.910) | (0.906) | (1.267) | (1.272) |
| EMPL | 1.897* | 1.888* | 1.887* | 1.797 | 1.996* | 1.93* | -0.256 | 2.401 |
| | (0.947) | (0.942) | (0.951) | (0.927) | (0.957) | (0.953) | (0.936) | (1.309) |
| ENVI | -1.013 | -0.998 | -0.994 | -0.977 | -0.937 | -0.954 | -1.208 | -0.979 |
| | (0.721) | (0.723) | (0.713) | (0.699) | (0.757) | (0.743) | (0.747) | (1.210) |
| ITRE | 1.753* | 1.763* | 1.876* | 1.700* | 1.780* | 1.802* | -0.028 | 2.361 |
| | (0.837) | (0.835) | (0.814) | (0.810) | (0.853) | (0.850) | (0.723) | (1.206) |
| IMCO | 0.008 | 0.015 | 0.018 | -0.050 | 0.048 | 0.074 | -0.328 | 0.018 |
| | (0.815) | (0.814) | (0.802) | (0.780) | (0.838) | (0.835) | (0.798) | (1.249) |
| TRAN | -0.110 | -0.122 | -0.095 | -0.132 | 0.006 | -0.038 | -0.033 | -0.264 |
| | (0.768) | (0.768) | (0.757) | (0.742) | (0.806) | (0.792) | (0.735) | (1.322) |
| REGI | 1.099 | 1.099 | 1.179 | 1.263 | 1.055 | 1.148 | 1.050 | |
| | (0.780) | (0.784) | (0.770) | (0.774) | (0.776) | (0.783) | (0.647) | |
| AGRI | -1.287 | -1.266 | -1.287 | -1.319 | -1.436 | -1.285 | -0.622 | -2.630 |
| | (0.891) | (0.896) | (0.874) | (0.901) | (0.892) | (0.906) | (0.969) | (1.477) |
| JURI | -0.086 | -0.076 | -0.095 | 0.034 | 0.088 | 0.003 | -1.791 | 1.753 |
| | (0.984) | (0.988) | (0.976) | (1.015) | (1.014) | (0.996) | (0.929) | (1.485) |
| LIBE | 0.936 | 0.916 | 0.871 | 0.869 | 1.103 | 1.028 | 0.535 | 1.374 |
| | (0.900) | (0.897) | (0.899) | (0.855) | (0.955) | (0.927) | (0.736) | (1.554) |

| | M1 | M2 | M3 | M4 | M5 | M6 | M7_not early | M8_early |
|---|---|---|---|---|---|---|---|---|
| AFCO | 0.707 | 0.714 | 0.688 | 0.985 | 0.721 | 0.637 | | 1.374 |
| | (0.871) | (0.872) | (0.879) | (0.897) | (0.881) | (0.895) | | (1.345) |
| FEMM | -0.837 | -0.830 | -0.755 | -0.696 | -0.917 | -0.783 | -1.565* | |
| | (0.710) | (0.711) | (0.696) | (0.690) | (0.735) | (0.733) | (0.624) | |
| Constant | 2.826** | 2.720** | 2.649** | 2.517** | 2.444** | 2.733*** | 2.965** | -1.006 |
| | (0.724) | (0.640) | (0.618) | (0.610) | (0.713) | (0.659) | (0.553) | (1.096) |
| Pseudo LL | -109.1 | -109.2 | -108.8 | -108.6 | -108.6 | -109.0 | -37.9 | -62.7 |
| Deviance | 142.0 | 142.1 | 141.4 | 141.0 | 141.0 | 141.7 | 30.5 | 94.3 |
| N | 333 | 333 | 333 | 333 | 333 | 333 | 160 | 173 |

*Note:* Dependent variable: proportion of adopted amendments in the first reading EP opinion derived from a committee report on a codecision proposal in the period 2004-2009. Robust standard errors displayed in brackets, * significance at 5%, ** significance at 1%. Abbreviations: AFET: Foreign Affairs; DEVE: Development; INTA: International Trade; BUDG: Budgets; CONT: Budgetary Control; ECON: Economic and Monetary Affairs; EMPL: Employment and Social Affairs; ENVI: Environment, Public Health and Food Safety; ITRE: Industry, Research and Energy; IMCO: Internal Market and Consumer Protection; TRAN: Transport and Tourism; REGI: Regional Development; AGRI: Agriculture; JURI: Legal Affairs; LIBE: Civil Liberties, Justice and Home Affairs; AFCO: Constitutional Affairs; FEMM: Women's Rights and Gender Equality.

**Appendix J Chapter 5: Negative binomial regression of the number of adopted changes to committee reports in plenary (committee fixed effects displayed)**

| | M1 | M2 | M3 | M4 | M5 | M6 | M7_not early | M8_early |
|---|---|---|---|---|---|---|---|---|
| Early | 1.942** | 1.938** | 1.910** | 1.907** | 1.600** | 1.971** | | |
| | (0.129) | (0.128) | (0.140) | (0.154) | (0.180) | (0.148) | | |
| Related interest | -0.065 | -0.095 | -0.203 | -0.103 | -0.143 | -0.111 | -0.285 | 0.013 |
| | (0.194) | (0.192) | (0.324) | (0.191) | (0.192) | (0.190) | (0.380) | (0.190) |
| Early*Related interest | | | 0.188 | | | | | |
| | | | (0.355) | | | | | |
| Related expertise | -0.270 | -0.281 | -0.287 | -0.329 | -0.273 | -0.272 | -0.496 | 0.132 |
| | (0.196) | (0.197) | (0.198) | (0.294) | (0.191) | (0.188) | (0.264) | (0.170) |
| Early*Related expertise | | | | 0.094 | | | | |
| | | | | (0.322) | | | | |
| National party delegation size | 0.003 | 0.004 | 0.004 | 0.004 | 0.003 | 0.003 | 0.005 | 0.005 |
| | (0.005) | (0.005) | (0.005) | (0.005) | (0.005) | (0.005) | (0.009) | (0.006) |
| EPP–ED | -0.388 | -0.551** | -0.555** | -0.557** | -0.965** | -0.554** | -1.083** | -0.173 |
| | (0.245) | (0.166) | (0.166) | (0.164) | (0.234) | (0.165) | (0.279) | (0.170) |
| Early*EPP-ED | | | | | 0.746** | | | |
| | | | | | (0.240) | | | |
| PSE | -0.186 | -0.355 | -0.352 | -0.361 | -0.348 | -0.287 | -0.669* | -0.137 |
| | (0.259) | (0.192) | (0.192) | (0.187) | (0.181) | (0.322) | (0.313) | (0.130) |

| | M1 | M2 | M3 | M4 | M5 | M6 | M7_not early | M8_early |
|---|---|---|---|---|---|---|---|---|
| Early*PSE | | | | | | | | |
| ALDE | 0.299 | | | | | -0.130 | | |
| | (0.276) | | | | | (0.320) | | |
| Num. valid comm. ams. | 0.016** | 0.016** | 0.016** | 0.016** | 0.016** | 0.016** | 0.012** | 0.019** |
| | (0.002) | (0.002) | (0.002) | (0.002) | (0.002) | (0.002) | (0.002) | (0.002) |
| Num. consul. committees | 0.105** | 0.099** | 0.100** | 0.099** | 0.103** | 0.098** | 0.136* | 0.107* |
| | (0.035) | (0.034) | (0.035) | (0.035) | (0.037) | (0.035) | (0.064) | (0.054) |
| Regulation/Directive | 0.216 | 0.217 | 0.215 | 0.217 | 0.227 | 0.220 | 1.173** | -0.173 |
| | (0.180) | (0.182) | (0.183) | (0.181) | (0.178) | (0.183) | (0.320) | (0.194) |
| AFET | 0.107 | 0.057 | 0.075 | 0.031 | -0.042 | 0.030 | | -0.234 |
| | (0.450) | (0.438) | (0.445) | (0.431) | (0.426) | (0.422) | | (0.447) |
| DEVE | -1.335* | -1.302* | -1.293* | -1.299* | -1.576* | -1.325* | -3.798** | -0.290 |
| | (0.643) | (0.640) | (0.645) | (0.645) | (0.629) | (0.635) | (0.979) | (0.400) |
| INTA | -0.336 | -0.212 | -0.196 | -0.205 | -0.205 | -0.246 | -24.46** | 0.679 |
| | (0.678) | (0.683) | (0.688) | (0.688) | (0.703) | (0.679) | (1.154) | (0.349) |
| BUDG | 0.331 | 0.328 | 0.321 | 0.310 | 0.441 | 0.330 | -0.180 | |
| | (0.295) | (0.295) | (0.296) | (0.302) | (0.300) | (0.297) | (0.449) | |
| CONT | -18.16** | -23.00** | -23.36** | -19.13** | -18.10** | -20.21** | -23.55** | |
| | (0.865) | (0.864) | (0.866) | (0.865) | (0.916) | (0.887) | (0.920) | |

| | M1 | M2 | M3 | M4 | M5 | M6 | M7_not early | M8_early |
|---|---|---|---|---|---|---|---|---|
| ECON | -0.522 | -0.499 | -0.503 | -0.495 | -0.603 | -0.504 | -1.119 | -0.686 |
| | (0.323) | (0.316) | (0.319) | (0.318) | (0.323) | (0.317) | (0.895) | (0.378) |
| EMPL | -0.570 | -0.544 | -0.539 | -0.540 | -0.687* | -0.555 | -1.570** | -0.541 |
| | (0.323) | (0.319) | (0.321) | (0.321) | (0.325) | (0.320) | (0.583) | (0.353) |
| ENVI | -0.009 | -0.015 | -0.002 | -0.019 | -0.096 | -0.028 | -0.226 | -0.308 |
| | (0.299) | (0.298) | (0.302) | (0.298) | (0.303) | (0.295) | (0.512) | (0.360) |
| ITRE | -0.722* | -0.697* | -0.705* | -0.699* | -0.864** | -0.722* | -1.010 | -1.301** |
| | (0.332) | (0.335) | (0.332) | (0.333) | (0.330) | (0.334) | (0.532) | (0.392) |
| IMCO | -0.265 | -0.271 | -0.265 | -0.265 | -0.329 | -0.289 | -0.196 | -0.287 |
| | (0.287) | (0.285) | (0.287) | (0.287) | (0.294) | (0.286) | (0.602) | (0.350) |
| TRAN | -0.108 | -0.083 | -0.073 | -0.077 | -0.222 | -0.104 | -1.100* | 0.437 |
| | (0.321) | (0.318) | (0.321) | (0.319) | (0.327) | (0.318) | (0.543) | (0.392) |
| REGI | -1.004* | -0.993* | -1.007* | -1.009* | -1.025* | -1.015* | -1.544** | |
| | (0.424) | (0.419) | (0.423) | (0.423) | (0.471) | (0.430) | (0.544) | |
| AGRI | -0.114 | -0.170 | -0.213 | -0.151 | -0.135 | -0.168 | -0.372 | -0.083 |
| | (0.352) | (0.356) | (0.347) | (0.358) | (0.359) | (0.359) | (0.645) | (0.424) |
| JURI | 0.208 | 0.200 | 0.204 | 0.191 | -0.036 | 0.168 | -0.151 | -0.786 |
| | (0.516) | (0.513) | (0.512) | (0.513) | (0.492) | (0.490) | (0.661) | (0.484) |
| LIBE | -0.770 | -0.701 | -0.690 | -0.703 | -0.861* | -0.721 | -1.290* | -0.423 |
| | (0.407) | (0.413) | (0.413) | (0.412) | (0.413) | (0.416) | (0.547) | (0.552) |

|  | M1 | M2 | M3 | M4 | M5 | M6 | M7_not early | M8_early |
|---|---|---|---|---|---|---|---|---|
| AFCO | -0.640 | -0.619 | -0.600 | -0.657 | -0.598 | -0.599 | | -0.849* |
|  | (0.383) | (0.386) | (0.391) | (0.398) | (0.381) | (0.395) | | (0.417) |
| FEMM | 0.658 | 0.660 | 0.650 | 0.644 | 0.700 | 0.650 | 0.410 | |
|  | (0.418) | (0.417) | (0.418) | (0.421) | (0.459) | (0.425) | (0.459) | |
| Constant | 0.988** | 1.159** | 1.163** | 1.184** | 1.450** | 1.162** | 1.282* | 3.009** |
|  | (0.360) | (0.318) | (0.319) | (0.322) | (0.348) | (0.319) | (0.515) | (0.352) |
| Pseudo LL | -1259.7 | -1260.5 | -1260.3 | -1260.4 | -1256.0 | -1260.4 | -452.7 | -755.0 |
| Pseudo R2 | 0.101 | 0.101 | 0.101 | 0.101 | 0.104 | 0.101 | 0.109 | 0.103 |
| Alpha | 0.992 | 0.997 | 0.996 | 0.997 | 0.97 | 0.996 | 1.372 | 0.479 |
| lnalpha | -0.008 | -0.003 | -0.004 | -0.003 | -0.03 | -0.004 | 0.316 | -0.737 |
| N | 334 | 334 | 334 | 334 | 334 | 334 | 161 | 173 |

*Note*: Dependent variable: number of changes to a committee report in the first reading EP opinion on a codecision proposal in the period 2004-2009 (rejected committee amendments plus adopted non-committee amendments). Robust standard errors displayed in brackets, * significance at 5%, ** significance at 1%. Abbreviations: AFET: Foreign Affairs; DEVE: Development; INTA: International Trade; BUDG: Budgets; CONT: Budgetary Control; ECON: Economic and Monetary Affairs; EMPL: Employment and Social Affairs; ENVI: Environment, Public Health and Food Safety; ITRE: Industry, Research and Energy; IMCO: Internal Market and Consumer Protection; TRAN: Transport and Tourism; REGI: Regional Development; AGRI: Agriculture; JURI: Legal Affairs; LIBE: Civil Liberties, Justice and Home Affairs; AFCO: Constitutional Affairs; FEMM: Women's Rights and Gender Equality

# | index

www.ingramcontent.com/pod-product-compliance
Lightning Source LLC
Chambersburg PA
CBHW072124020426
42334CB00018B/1706